Mircea Trifu

Tool-Supported Identification of Functional Concerns in Object-Oriented Code

Tool-Supported Identification of Functional Concerns in Object-Oriented Code

by
Mircea Trifu

 Scientific Publishing

Dissertation, Karlsruher Institut für Technologie
Fakultät für Informatik,
Tag der mündlichen Prüfung: 20.01.2010

Impressum

Karlsruher Institut für Technologie (KIT)
KIT Scientific Publishing
Straße am Forum 2
D-76131 Karlsruhe
www.uvka.de

KIT – Universität des Landes Baden-Württemberg und nationales
Forschungszentrum in der Helmholtz-Gemeinschaft

KIT Scientific Publishing 2010
Print on Demand

ISBN 978-3-86644-494-2

Tool-Supported Identification of Functional Concerns in Object-Oriented Code

Zur Erlangung des akademischen Grades eines

Doktors der Ingenieurwissenschaften

von der Fakultät für Informatik
des Karlsruher Instituts für Technologie (KIT)

genehmigte
Dissertation

von

Mircea Dan Lucian Trifu

aus Satu Mare, Rumänien

Tag der mündlichen Prüfung: 20. Januar 2010
Erster Gutachter: Prof. em. Dr. Dr. h.c. Gerhard Goos
Zweiter Gutachter: Prof. Dr. Ralf Reussner

Acknowledgements

First of all I would like to express my deepest appreciation and gratitude to my supervisor Prof. Gerhard Goos for his guidance, continued support, and for giving me the opportunity to work in a very stimulating research environment. With his encyclopedic knowledge and comprehensive perspective on software engineering, he shaped my development as a scientist, and with his insightful questions and invaluable comments, he helped me improve this work. Prof. Goos has been a true mentor and I am privileged to call myself his student.

I would also like to express my gratitude to my second supervisor Prof. Ralf Reussner for his constructive suggestions and invaluable advice, while preparing my dissertation, for his unwavering support, and for giving me the opportunity to continue my scientific career as a postdoctoral researcher. His tireless quest for knowledge and scientific excellence inspired me to challenge myself.

I owe a lot of gratitude to my brother Dr. Adrian Trifu for his continued support throughout the years. He has always been a forerunner, whose footsteps I also followed to Karlsruhe. I am especially grateful for the many opportunities he created for me and for the excellent collaboration and discussions we had, while working side by side as colleagues at FZI.

A special thank you goes to my dear friend Dr. Radu Marinescu, who awoke my interest for genuine scientific research with his unwavering convictions and his uncurbed enthusiasm, and set me on the course, which brought me where I am today. I am also grateful for the energizing discussions we had, especially during my visits to Timişoara.

I am also indebted to my brother Dr. Adrian Trifu and to my dear friend Dr. Daniel Raţiu for patiently and thoroughly reviewing my dissertation.

Many thanks to my students: Marius Muja and Johannes Stammel, who helped me try our some of my ideas in practice, and to my close colleagues at FZI: Dr. Christoph Andriessens, Christian Bartsch, Dr. Holger Bär, Dr. Markus Bauer, Dr. Steffen Becker, Franz Brosch, Zoya Durdik, Dr. Thomas Genssler, Thomas Goldschmidt, Henning Groenda, Dr. Jens Happe, Michael Hauck, Stefan Hellfeld, Lucia Kapova, David Karlin, Dr. Jan Kofron, Dr. Samuel Kounev, Klaus Krogmann, Dr. Volker Kuttruff, Martin

Küster, Prof. Dr. Marco Mevius, Dr. Christof Momm, Dr. Pierre Parrend, Christoph Rathfelder, Thomas Schuster, Dr. Olaf Seng, Johannes Stammel, Gábor Szeder, Peter Szulman, Dr. Adrian Trifu, and Jan Wiesenberger, for the fruitful discussions and the very pleasant and constructive work environment they help to create.

Special thanks also go to Andreea Cosma, for her understanding and support, while writing my dissertation.

And last but not least, my wholehearted thanks go to my parents, Lucia and Ioan, who have encouraged and supported me unconditionally in every possible way throughout the years. I am especially grateful for the excellent education they gave me as a child and the sacrifices they made so that I can pursue my dreams. None of this would have been possible without their support. For always being there for me, all through my ups and downs, and for believing in me even when I didn't, I dedicate this work to them.

Karlsruhe, March 2010

Mircea Trifu

Contents

Contents

Contents

Chapter 1.

Introduction

This work is intended to support program understanding of object-oriented code, by creating direct traceability links between functional concerns and their implementations in code. The traceability links are discovered by an automated tool, based on a high-level specification of these concerns, provided by the software engineer.

The term *concern* is highly overloaded and has a very broad meaning, with typical examples including requirements, features, data structures, and extra-functional properties. Within the context of this work, we restrict this broad meaning and basically regard concerns as requirements. The term concern will be defined more precisely in section 2.1, but for the time being this intuitive definition should be sufficient to define the goal of this thesis, and to present an overview of our approach.

1.1. Problem Definition

In general, the lack of direct traceability between concerns and their implementations makes program understanding significantly harder, and contributes to increased software evolution costs. In particular, the understanding of object-oriented code is especially hindered by crosscutting concerns, whose implementations are typically scattered over many locations and tangled with the implementations of other concerns.

1.1.1. Context of the Work

Program understanding is a prerequisite for any software evolution activity, and because it has a strong reasoning component, it is difficult and time-consuming. According to Brooks, program understanding involves "the reconstruction of the

1

domain knowledge used by the initial developer. Understanding involves recreating the mappings from the problem domain into the programming domain" (Brooks 83). A similar view is shared by Biggerstaff, who sees program understanding as a *concept assignment problem* and defines it as "the problem of discovering human oriented concepts and assigning them to their implementation oriented counterparts" (Biggerstaff 93).

According to Mens and Demeyer (Mens 08b), on average 50% of the costs associated with software evolution are spent on program understanding. The percentage is estimated based on data collected in the industry (Corbi 89), and agrees with estimates from Ben-Menachem and Marliss (Ben-Menachem 97). As for the software evolution costs, "for long-lifetime systems, these costs are likely to exceed the development costs by a factor of 3 or 4" (Sommerville 06). The same view is shared by Pressman (Pressman 01), and supported by empirical data from the industry (Koskinen 04; Erlikh 00; Putnam 97; Jones 91; Moad 90; Lientz 80), suggesting that software evolution costs represent between 60% and 80% of the total costs associated with a software system over its entire life cycle. This means that program understanding alone accounts for roughly a third of the total costs, thus making it the most expensive activity of the entire software life cycle.

One of the causes of these high costs is that software systems do not exhibit a clear separation of concerns at the implementation level. The term *separation of concerns*, attributed to Dijkstra (Dijkstra 82), denotes a fundamental principle in programming, which enables software developers to master the complexity of a software system, by decomposing it into a set of distinct concerns, which are addressed in turn, one at a time. Concern separation is very effective, because it allows developers to focus their attention on a single concern and ignore the details of other concerns. Nowadays, it is widely accepted as justified to invest more effort in the initial development of a system, if this investment improves the separation of concerns. Even though this doesn't always happen in practice, the previous data on program understanding costs suggests that such an investment eventually pays off manifold.

Over the years, the evolution of programming paradigms and programming best practices brought new ways to achieve better separation of concerns. Programming language constructs such as procedures, abstract data types and classes facilitate this separation by means of encapsulation and information hiding, whereas architectural styles and design patterns provide rudimentary solutions for typical concern decomposition problems. The IEEE Standard Glossary of Software Engineering Terminology defines encapsulation as "a software development technique that consists of isolating a system function or a set of data and operations on those data within a module and providing precise specifications for the module" (IEEE 90), and information hiding as "a software development technique in which each module's interface reveals as little as possible about the module's inner workings and other modules are prevented from using information about the module that is not in the module's interface specification" (IEEE 90). In his seminal paper, Parnas pointed out that both encapsulation and information hiding are essential to achieve a good separation of concerns (Parnas 72).

Because different language constructs favour the encapsulation of different types of concerns, and because different architectural styles and design patterns impose different concern decompositions, the implementation of a concern in an existing system is constrained by the capabilities of the programing language and by the previously made architectural, design and implementation decisions.

Research on morphogenic software at the IBM T. J. Watson Research Center showed that concerns take many forms and shapes, and while their separation is highly desirable, it is also very hard to achieve at the implementation level. At the requirements level, concerns may overlap, vary from very general to very specific and even contradict one another. They define a decomposition of the system across multiple dimensions. Because traditional (object-oriented) programming languages suffer from a problem known in the literature as the *tyranny of the dominant decomposition* (Tar 99), meaning that they support only a single dominant dimension of decomposition at a time, it is impossible to simultaneously encapsulate all concerns using the available language constructs, regardless of architectural, design and implementation decisions. Concerns, which cannot be encapsulated, are called *crosscutting concerns*, because their implementations crosscut the implementations of other concerns.

1.1.2. Problem Statement

Although working with concern decompositions at the requirements level is very useful and accessible to developers, the implementations of these concerns in object-oriented code is typically interleaved to form an integrated software system. The implementation of a new concern may also produce new classes, but it will also require inserting some program fragments in the existing classes. And because the existing class structure supports a single dimension of decomposition at a time, the implementations of crosscutting concerns end up "scattered over many locations and tangled with the implementations of other concerns, resulting in a system that is hard to explore and understand" (Ceccato 05).

In the general case the relationships between concerns and classes are complex many-to-many relationships, typically known only by the developers. In the rare cases, when these relationships are partially documented, it is usually done in the form of a *traceability matrix*. Commonly used in *traceability analysis*, a traceability matrix is "a matrix that records the relationship between two or more products of the development process; for example, a matrix that records the relationship between the requirements and the design of a given software component" (IEEE 90). In case of an encapsulated concern, the traceability matrix may also contain the names of the major classes involved in its implementation, but not the level of detail required to support program understanding.

Existing approaches to traceability analysis typically require a rigourous requirements engineering process and the existence of detailed up-to-date traceability information. And because maintaining these traceability links is a difficult and time-consuming activity requiring a lot of manual effort, it is not considered cost-effective by developers and managers (Gotel 94). What is needed are methods and tools to automatically identify such traceability links.

1.2. Goal and Criteria

The goal of the present work is to support program understanding of object-oriented code during software evolution, by creating and maintaining direct traceability links between functional concerns defined at the requirements level and their respective implementations in code. The focus of this work is on functional concerns, because functional concerns are typically addressed by the code alone, whereas non-functional concerns are typically addressed by both the code and its execution environment. We achieve this goal by developing a tool-supported method to identify the implementations of functional concerns in object-oriented code, which uses:

- a high-level manual specification of functional concerns, and
- an automated discovery of functional concern implementations.

In order to be useful in practice, our approach must fulfill the following criteria, which we regard as being essential for any approach of this nature.

- **Expressiveness:** The method should be able to capture functional concerns and the typical relationships between them, including concern overlaps and hierarchic refinements.

- **Accuracy:** The concern identification method should be accurate, meaning that the results it produces should be similar to those produced by a human expert, after a careful examination of the code and a manual identification of the concern implementations.

- **Practicability:** The method should be able to handle the typical language features found in most object-oriented languages: structured data types, object aliasing, exception handling, dynamic dispatch, and polymorphism.

- **Scalability:** The method should be applicable to realistic software systems, having at least the size of a typical subsystem (around 200 classes).

- **Automation:** The method should allow a high degree of automation, meaning that it should allow the creation of tools to automate as much as possible of the concern identification process.

  Note that a full automation is not possible, because the creation of an initial subset of the traceability links requires semantic knowledge about and a deeper understanding of the software system.

1.3. Application Scenario

The application scenario targeted in this work is the evolution of an existing object-oriented software system. As pointed out by Lehman's Law of Continuing Change (Lehman 74), a software systems must undergo a continuous process of change in order to avoid becoming progressively less satisfactory. Software changes may occur due to many causes, extensively documented in the literature (Sommerville 06), but they are always expressed at the requirements level.

While expressing a change at the requirements level is natural and straight-forward, typically affecting a single concern, due to the fact that concern implementations may be scattered over many locations and tangled with the implementations of other concerns, reflecting the change at the code level may turn out to be very difficult. A software engineer must first find all the code fragments affected by the change, which in the case of cross-cutting concerns can be very time consuming when done manually. Then he must study the code in order to understand not only every fragment in isolation, but also the interdependencies between those fragments.

The approach presented in this work allows a software engineer to specify a set of hierarchically refined functional concerns in a persistent form, using a simple data-oriented abstraction, and for each such concern a minimal set of direct code traceability links, which are then processed by an automated tool to identify the code fragments, belonging to the implementation of this particular concern. Furthermore, identified concern implementations are presented at a level of abstraction suitable for program understanding.

The main advantage of this approach is that it makes no assumptions about the initial development of the analyzed software system and it does not require the use of a formal requirements engineering process. The above-mentioned concern intent specification consists of a small subset of the traceability links, which must be defined only once, either during the initial implementation of the concern or during the implementation of an evolutionary change affecting the concern. Once created this specification can be reused for subsequent evolution activities targeting the same concern, if the concern definition itself, but not its implementation, remains unchanged.

1.4. Approach Summary and Contributions

Concern identification aims at identifying the implementation of a concern in existing code. While being part of program understanding, concern identification received special attention because it is the part that can be automated, whereas the actual understanding is inherently a human activity. Concern identification typically consists of two steps: the specification of *concern seeds* and the identification of concern implementations. A concern seed is a well-chosen program element from the implementation of a concern, used as as a starting point for the identification of concern implementations. Each concern is delimited by a small set of concern seeds, which are then expanded using some predefined expansion rule to obtain a larger set of program elements, used in the concern's implementation, called the *concern extent*. The concern extent is a more or less abstract representation of the identified concern implementation.

The concern identification approach, described in the present work, uses a tool-supported but manual concern seed specification, and a fully automated identification of concern extents.

Concerns are described using the Hierarchic Concern Model, where each concern is treated as a gray-box and defined in terms of its subconcerns, the inputs it uses and the outputs it produces. The model allows a very accurate representation of the concern space, because it supports a hierarchic decomposition of concerns and a natural way to express overlapping concerns.

At the implementation level, the inputs of a concern are represented by abstract locations called *information sources*, and its outputs by abstract locations called *information sinks*. Abstract locations are statically distinguishable variables and represent all kinds of named or unnamed entities, capable of storing values, such as class fields, local variables, formal parameters, exception parameters, return value variables, object context variables, and object creation variables. Note that an abstract location represents all the variables defined at a given location in code. For example, a class field will be represented by a single abstract location regardless of the number of created class instances.

Although finding abstract locations in code actually amounts to creating a mapping between the requirements level and the implementation level, this mapping is much easier to create than the mapping between concerns and classes, because the relationships between inputs and outputs on the one hand and their corresponding information sources and sinks on the other, are simple one-to-one relationships. The mapping is typically specified manually by the developer, but its discovery is often supported by tools. And although finding the information sources and sinks usually requires detailed knowledge about what the system does at the requirements level, it requires very little knowledge about how it does it at the implementation level.

The concern identification approach, described in the present work, operates on a concern graph, consisting of abstract locations as nodes and labelled direct flow relations as edges. A direct flow relation between two abstract locations means that the value of the source abstract location is used to produce the value of the target abstract location. In order to differentiate between different call or object contexts of the involved abstract locations, we encode these contexts into the labels of the corresponding edge in the concern graph.

Depending on the type of value influence between abstract locations, we define three categories of direct flow relations: dataflow relations to capture direct value transfer between abstract locations, inheritance relations to capture potential value transfer to and from overriding methods as a result of dynamic binding, and direct dependency relations to capture data dependencies other than value transfer between abstract locations.

Our approach treats the identification of concern implementations as a context-free language reachability problem (Reps 97) in the concern graph. For each concern, it uses the manually specified information sources and sinks as concern seeds, and

7

determines a data-oriented abstraction of the concern at the implementation level, called the *concern skeleton*, which contains all the *flow paths* from the information sources to the information sinks.

A *flow path* is defined as a valid path inside the concern graph, such that the word obtained by concatenating the sequence of edge labels in the path is a word in the associated context-free language. The intuitive meaning of such a path between two abstract locations is that the value of the start abstract location is potentially used to produce the value of the end abstract location. The algorithm to extract flow paths is based on a demand-driven context-sensitive and object-sensitive analysis of the concern graph.

Given how they are obtained, it may happen that two concern skeletons are not completely disjoint. Their intersection is considered to represent a shared subconcern of the initial concerns, and as such is extracted as a separate concern skeleton and aggregated by both parent concern skeletons. After performing this extraction on all overlapping pairs of concern skeletons, a hierarchic decomposition of the concern skeletons is obtained, which facilitates a modular understanding of the code.

Because program understanding also involves understanding the interaction between concerns, we define a number of simplified representations of the system, called *concern maps*. Concern maps are meant to provide overviews of the entire system on a particular aspect. Particularly useful for program understanding are: the *concern aggregation map*, highlighting the hierarchic decomposition of concern skeletons, the *concern interaction map*, highlighting the data dependencies between concern skeletons, and the *concern dispersion map*, highlighting the scattering and tangling of concerns with respect to classes.

The above described approach is implemented by a prototype tool called CoDEx. The validation, carried out with CoDEx, shows that the concern skeleton, defined in the Hierarchic Concern Model, is a suitable abstraction, capable to express functional concerns in object-oriented code (Expressiveness). Furthermore, the evaluation shows that our approach is able to accurately identify concern skeletons (Accuracy) in a real object-oriented software system (Practicability), having at least the size of a typical subsystem (Scalability). Moreover, our approach handles the identification of concern skeletons in a fully automated fashion, and although creating the initial concern intent specification is largely manual, the specification contains only a small set of concern seeds, which can also be reused in subsequent revisions of the code, provided that the specified concerns, but not their implementations, remain unchanged (Automation).

The main contributions of this work can be summarized as follows:

- The **Hierarchic Concern Model**, supporting multiple simultaneous hierarchic concern refinements across overlapping dimensions. The model defines a concern skeleton as a gray-box abstract representation of a concern at the implementation level, consisting of a manually specified concern intent, which defines its inputs, outputs, and contained subconcerns, and an automatically identified concern extent.

- The **CoDEx language** for specifying concern intents. Featuring a simple straight-forward syntax, the language allows a very precise and at the same time very concise delimitation of functional concerns, which can be reused for multiple versions of the code base.

- A method for **automated identification of concern skeletons**, based on context-free language reachability in a directed multigraph structure, called the concern graph. In order to address the accuracy-scalability tradeoff, the method supports multiple flow analysis techniques (insensitive, context-sensitive, and object-sensitive), and a configurable precision factor for the object-sensitive flow analysis.

- A technique for the **detection and separation of superimposed class roles**, resulted from multiple interface inheritance. The detection is based on a heuristic rule inspired by the Interface Segregation Principle (Martin 96a), and the separation is achieved by creating dedicated copies of each abstract location for each superimposed class role.

- The **Reduced Concern Graph** and the **Growing Flow Sets** techniques, which support the selection of concern seeds, by filtering and significantly reducing the search space investigated manually by the software engineer.

- An **extensible tool (CoDEx)**, implementing the above mentioned method for the Java programming language.

1.5. Outline of the Thesis

The rest of this thesis is structured as follows. Chapter 2 introduces the basic terminology used in the field of concern identification and provides a concise overview of related work, both background work used by our approach and competing approaches. The competitive state of the art is classified and assessed based on the criteria defined in section 1.2.

Chapters 3 through 5 constitute the core of the thesis, with chapter 3 providing the theoretical foundation of our approach. The chapter defines the basic theoretical concepts such as the flow relations, and the traceability function, and introduces the Hierarchic Concern Model, used for expressing functional concerns in object-oriented code.

Chapter 4 defines the concern graph used by our concern identification approach, and provides a concrete mapping from the Java programming language to this structure. It also discusses a technique to deal with software libraries, which can be applied even if the source code of the library is not available.

Chapter 5 presents our concern identification approach, which uses a manual concern intet specification, consisting of concern seeds and subconcern definitions, to automatically identify abstract representations of the concern implementations, called concern skeletons. The chapter also discusses the selection of suitable concern seeds, and introduces three concern maps to support the understanding of the interdependencies between concern skeletons.

The implemented tool-support and the case-study based validation of our approach are covered in chapter 6, which also contains an overall assessment of the approach using the criteria discussed above. The details of the experimental setup used and the complete set of measurements collected during the validation are presented in appendix A.

Finally, chapter 7 provides a short summary of the contributions and results of this thesis, discusses the assumptions and limitations of our approach, and presents opportunities for future work.

Chapter 2.

Background and Related Work

Establishing traceability between functional concerns and their implementations in code is a classical problem, as old as software development itself. It has been tackled in many different ways by a multitude of approaches, spanning several research fields. The purpose of this chapter is to provide an overview of these research fields and the related work addressing this problem.

Because each research field has its own special focus, several approaches discussed in this chapter are only marginally related to our goal. But we chose to briefly discuss them anyway, because the techniques they employ are similar to the ones used in our approach. However, the main focus of this chapter is on competing concern identification approaches, which are examined critically with respect to the criteria presented in section 1.2.

2.1. Terminology

Before discussing related work, we have to introduce the most important terms used in this thesis, as follows:

Requirement is "a condition or capability that must be met or possessed by a system or system component to satisfy a contract, standard, specification, or other formally imposed documents" (IEEE 90).

Note that this definition does not make any assumptions about granularity and does not refer exclusively to high-level requirements, typically written using informal language in a requirements document.

Functional Requirement is "a requirement that specifies a function that a system or system component must be able to perform" (IEEE 90).

Note that this definition also does not make any assumptions about granularity, meaning that it also includes technical requirements, defined as a result of the already made architectural, design and implementation decisions. Note that a technical requirement is always a functional requirement, even if it addresses a higher-level non-functional requirement. For instance, the requirement to use a challenge-based authentication system is a technical requirement addressing the higher-level non-functional requirement of security. In order to distinguish between functional and non-functional requirements, we use the following mental model. If a requirement can be implemented using a Turing machine, without further refining it through additional design decisions, then it is a functional requirement, and if it cannot, then it is a non-functional requirement.

Concern is a very general term used to refer to "any matter of interest in a software system" (Sutton-Jr. 05), but for the purpose of this thesis we restrict its definition to denote a self-contained collection of one or more functional requirements, with explicitly specified required inputs and provided outputs. Being self-contained is the property enabling separation of concerns, and it just means that the functionality represented by a concern can be expressed, understood and addressed separately from other concerns.

Crosscutting Concern is a concern, whose implementation cannot be encapsulated in object-oriented code using the available language constructs in such a way, that this implementation is in line with the intended architecture, design and adopted implementation conventions of the software system. The implementation of a crosscutting concern in object-oriented code is said to "crosscut the implementations of other concerns" (Kiczales 97) and as a result, it is "*scattered* over many locations and *tangled* with the implementations of other concerns" (Ceccato 05).

Although intuitively suggestive, the name is somewhat misleading, because it suggests that being crosscutting is an attribute of the concern itself, and not an attribute of its implementation. In reality, the same concern may have a perfectly encapsulated implementation in one software system, and an alternate crosscutting implementation in a different system.

Homogeneous Concern is a crosscutting concern, whose implementation exhibits a broad scattering of very similar code in each location (Colyer 04). The classic examples of a homogeneous concern is the *Logging* concern (also called *Tracing*), which involves inserting a few statements at the beginning or the end of each selected method, in order to trace the runtime execution order of these methods.

Heterogeneous Concern is a crosscutting concern, whose implementation exhibits a broad scattering of different logic in each location (Colyer 04). As opposed to homogeneous concerns, heterogeneous concerns are usually larger and more difficult to understand, with typical examples including a custom serialization / persistency mechanism of an object hierarchy.

Concern Intent is "the objective of a concern" (Marin 07). It defines what the concern is supposed to do at the code level. In the context of this work, a formal definition of this term will be provided in section 3.2.4.

Concern Extent is "the concrete representation of a concern in source code" (Marin 07), the actual set of program elements contributing to its implementation. The extent describes how the concern intent is implemented. A formal definition of this term, used in the context of this work, will be provided in section 3.2.4.

Concern Identification, also referred to as *concept location* or *feature location*, is a research field aimed at finding the implementation of a concern in existing software systems. It is used to support program understanding and represents a necessary step for any software evolution activity.

Concern Seed is tyically a well-chosen program element, used as a starting point in concern identification. Concern seeds are usually specified manually by the user, but they can also be identified automatically using some heuristic rule. Automatically identified seeds are sometimes called candidate seeds, because they must be reviewed and confirmed by the user.

2.2. Static Program Analysis

Static program analysis reunites "compile-time techniques for predicting safe and computable approximations to the set of values or behaviours arising dynamically at run-time when executing a program on a computer" (Nielson 99). It represents one of the two large categories of program analysis techniques, the other one being dynamic program analysis.

Both categories of program analysis focus on the dynamic properties of the program, but as already suggested in the previous definition, static program analysis techniques obtain their results by analyzing the source code or sometimes the object code of the program in question, without executing it, whereas dynamic program analysis techniques obtain their result by executing the program in question on a set of input test cases.

Both categories have advantages and disadvantages, and choosing the right category is often a trade-off between precision and generality. As a general rule, static program analyses provide less precise but general results, whereas dynamic program analyses provide results, which are more precise but restricted to the set of input test cases.

Depending on the dynamic properties they address, static program analyses come in many shapes and forms, with typical examples including data flow analysis, control flow analysis, type analysis, and pointer analysis. Note that there are many kinds of static program analyses, but we concentrate on data flow and pointer analyses, because they are more relevant in the context of this thesis.

As pointed out by Nielson et al. (Nielson 99), static program analyses can be classified according to the following criteria:

- Scope of analysis. Based on this criterion, there are two kinds of static program analysis: *intraprocedural* analysis, localized to the body of a single procedure, and *interprocedural* analysis, supporting the analysis of entire programs across procedure boundaries. Interprocedural analysis is significantly harder, because it has to deal with the calling of procedures and the returning from calls.

- Flow-sensitivity. A static program analysis can be *flow-sensitive*, meaning that it takes into account the execution order of the statements of a program, or *flow-insensitive*, meaning that it ignores this execution order.

Depending on the way they handle different call and object contexts, interprocedural analyses can be further classified based on the following criteria:

- Context-Sensitivity. A *context-sensitive* analysis takes into account the call context of a procedure and differentiates between different call sites, whereas a *context-insensitive* ignores the call context and merges together all the different call sites for a given procedure.

- Object-Sensitivity. Based on this criterion, an analysis may be *object-sensitive*, in which case it takes into account the object context of a field and differentiates between different instances of a field contained in different objects, and *object-insensitive*, in which case it ignores the object context and merges together all instances of a field from all containing objects of a given class.

Note that context-sensitivity and object-sensitivity are independent of each other, and can theoretically appear in all combinations. However, because object-sensitivity appeared much later, out of necessity to improve the precision of the static program analyses of object-oriented languages, the combination context-insensitive and object-sensitive is not very common. In order to simplify the formulation within this thesis, we use the term *insensitive* to refer to an analysis, which is both context-insensitive and object-insensitive.

Static program analyses are typically implemented using a wide range of techniques, one of which being particularly relevant to our tool-supported concern identification approach. The technique was introduced by Reps (Reps 97; Reps 98) and is based on context free language reachability (CFL-reachability), a generalization of ordinary graph reachability. Reps showed that several static program analysis problems, such as interprocedural dataflow analysis, flow-insensitive pointer analysis, and program slicing, can be formulated as CFL-reachability problems and solved using a simple dynamic programming algorithm.

The CFL-reachability problem is the problem of identifying a path in a labelled graph, such that the word obtained by concatenating the arc labels is a valid word in a given context-free language. Reps introduced a context free language of balanced parentheses to label the arcs of a graph, and showed that this language can be used to compute precise context-sensitive solutions to the above mentioned static program analysis problems.

2.2.1. Data Flow Analysis

Data flow analysis is an important part of static program analysis, concerned with deriving information about the flow of data along program execution paths. Data flow analysis can answer whether a value computed at a given point in a program can reach another point without being altered.

Because not all points in the execution of a program are equally interesting, data flow analysis is typically performed on an abstract representation of the program, called the control flow graph, whose nodes are basic blocks and the edges represent the flow of control between them during execution. A basic block is a maximal group of consecutive statements in a program, having a single control flow entry point at the beginning of the block, and a single control flow exit point at the end of the block. This means that a basic block may not contain a control flow altering statement except as its last statement, and cannot contain targets of jump or branch statements except as its first statement.

Because data flow analysis is mostly used for compiler optimizations, it is covered extensively in the classic compiler construction textbooks (Aho 86).

15

Data flow analyses can be classified as forward analyses or backward analyses. The typical example of a forward data flow analysis is the *reaching definitions* analysis, which determines for each basic block the variable definitions reaching its first statement. The analysis is used for the determination of a definition-use (DU) chain, which links a block defining a variable to all the blocks using it. The typical example of a backward data flow analysis is the *live variables* analysis, which determines for each basic block which variables are live after the last statement of the block. This analysis has applications in the elimination of dead code.

The first efficient solution to a data flow analysis problem was proposed by Kildall (Kildall 73) and is based on a fixed point iteration, solving a set of data flow equations for each basic block. The actual equations depend on the concrete data flow analysis and the structure of the control flow graph, but as a general rule there are two types of equations: equations which derive the exit information of a node from its entry information, and equations which derive the entry information of a node from the exit information of its predecessors.

In the classic literature, Kildall's solution is called the Maximal Fixed Point (MFP) solution, and although it is always easily computable, it is not always precise. A more precise solution is the Meet Over all Paths (MOP) solution, which directly propagates data flow information along the paths of the control flow graph, but as proven by Kam and Ullman (Kam 77), this solution is not always computable. A detailed theoretical presentation of both MFP and MOP solutions is covered by Nielson et al. (Nielson 99).

2.2.2. Pointer Analysis

Pointer or points-to analysis is a type of static program analysis, concerned with determining the set of possible variables (storage locations) a pointer or a reference can point to, during the execution of a program. This set is called the *points-to* set of the pointer.

Another analysis, which is strongly related to pointer analysis and is solvable using the same techniques, is the so called alias analysis, which determines whether two pointers may point to the same variable. Alias analysis can answer if two pointers are unaliased, meaning that the two pointers can never point to the same variable, may-aliased, meaning that there is at least one execution path on which the two pointers point to the same variable, or must-aliased, meaning that the two pointers must point to the same variable on every execution path.

With the advent of object-oriented languages, encouraging the heavy use of dynamic memory allocation on the heap, the importance of pointer analysis increased significantly, which is also reflected by the great attention it received in the last decades, since its introduction by Weihl (Weihl 80).

The first scalable pointer analysis was introduced by Steensgaard (Steensgaard 96), who proposes a context-insensitive equality-based solution, in which the points-to sets of two pointers are either equal or disjoint. The approach creates equivalence classes for pointers by repeatedly merging the points-to sets of aliased pointers and making them point to the merged set. Steensgaard's analysis can be implemented in near-linear time, but it is rather imprecise.

A more precise but still context-insensitive pointer analysis was introduced by Andersen (Andersen 94). Andersen's analysis is called inclusion-based or subset-based, because an assignment between two pointers results in the points-to set of the R-value pointer to be included in the points-to set of the L-value pointer. Despite being more expensive than equality-based approaches, inclusion-based approaches are more popular because of their increased precision, which is why Andersen's analysis was used as basis for hundreds of increasingly better pointer analyses.

Flow-sensitive pointer analysis was first presented by Choi et al. (Choi 93), but their analysis was context-insensitive. One of the earliest influential papers, describing a flow-sensitive context-sensitive pointer analysis, was published by Emani et al. (Emami 94). Milanova et al. (Milanova 02; Milanova 05) were the first to introduce object-sensitivity, while Shridharan et al. (Sridharan 05) were the first to present a demand-driven pointer analysis, which only calculates the points-to set for a single user-specified pointer.

2.2.3. Static Program Slicing

Static program slicing is an important technique used in static program analysis to determine an executable subset of the statements, which may affect or may be affected by the computation at a given point, during the execution of a program. This subset of statements is called a program slice, and it was first defined by Weiser (Weiser 79; Weiser 84).

As suggested by the previous definition, it is possible to compute two types of program slices: a backward slice, consisting of an executable set of statements, which may affect the values of a set of variables at a given statement, and a forward slice,

consisting of the set of statements, which may be affected by the variable definitions at a given statement. The pair consisting of a statement and a set of variables
of interest is called a *slicing criterion*, and is used to define a program slice.

Initially, static program slicing was designed to support debugging of programs
(Weiser 82), but it was since used for various purposes, including testing, information flow control, and software maintenance. There are literally hundreds of papers
dealing with static program slicing, which is why giving a complete overview of the
entire field is nearly impossible. Comprehensive surveys of program slicing techniques were presented by Tip (Tip 95), Xu et al. (Xu 05) and Krinke (Krinke 03).

Program slicing is typically performed on system dependence graphs (Horwitz 88;
Horwitz 90), which are an extension of program dependence graphs supporting
multiple procedures. The program dependence graph is an intermediate program
representation, which "makes explicit both the data and control dependences for
each operation in a program" (Ferrante 87). Although program dependence graphs
were originally designed to support the implementation of various compiler optimizations, they turned out to be a suitable data structure for static program slicing
(Ottenstein 84).

Gallagher et al. (Gallagher 06) present an improved version of program slicing,
called *stop-list slicing*, which extends the classic slicing criterion with a list of variables acting as termination points for the analysis, called the stop-list. The purpose
of this list is to enable a better control over the scope of the analysis, and thus allow
software engineers to focus on the computation of interest. The idea to use a stop-
list was also used in our bounded flow set extraction algorithm, discussed in chapter
5.3.3.

From the above-mentioned application fields of program slicing, we briefly discuss
information flow control, because of its relevance in the context of this thesis. Information flow control is a technique for identifying security leaks in programs, which
may affect either the confidentiality of data or the integrity of certain computations
(Hammer 09a; Hammer 09b). Of particular interest is language-based information
flow control, which can answer whether there is a flow of information from a source
abstract location to a target abstract location. Information flow can either be *explicit*, resulting from direct value transfer, or *implicit*, resulting from conditional execution.

As in the case of static program slicing, information flow control typically uses system dependence graphs as internal representation (Hammer 09a; Hammer 09b),
but if the focus lies on data confidentiality alone, the analysis can also be performed

on a flow graph, consisting of abstract locations and flow edges (Liu 08; Liu 09), which is similar to our concern graph, discussed in chapter 4.

Despite this similarity, we do not regard information flow control approaches as competition for our approach, because their goals are very different from ours.

2.3. Traceability Analysis

In software engineering, traceability refers to "the ability to trace between software artefacts, generated and modified during the software life-cycle" (Bohner 96). These artefacts are sometimes called software life-cycle objects (SLOs), and can represent almost anything from a piece of requirement to a software component or a test case.

Although traceability analysis can also be used for other software engineering activities, Bohner and Arnold (Bohner 96) regard traceability analysis as an important part of change impact analysis, concerned with "examining the dependency relationships between all types of SLOs", for the purpose of "identifying the potential consequences of a change or estimating what needs to be modified to accomplish a change".

Traceability links can involve any type of SLOs, but because of its obvious importance to software verification and validation, traceability analysis involving requirements received a great deal of attention in the past decades. Gotel and Finkelstein define requirements traceability as "the ability to describe and follow the life of a requirement, in both a forward and a backward direction" (Gotel 94).

Being a part of requirements engineering, requirements traceability analysis was extensively covered in many textbooks dealing with this topic (Wiegers 03; Kotonya 98), and based on the direction in which the traceability links are traversed, we distinguish between: *forward traceability* analysis, concerned with tracing a requirement to the artefacts derived from it (design documents, code, test plans, etc.), and *backward traceability* analysis, concerned with tracing a requirement to the source (person, institution, law, argument, etc.) which produced the requirement (Wieringa 95).

Traceability links can be represented in a number of ways, ranging from simple textual cross-references inserted in a requirements document, to full-blown entity-relationship models stored in relational databases. A very popular approach is to use a *traceability matrix*, which is basically a large table capturing the traceability links between two types of SLOs such as requirements and software components, or requirements and test cases.

Note that the two dimensions of this matrix need not necessarily be different. It is entirely possible and quite common practice to create a traceability matrix, capturing the traceability links between SLOs of the same type, such as the relationships between requirements, or the relationships between software components. In such cases, the traceability matrix can either be a connectivity matrix, capturing only direct relationships, or a reachability matrix, capturing the transitive closure of the direct traceability relationships.

The main difficulty faced by requirements traceability is the need to keep traceability links always in sync with the changes in requirements and implementation. This is rarely the case, because although there are many tools to support traceability analysis, maintaining these links is still a largely manual effort, and it is not perceived by developers and managers as being cost-effective (Gotel 94).

The above mentioned problem, combined with the fact that the granularity of SLOs typically used in traceability analysis is too high to support program understanding, constitutes the key motivator behind this thesis.

2.4. Concern Encapsulation

Concern encapsulation approaches try to circumvent the traceability problem between functional concerns and their implementations in code altogether, by providing the means to capture and encapsulate each concern separately. As pointed out in section 1.1.1, because it is impossible to simultaneously encapsulate all concerns using the typical object-oriented language constructs, some concerns end up having a crosscutting implementation in object-oriented code. Given the fact that it is particularly difficult to create and maintain traceability links between crosscutting concerns and their respective implementations in code, most concern encapsulation approaches explicitly target these concerns.

One of the most prominent such approaches is called Aspect Oriented Programming (AOP), and was introduced by Kiczales et al. (Kiczales 97). AOP is "a programming paradigm of the post-OOP era" (Hayes 03), which extends the Object Oriented Programming (OOP) paradigm with new language constructs, called *aspects*, especially designed to encapsulate crosscutting concerns.

Although AOP achieves a good encapsulation of homogeneous concerns, it often does so at the expense of information hiding. A software system developed using AOP typically consists of an object-oriented core, implementing the main concerns, and a number of aspects, implementing the crosscutting concerns. An aspect is basically a set of object-oriented code fragments together with the associated rules to inject these fragments into the object-oriented core. With the exception of the most trivial programming tasks, the specification of the injection rules requires intimate knowledge about the object-oriented code, including its inner workings, which makes aspect code fragile with respect to changes in the object-oriented core. This non-uniform treatment of functional concerns severely limits the capability of AOP to explicitly capture interactions between crosscutting concerns, thus seriously hindering the maintainability and understandability of AOP code.

Recognizing this drawback, Rajan and Sullivan (Rajan 05) introduce a new language construct, which they call *classpect*, intended to merge into a single unifying concept both the characteristics of a class and those of an aspect. Unfortunately, this unification was done only at the syntactic level and it resulted in a language construct with poor information hiding capabilities, which essentially uses the same fragment injection mechanism as AOP. As a result, the approach failed to achieve a significant impact.

A very ambitious approach, concerned not only with the syntactic aspects of concern encapsulation, but also with defining a true concern-oriented software engineering was developed at IBM T. J. Watson Research Center (Ossher 99; Tar 99). The approach is called Multi-Dimensional Separation of Concerns (MDSOC) and it allows a separation and encapsulation of concerns over multiple simultaneous and possibly overlapping dimensions. The implementation of a concern is captured by a *hypermodule*, consisting of a set of object-oriented program fragments called *hyperslices* and a set of composition relationships between hyperslices. Given the fact that the result of composing hyperslices is also a hyperslice, MDSOC allows a hierarchic definition of concerns.

This approach is a generalization of Subject Oriented Programming (Harrison 93), and was implemented in the Concern Manipulation Environment (CME) (Harrison 04), an integrated environment for aspect-oriented software development (AOSD). The CME supports the definition, encapsulation, extraction, and composition of concerns. It also offers concern identification support through an integrated query-based search framework, called PUMA (Tarr 04).

Although the approach is quite ingenious and has a very powerful concern model, it is limited by the capabilities of the composition language, which supports concern composition only at the level of class members. As a result, its applicability to existing object-oriented systems, exhibiting tangling of concern implementations inside method bodies, is rather limited.

Strongly related to AOP and MDSOC is the Feature Oriented Programming (FOP) paradigm, which is a forward engineering methodology, supporting the development of software product lines. As defined by Clemens and Northrop (Clements 01), a software product line (SPL) is "a set of software-intensive systems sharing a common, managed set of features that satisfy the specific needs of a particular market segment or mission and that are developed from a common set of core assets in a prescribed way".

A feature is basically a functional concern, representing a clearly defined piece of functionality of the application domain. The set of features shared by the members of a software product line are obtained through a process called domain analysis, whose outcome is a domain model that explicitly capture "the common and variable properties of the systems in a domain, the semantics of the properties and domain concepts, and the dependencies between the variable properties" (Czarnecki 00). Within this domain model, features are represented using feature diagrams, capturing not only the refinement of features, but also information about which combinations of features are valid.

Features are implemented by reusable software assets, called feature modules, which can be composed using declarative configuration languages, to produce a concrete member of the software product line. The actual technique used for the implementation and composition of feature modules depends on the chosen FOP approach. For example, the first implementation of GenVoca (Batory 92) used rudimentary C preprocessor directives, but was later replaced by mixin-layers (Smaragdakis 99; Smaragdakis 02). Mixin-layers were also used in the Algebraic Hierarchical Equations for Application Design (AHEAD) approach (Batory 03), which is basically a generalization of the GenVoca approach.

Strongly related to FOP is Kuttruff's approach (Kuttruff 09) for constructing software product lines, through invasive composition of concern implementations. The approach defines an implementation-oriented concern and composition model, more general than the mixin-based feature models of GenVoca and AHEAD, consisting of a set of typed program fragments and an associated construction plan, specifying in an algorithmic form the composition of these fragments.

The approach makes a very strict distinction between domain engineering (the engineering of the product line) and application engineering (the engineering of a concrete member of the product line), and was designed with the expressed intent to facilitate the latter. Towards that end, it defines a simple declarative configuration language, which also supports the automatic detection of invalid configurations.

2.5. Concern Identification

Concern identification is a relatively new but fervent research area. As defined in section 2.1, it is aimed at finding the implementations of functional concerns in existing software systems. Concern identification has its origins in the concept assignment problem (Biggerstaff 93), which is why the earliest approaches refer to it as *concept or feature location*. After the appearance of AOP, a new subfield of concern identification, called *aspect mining*, focusing on the identification of crosscutting concerns, emerged from within this community.

Nowadays, concern identification reunites a large number of related approaches, which can be classified based on: the information used for the identification, the identification strategy, and the concern extraction technique.

Existing approaches use a wide range of information such as:

- Structural and cross-referencing information, including member containment, inheritance, method calls, and variable accesses.
- Semantic information, encoded in the identifiers of named program elements, or contained in code comments.
- Various metrics and heuristics, including coupling and cohesion metrics, method call fan-in, and interface segregation.
- Dynamic information, typically in the form of execution traces.

We distinguish between two identification strategies:

- Decompositional strategy, designed to produce a decomposition of the software system into concerns, meaning that it identifies all concerns at once. Approaches using this identification strategy typically require no user-specified concern seeds and are fully automated, but they usually require more effort for understanding the identified concerns.
- Goal-oriented search strategy, designed to identify specific concerns, one at a time, starting from a set of concern seeds. The concern seeds can be either manually specified by the software engineer or they can be suggested automatically by a tool, based on some heuristics, and confirmed by the software engineer.

Note that an approach using the goal-oriented search strategy can also simulate the decompositional strategy, by skipping the confirmation step of the candidate concern seeds.

And finally, based on the concern extraction technique, concern identification approaches can be assigned to one of the following categories: *manual identification, pattern search, pattern recognition, clustering and formal concept analysis, clone analysis,* and *static program analysis.* The remainder of this section is structured according to these categories, and contains in addition a subsection about comparative studies of concern identification approaches.

2.5.1. Manual identification

Early work on concern identification had a strictly manual character, despite occasional support from general purpose text processing tools such as the popular Unix tool *grep*. Within this category we include all concern identification approaches, where the user has to map each program element or set of program elements to a concern manually. Manual approaches typically use a combination of structural, cross-referencing and semantic information, and employ a goal-oriented search strategy.

Chen and Rajlich (Chen 00) present a case study on feature location in a software dependence graph, extracted from the source code of the *NCSA Mosaic* web browser. The approach is based on the systematic manual exploration of the source code, dependence graph, and documentation of the system, in order to decide if the investigated program elements should be included in the feature or not. The paper envisions a scenario, where this activity is supported by an integrated tool, and identifies concrete requirements for this tool.

One of the earliest mention of crosscutting concern identification is by Robillard and Murphy (Robillard 99), who report on the successful migration of a static analysis tool, called *Jex*, to AspectJ, the flagship language of the AOP community. The paper presents a number of identified aspects, but it does not describe the method used for their identification. However, given the fact that AOP itself was only two years old at the time, we assume it was an ad-hoc manual method.

A more systematic, but still manual concern identification method was presented by Murphy et al. (Murphy 01), as part of an exploratory study on separating user-relevant features in the source code of *gnu.regexp* and *jFTPd*, using three approaches for concern encapsulation: AspectJ, Hyper/J, and a lightweight concern separation method proposed by the authors. Although the main focus of the paper is on comparing these three concern encapsulation approaches, the authors also describe the method used for identifying the concerns, which is based on a manual tagging of source code segments, using the *Feature Selection Tool* (Lai 99).

A significant improvement in tool support was presented by Lai and Murphy (Lai 02). The paper defines a methodology and a supporting tool for creating a behavioural model of a concern, with direct traceability links to the code. The approach is centered around the notion of *conceptual module*, representing a logical unit, consisting of a collection of non-contiguous source code lines. The approach was applied to manually construct a state transition model for *jFTPd*, an FTP server implemented in Java.

One of the first large-scale experiments on refactoring members of an industrial middleware product-line from IBM was conducted and documented by Colyer and Clement (Colyer 04). The paper introduces the classification of crosscutting concerns into *homogeneous* and *heterogeneous*, an presents an iterative refactoring process, involving a gradual manual discovery of concern implementations. The experiment gives valuable insights into the process of separating both homogeneous and heterogeneous concerns, and provides first evidence that heterogeneous concerns are much more difficult to identify and separate than homogeneous concerns.

Despite the fact that nowadays many different concern identification tools are available, manual identification is still used, because it can provide valuable reference concern implementations, which can be used as an evaluation base line for different concern identification approaches. Such is the case of a more recent paper by Eaddy et al. (Eaddy 07), presenting a systematic methodology for identifying concern implementations, and a suite of metrics for quantifying the crosscutting nature of the source code. Concern identification is done manually, based on a set of concern assignment guidelines, defined by the authors.

A general critique, which is a direct consequence of their lack of automation, and applies to all approaches in this category, is that they are difficult to use on a large scale. With one notable exception, all of the approaches discussed above have only been applied to small software systems, having around 10 KLOC. Furthermore, because most of these approaches rely on a manual exploration and marking of code fragments, they include only a rudimentary concern model, representing concerns as sets of program elements arranged in a flat concern space. And although, this is not a conceptual limitation of the entire category, all of the approaches discussed in this section were based on such concern models, which are incapable of capturing the relationships between functional concerns, described in section 3.1.

2.5.2. Pattern search

Pattern search approaches employ a goal-oriented search identification strategy and use primarily the semantic information encoded in the identifiers of named program elements, which some of them complement with structural and cross-referencing information.

One of the first automated concern identification approaches was presented by Hannemann and Kiczales (Hannemann 01). The approach is supported by the Aspect Mining Tool (AMT), which combines a textual search for a user-defined pattern with the extraction of type usage information, to identify homogeneous crosscutting concerns in existing object oriented code. The approach accepts queries based on type usage and regular expressions, and identifies the matching source code lines.

Although this combination of techniques arguably produces better results than each of them separately, it is still rather crude and its accuracy is not very good. The approach has a severely limited capability of expressing complex concerns, and basically regards them as flat sets of source code lines, which is why the applicability of this approach on a large scale is very difficult.

Recognizing this difficulty, Zhang and Jacobsen (Zhang 03a; Zhang 03b) built an extension of this tool, which they call the Extended Aspect Mining Tool (AMTEX), and used it for a large-scale crosscutting concern identification experiment, involving several open implementation of the *CORBA 2.0* standard: JacOrb, Orbacus and OpenORB. The proposed extensions addressed the possibility to combine several queries, and the addition of a simple type ranking feature based on usage frequency, intended to support the software engineer in writing better type usage queries.

AMTEX was quickly replaced with an own development from Zhang and Jacobsen, called PRISM (Zhang 03c; Zhang 04). Despite being newer and integrated in the Eclipse framework, PRISM presents no significant improvements over AMTEX with respect to concern identification. It supports a very similar search for user-defined textual and type usage patterns, which the authors call *fingerprints* and produces a result called a *footprint* consisting of a set of source code lines. As pointed out by the authors themselves, the prerequisite for this approach is to have semantically rich identifiers, reflecting domain concepts.

Based on the heuristic that the implementations of an interface in subclasses can, under certain conditions, represent an aspect, Tonella and Ceccato (Tonella 04b) propose an aspect mining and refactoring approach, which combines a textual pattern search for interface names with a simple coupling metric. The approach specifically looks for an interface, having a name that ends with the suffix "able" such as

`Serializable` or `Cloneable`, and if the implementations of this interface have both a low afferent and a low efferent coupling to the rest of their respective containing classes, the interface together with its implementations is considered a candidate aspect.

The main weakness of this approach is that it can only be used for a small subset of concerns, which match the above described pattern. Also, because it uses concrete name patterns, its accuracy is in general not very good, and highly dependent on interface naming conventions.

As pointed out in section 2.1, a homogeneous concern is characterized by the scattering of very similar logic in many locations across the entire code base. As in the case of the widely known *Logging* example, the scattered code of such a concern often takes the form of a single call to the same method. Exploiting this observation, Marin et al. (Marin 04; Marin 07) present an interesting approach, which identifies this invocation pattern based on the value of the fan-in metric of the target method. The approach actually calculates the fan-in metric for all methods in a system, and if the value of the fan-in metric for a given method exceeds a threshold, the method in question is considered a candidate concern seed. Because the candidate seeds can be reviewed and filtered manually, this approach can use both concern identification strategies.

Although the idea is quite original, the approach is only able to identify simple homogeneous concerns or in some cases only fragments of such concerns. Another weakness of the approach is that it provides no support for combining search patterns, meaning that the identification of complex concerns requires manual effort.

In order to facilitate the identification, understanding, and refactoring of crosscutting concern implementations Marin et al. (Marin 05; Marin 06) propose a classification of crosscutting concerns into sorts, which they describe using a fixed template, similar to the one used by Gamma et al. (Gamma 95) to describe design patterns. The template includes an informal textual description of a structural pattern, representing the typical implementation of a concern of this sort in the Java language, which is used as search pattern for the identification of crosscutting concerns of this sort.

Although the approach based on concern sorts can be used to search for several different patterns, these patterns have the same complexity level as the typical invocation pattern of a homogeneous concern, meaning that the approach suffers from the same weaknesses as the one using the fan-in metric. Furthermore, both approaches use very simple concern models, incapable of expressing concern refinement and overlap.

An important step forward in pattern specification was achieved by Robillard and Murphy (Robillard 02; Robillard 07), who propose a way to express complex search patterns based on structural dependencies between program elements. When matched against the source code of a software system, these patterns result in a program fragment consisting of named program elements such as classes, methods, and fields, as well as different kinds of cross-references such as method calls, variable reads and writes, and various type references. These patterns are specified in a tool called *FEAT*, and are captured in a structure, the authors call a *concern graph*. Note that this structure has nothing to do with our concern graph, described in chapter 4.

The above mentioned approach is very similar to the one presented by Kozaczynski and Ning (Kozaczynski 94), who also used complex pattern search to identify concepts in COBOL code. Kozaczynski and Ning define a hierarchic concept model, which allows them to specify a recognition rule, called a *plan*, for a given concept based on the set of contained subconcepts and a set of constraints, expressing structural and cross-referencing dependencies between these subconcepts.

Both approaches allow a very fine-grained specification of concern implementations, but they both use rather rudimentary concern models, incapable of expressing concern overlap. Furthermore, because the user-specified patterns are rather large and refer directly to program elements in the source code, they are not reusable for subsequent versions of the code base, making both approaches very difficult to apply on a large scale.

A somewhat similar approach, suffering from the same weaknesses, was presented by Janzen and De Volder (Janzen 03). They propose an interactive code exploration approach, supported by a tool called *JQuery*. The tool is implemented as an Eclipse plugin and incorporates an advanced query language, similar to Prolog, which can be used to express search patterns related to structural, cross-referencing, and semantic information. The results of the search are displayed in a tree structure, which can be navigated and extended by additional queries.

As briefly mentioned in section 2.4, the Concern Manipulation Environment (CME) also supports concern identification through its integrated query-based search framework called *PUMA* (Tarr 04). Queries are expressed in a powerful query language, called *Panther*, and can refer to both semantic information as well as structural and cross-referencing information.

Although the approach has a flexible hierarchic model behind it, this model and implicitly the concern identification approach are limited by the capabilities of the composition language, which supports concern composition only at the level of class members. As a result, the applicability of this approach to existing object-oriented systems, exhibiting tangling of concern implementations inside method bodies, is rather limited. Furthermore, as in the case of the two previous approaches, the specified patterns tend to be very large and strongly coupled with the existing source code, making them difficult to evolve, when the code changes.

Marcus and Maletic (Marcus 03) use an information retrieval technique called *latent semantic indexing* (LSI) to calculate the similarity between documentation and source code. Towards that end, the documentation is divided into so called external documents, where each external document represents a section in the original documentation, and the source code into source code documents, where each source code document represents a separate source file. LSI uses a term-document matrix, where each unique term is represented by a row and each document by a column, and determines the conceptual correlations between terms, given by their common occurrence in similar contexts. Based on these correlations and the terms encountered in each document, the approach calculates a similarity metric between external documents and source code documents, and if the value of this metric exceeds a predefined threshold, a traceability link is created between the external document and the source code document.

Technically speaking, this approach is not a concern identification approach, but it can be used for concern identification, if the external documents contain textual concern descriptions, taken from the documentation of the analyzed system. The main weakness of this approach is that the recovered traceability links are too coarse-grained, and even if the granularity could be increased as the authors suggest, the approach can only provide an approximate localization of concern implementations in code.

An interactive version of the above mentioned approach, suffering from the same weaknesses, was proposed by Marcus et al. (Marcus 04) to calculate the similarity between a user-specified query, expressed in natural language, and the source code of a software system. The approach works much like a search engine and returns a set of source code documents, with the property that the value of the similarity metric between each such document and the user query exceeds a certain threshold. As for the granularity of source code documents, the approach considers each function to be a separate document, and all the remaining declaration blocks in each file as an extra document.

Most of the approaches presented above rely on textual pattern search, which is why their accuracy is in general not very good, and highly dependent on a consistent and semantically rich naming scheme of the identifiers in the source code. Furthermore, because they rely on rather rudimentary concern models, none of them is able to express complex relationships between concerns, such as the ones discussed in section 3.1.

2.5.3. Pattern recognition

Pattern recognition approaches often represent fully automated versions of similar pattern search approaches, using decompositional identification strategies. These approaches do not look for specific patterns, but rather try to find frequently recurring patterns in large data sets consisting of structural, semantic, or dynamic information.

Shepherd et al. (Shepherd 05b) present an approach, based on a natural language processing technique called *lexical chaining*, to identify crosscutting concerns in existing source code. Since lexical chaining computes the semantic distance between words, based on a database of known relationships between words, the authors apply this technique to a filtered textual representation of the source code, containing only class names, method names, filed names, and comments, in order to identify semantically related sections of the source code.

The approach has a highly explorative nature and it can only be used to identify initial concern seeds. Its main weakness results from the inability of lexical chaining to handle equivocal words, for which a prior word disambiguation is needed. But because this often depends on the context, it may require human intervention. The authors themselves recognize that although the approach seems promising, it requires a significant manual effort to find the interesting lexical chains, which makes it difficult to use on a large scale.

Breu and Krinke (Breu 03; Breu 04) presents a method for recognizing recurring invocation patterns in program execution traces, based on textual matching of method signatures at entries into and exits from method executions. And because the recognized patterns represent basic building blocks for AOP aspects, the authors call them accordingly. They distinguish between two kinds of patterns: outside-aspects, representing sequences of consecutive method calls, and inside-aspects, representing sequences of nested calls. The approach was implemented in the Dynamic Aspect Mining Tool (DynAMiT) and applied on various middle-sized case studies.

A very similar but slightly improved approach for recognizing arbitrary invocation patterns in program execution traces was presented by Safyallah and Sartipi

(Safyallah 06), who apply a data mining technique, called sequential pattern mining, to recover features in the source code of the Unix drawing tool *Xfig*.

Antoniol and Guéhéneuc (Antoniol 05) propose a feature identification technique, which relies on a scenario based probabilistic ranking of events, observed in an execution trace. The approach requires two sets of test cases: one exercising the feature of interest and another not exercising it. By analyzing the execution traces obtained for each test case, the approach calculates a relevance index for each event interval, quantifying the probability that the considered event interval is relevant for the feature.

As is the case with all approaches using execution traces, the above mentioned approaches are highly dependent on the quality of the test scenarios, used for the extraction of the execution traces. Furthermore, the recognized patterns are often very small and may represent only fragments of concern implementations at best. And since the above mentioned approaches provide no suggestions on how to aggregate such patterns, their usefulness is limited to simple homogeneous crosscutting concerns.

An interesting approach, combining semantic and dynamic information to identify features, was proposed by Poshyvanyk et al. (Poshyvanyk 06; Poshyvanyk 07a). The approach not only combines two types of information, but it also combines two different techniques: a technique based on latent semantic indexing, similar to the one presented by Marcus et al. (Marcus 04), and the previously mentioned technique for scenario based probabilistic ranking of events in execution traces.

Since both techniques provide ranked facts about features, these rankings are treated as the distinct opinions of two experts, and are combined using a weighted sum, where each weight is the product of two factors: a normalization factor for the ranking, and a coefficient representing the confidence level of the corresponding expert.

Pattern recognition was also used by Breu and Zimmermann (Breu 06) to identify crosscutting concerns based on version histories. The proposed approach works by identifying insertions of method calls in each revision. It first identifies simple aspect candidates, consisting of a single target method and the corresponding calls to it, which are then combined into complex aspect candidates based on the locality of the contained calls.

Because the approach combines two simple aspect candidates only if their sets of call locations are identical, it is not very likely to identify complex aspect candidates, consisting of more than a single pair of methods, such as the typical synchronization example, consisting of a method `lock` called upon entering a critical region of code, and a method `unlock` called upon exiting the region.

The main weakness of the approach is that it is highly dependent on a very systematic programming style, with a rigorous versioning of the code. It assumes that the implementation of a crosscutting concern changes over time, and that programmers work on a single concern at a time. Although plausible, these hypothesis cannot be verified in any way, nor can such a practice be enforced. The approach requires a complete version history, covering the entire implementation of a concern from its first statement, and it only works if the primary object-oriented decomposition remains unchanged. Furthermore, the approach is able to identify only homogeneous concerns.

Another interesting approach was described by Robillard and Murphy (Robillard 03), who propose to automatically infer the implementation of a concern, based on a recorded log of program investigation activities. Although the idea is very original, technically speaking the approach does not identify concerns. It only records the source code locations visited by a human expert, when trying to manually identify a concern implementation. Its main weakness is that the recorded concern implementations unavoidably contain noise, thus reducing the accuracy of this approach.

A general critique, which applies to all approaches in this category is that their accuracy is not very good. The approaches based on textual pattern recognition are highly dependent on the naming scheme of the identifiers, while the approaches based on dynamic information are dependent on the quality of the test cases. And because the recognized patterns are rather simple, the use of these approaches is mostly limited to simple homogeneous concerns. Furthermore, the approaches in this category typically lack an expressive concern model, capable of capturing concern refinement and concern overlap.

2.5.4. Clustering and formal concept analysis

This subsection describes several decompositional concern identification approaches, which produce as result a set of clusters of related program elements. The category includes approaches based on clustering (Hartigan 75), but also approaches based on formal concept analysis (FCA) (Ganter 99), which can be regarded as a form of clustering in a bipartite graph, called the formal context, consisting of a set of objects, a set of attributes of these objects, and a set of edges, each connecting an object with an attribute. FCA identifies a family of concepts, each consisting of a maximal subset of the objects and a subset of the attributes, representing the set of all shared attributes of the objects in the first subset. The identified family of concepts represents a lattice, called the concept lattice.

Maletic and Marcus (Maletic 00; Maletic 01) present an approach, based on clustering, for identifying concepts in a program. They use latent semantic indexing to calculate a semantic similarity between source code documents, representing in this case function bodies. The set of source code documents and the computed semantic similarities between them are then represented as a weighted graph, where the weight of each edge represents the semantic similarity between the source code documents represented by the connected nodes, and a minimal spanning tree (MST) algorithm is used to cluster these source code documents. The MST algorithm is one of the simplest iterative clustering algorithms, which starts with an initial set of clusters, each containing a single source document, and in each iteration it joins two clusters if these clusters have an inter-cluster edge between them, whose weight exceeds a given threshold.

A very similar approach for recovering architectural concepts was presented by van der Spek et al. (van der Spek 08). The approach uses a complete-link hierarchical clustering algorithm to cluster methods, based on the semantic similarity between identifiers, calculated using latent semantic indexing.

Latent semantic indexing was also used by Poshyvanyk and Marcus (Poshyvanyk 07b) for locating concepts in source code. The approach is remarkably similar to the one presented by Maletic and Marcus (Maletic 00; Maletic 01), but instead of using normal clustering, it uses formal concept analysis, capable of also recovering an intentional description for each identified cluster. The approach uses a formal context, where objects are represented by the program elements, and attributes are represented by the terms obtained from the latent semantic indexing.

The main weakness of these approaches is that they can only provide an approximate localization of concern implementations in code, depending on the granularity of the considered source code documents. And since this granularity is chosen in such a way that a source code document is a function / method body, these approaches are unable to distinguish crosscutting concerns tangled within the same function / method. Furthermore, being based on the semantic information encoded in identifiers and comments, their accuracy depends on the quality of this information.

Semantic information encoded in identifiers was also used by Tourwé and Mens (Tourwé 04) to mine aspectual views in existing source code. As defined by the authors of this paper, an aspectual view is a set of structurally related named source code entities such as classes, methods, formal parameters, and fields. The approach splits identifiers into distinct words, based on the Java naming conventions (Inc. 97), and applies formal concept analysis to the set of named source code entities, using the individual words making up the identifiers as attributes. The result of the analysis is a set of natural clusters of source code entities, each cluster representing an aspectual view, semantically characterized by a common set of words.

Note that the source code entities in an aspectual view do not represent the complete implementation of an aspect, but rather a set of concern seeds, which can be used to identify an aspect candidate. The accuracy of the approach is not very good and highly dependent on the quality of identifier names. Furthermore, because the approach splits identifier names based on the Java naming conventions, its accuracy also depends on the rigorous application of these conventions.

Tonella and Ceccato (Tonella 04a) apply formal concept analysis (FCA) to program execution traces in order to mine candidate aspects in the source code. The execution traces are generated for a set of test scenarios, which exercise the main functionalities of the analyzed software system, using an instrumented version of the code base. The approach uses a formal context consisting of scenarios as objects and called class methods as attributes, and identifies potential aspect candidates in the resulting concept lattice, based on the scattering and tangling of methods with respect to the use cases. Concretely, the approach considers as a potential aspect candidate each concept labelled by methods from different classes, which in turn contain other methods that label other concepts.

A very similar approach was introduced by Eisenbarth et al. (Eisenbarth 01), and enhanced in subsequent papers (Eisenbarth 03; Koschke 05), presenting an approach, capable of refining the results obtained through the formal concept analysis of execution traces, by using a subsequent analysis of the static cross-referencing dependencies between computational units. A computational unit can be specified at various levels of granularity, including: basic blocks, methods, classes, compilation units, components, or subsystems. As opposed to the approach of Tonella and Ceccato, this approach does not assume a one-to-one correspondence between features and test scenarios, thus being able to use test scenarios, which exercise more than one feature at a time.

As is the case with all approaches using dynamic information, the approaches described above are highly dependent on the quality of the test cases used to extract the execution traces. And although the last approach we discussed tries to compensate for this weakness, by introducing a subsequent static dependency analysis step, this step can only provide a limited refinement of the initial results obtained from the execution traces.

A general critique, which applies to all approaches from this category is that they typically operate at a higher granularity level, and are not able to precisely pinpoint the implementation of a concern in source code. Most of them are only able to point at code blocks such as a method body, containing parts of this implementation, thus preventing them to distinguish between crosscutting concerns tangled within the same method body.

Another important critique is that these approaches lack expressive concern models, capable to capture complex relationships between concerns. And even though FCA is capable of identifying a family of concepts organized in a lattice, which potentially could be used to recover a hierarchic decomposition of overlapping concerns, the above mentioned approaches do not exploit this information, and only extract a flat decomposition of disjoint concerns. As for the approaches based on clustering, they are by definition unable to recover overlapping concerns.

2.5.5. Clone analysis

Clone analysis is a type of static code analysis, aimed at finding identical or nearly identical sections of source code, occurring within the code base of a single software system or a set of software systems, maintained by the same entity. Clone analysis is performed using a myriad of techniques, based on comparing textual representations, tokens, abstract syntax trees (AST), and even program dependence graphs (PDG). Although the primary application domain of clone analysis is not concern identification, several clone analysis approaches were used for the identification of homogeneous concerns. The approaches discussed below use semantic, structural and cross-referencing information, and employ decompositional identification strategies.

Bruntink et al. (Bruntink 04; Bruntink 05) apply three clone analysis techniques: one token-based, one AST-based and one PDG-based, to identify crosscutting concerns in an industrial application written in C. In order to evaluate the suitability of these techniques, the authors calculate the recall and precision values for each of the five crosscutting concerns considered, based on a set of reference concerns, annotated manually in the code. The evaluation shows that each of the techniques has its strengths and weaknesses, even though the PDG-based technique performs slightly better on average.

Clone analysis was used by Shepherd et al. (Shepherd 04) for aspect mining. The approach is very similar to the one presented above, although it concentrates more on the identification of AOP-style before aspects. It is supported by a tool called Ophir, which uses an initial PDG-based clone analysis technique, to identify potentially similar methods, followed by an AST-based clone analysis for the comparison at statement level. The combination of these two techniques makes the approach capable of identifying clones, using different variable names, exhibiting a different ordering of the statements, or containing intermingled statements. In order to improve its accuracy, this approach was later combined with the previously discussed approach from Marin et al. based on the fan-in metric, using the Timna framework (Shepherd 05a).

A general critique, which applies to all approaches based on clone analysis is that they can only be used for homogeneous concerns. Furthermore, these approaches do not identify complete concern implementations, but rather only fragments of these implementations. And because they lack an expressive concern model, they are unable to recover the complex relationships between concerns, described in section 3.1.

2.5.6. Static program analysis

Concern identification approaches based on static program analysis rely on structural and cross-referencing information, and typically employ a goal-oriented search strategy, which means that they require a set of concern seeds as input.

One of the earliest approaches in this category is an interesting extension of program slicing with application to software maintenance, presented by Gallagher and Lyle (Gallagher 91). They introduce the *decomposition slice*, which captures "all computation on a given variable" and not just the statements affecting or affected by the computation at a given statement. A decomposition slice is basically a union of all the program slices computable for a given variable. According to the authors, a decomposition slice represents a manageable piece of code, which can be studied and modified in isolation, without being influenced by, and without influencing other decomposition slices.

The approach is somewhat similar to our flow sets extraction, discussed in section 5.3.3, but it mostly concentrates on the technical aspects of extracting such slices. The approach can only identify flat decomposition slices, with no data dependencies between them. As we discuss in section 3.1, this is not the typical case of functional concern implementations. Furthermore, because the approach is based on slicing and thus it aims to recover executable code fragments, the identified decomposition slices tend to be much larger than the actual implementations of the functional concerns, making the approach difficult to apply to real software systems.

Another interesting approach, trying to unify concept location with program slicing, was presented by Harman et al. (Harman 02; Gold 05). The authors use a concept location approach called Hypothesis-Based Concept Assignment, to determine an initial set of statements related to a concept, based on the semantic information contained in identifiers and comments. This initial set is then augmented using backward program slicing to an executable concept slice, which represents the implementation of the concept in code. The approach is similar to ours, because it performs this slicing on the variables representing the results of the initial statement set, but it only supports procedural programming languages such as COBOL.

This approach basically suffers from the same weaknesses as the previous one. Executable concept slices are flat sets of statements and tend to be much larger than the actual implementation of the concept, which is why they are difficult to extract and to understand. Furthermore, because the approach relies on semantic information encoded in variable names and comments, its accuracy is highly dependent on the quality of this information.

Program slicing was also used by Ishio et al. (Ishio 07) for locating functional concerns in object oriented code. The approach uses as slicing criteria all the nodes in the program dependence graphs, constructed for a manually specified set of seed methods, and determines the union of all backward and forward slices, calculated for this criteria. What is interesting about this approach is that it uses a heuristic to limit the size of the identified slice, which works by skipping the slicing of a method, if the length of the shortest realizable path between this method and any seed method in the PDG is greater than a predefined distance threshold, or if the value of a similarity metric between this method and all seed methods is smaller than a predefined similarity threshold. The similarity metric between methods is defined based on the heuristic that similar methods refer to similar classes, methods and fields.

In order to evaluate the accuracy of the approach, the authors calculate the recall and precision values for each of the six functional concerns they consider, based on two sets of manually identified concern implementations. As shown in the paper, the accuracy of the approach is not very good, and the approach does not work for concern implementations tangled within the same method.

Krinke (Krinke 06) mines control flow graphs for recurring invocation patterns, representing basic building blocks of AOP aspects. This approach is strongly related to the previously discussed approach by Breu and Krinke (Breu 04), which identifies the same kind of invocation pattern in execution traces. The approach is supported by a tool implemented using the *Soot* framework, which was used to identify aspect candidates in the *JHotDraw* case study.

As pointed out by the author himself, the method is not very useful in practice, because most of the patterns it detects represent simple method delegations, which do not constitute suitable aspect candidates. Furthermore, because the approach gives no suggestions on how to aggregate such patterns, its usefulness is limited to trivial homogeneous crosscutting concerns.

Another interesting approach for mining crosscutting concerns, based on random walks in coupling graphs, is presented by Zhang and Jacobsen (Zhang 07). As suggested by its name, a coupling graph captures the usual structural and cross-referencing dependencies between program elements. The approach was designed to simulate the manual investigation of the coupling graph by a software engineer, having absolutely no semantic knowledge about the system, and it was implemented in a tool called the *Prism Aspect Miner* (PAM), which is the successor of the previously mentioned PRISM tool.

The main weakness of this approach is that the obtained results are very difficult to interpret, because they are void of any semantic information. And because the approach uses a wide range of structural and cross-referencing dependencies, including containment, its accuracy is poor, especially in the case of crosscutting concerns tangled within the same method.

A general critique, which applies to the approaches in this category, is that they are difficult to apply on a large scale, primarily because the presentation of the identified concerns is too large and too fine-grained to support their understanding. Furthermore, these approaches lack expressive concern models, capable to capture complex relationships between concerns, such as concern refinement and concern overlap.

2.5.7. Comparative studies

This subsection presents a summary of the conclusions reached by several independent studies, intended to compare different concern identification approaches.

One of the earliest comparative studies between concern identification approaches was done by Wilde et al. (Wilde 03). The study compares three approaches, when locating two features in legacy Fortran code. The first approach, called software reconnaissance, uses dynamic information recorded in execution traces, and identifies feature implementations based on comparing the traces obtained with and without the feature. The approach was found to be relatively quick, because it effectively focuses the analysis on a small portion of the code, but it is only usable, if the execution of the considered feature can be controlled by the input data. The second approach is the manual exploration of program dependence graphs, presented by Chen and Rajlich (Chen 00), which the authors of the study found to be very useful in understanding the investigated features, but also more difficult and time-consuming to use, due to its manual nature.

Both of these approaches were successful in identifying both of the considered concerns. However, this was not the case, of the third approach, which is based on a textual search for keywords using the *grep* tool. Despite being very quick, this last approach was found to be unreliable, and highly dependent on textual clues in the source code.

The results of the previous study were extended by a more comprehensive comparative study, conducted by Marcus et al. (Marcus 05). This study covers two of the above mentioned approaches, and instead of the software reconnaissance approach, it considers a previously discussed approach based on latent semantic indexing (Marcus 04). The main conclusion of the study is that, although the manual exploration of dependence graphs is most effective in focusing the identification effort, it is not always enough, and that especially in the case of crosscutting concerns, concern identification approaches based on textual pattern search can provide useful information.

Another conclusion of the study was that none of the investigated approaches is able to recover complete concern implementations, but rather they point to the relevant sections in the code. Summarizing the strengths and weaknesses of each approach, the authors noted that both the grep-based and the LSI-based approaches depend heavily on the developer's knowledge about the system and the problem domain, even though the LSI-based approach supports more flexible queries. The authors also noted that a mistake in the manual exploration of the program dependence graph can lead to "costly backtracks in the search".

A similar study, using a similar setup, was conducted by Ceccato et al. (Ceccato 05). The paper reports on a comparison between three different aspect mining techniques, applied to the *JHotDraw* open-source case study. The first one is the previously discussed approach, using the call fan-in metric to identify candidate aspect seeds (Marin 04). The other two approaches, covered in the study, have also been discussed above and are based on formal concept analysis of identifiers (Tourwé 04) and of execution traces (Tonella 04a). The study shows that the first approach and the one using execution traces produce largely complementary results, whereas the one using identifiers is especially useful in the initial identification of concern seeds. These observations lead the authors to the conclusion, that a combined approach could produce a better coverage than each of them alone.

The conclusion was validated in a subsequent study (Ceccato 06), which extended the scope of the previous one to include several combinations of the above mentioned three aspect mining approaches. The combined approaches always lead to better coverage, although in many cases this also meant a drop in the accuracy of the identification. In case of one of the four concerns considered in the study, this accuracy drop was drastic, suggesting that the combination of approaches is not always beneficial.

The same aspect mining approaches were also compared independently by Roy et al. in a more comprehensive study (Roy 07) on four case studies. The paper confirms the findings of the previous studies by Ceccato et al. (Ceccato 05; Ceccato 06), including the uncertainty regarding the usefulness of combining the approaches, but it also points out that all three aspect mining approaches require significant manual effort to use.

Mens et al. (Mens 08a) present a different kind of comparison between approaches. The paper makes a comprehensive and critical survey of aspect mining approaches, compiles a list of the shortcomings affecting these approaches, and identifies some of the root causes for these shortcomings. Among the identified shortcomings, the paper mentions: poor precision and recall of the obtained results, subjectivity in result interpretation, poor scalability due to manual effort, lack of solid empirical validations, and difficulty in comparing results. As root causes of these shortcomings, the study identifies: the use of inappropriate mining techniques, the lack of a precise definition of what constitutes an aspect, and the inadequate representation of the results.

An interesting observation of the study is that all aspect mining approaches lack a solid semantic foundation and are biased towards AOP-style syntactic definitions of crosscutting concerns, which basically confirms one of our frequently mentioned critiques, namely the lack of an expressive concern model, capable of expressing concerns from the problem domain and the typical relations between them.

2.6. Conclusions

The previous sections presented a critical overview of the existing concern identification approaches, pointing out their strengths but mostly their weaknesses. The discussed approaches have been grouped into six categories, based on the concern extraction technique they use, because we discovered that the approaches in a given category tend to share the same set of weaknesses, each of which traceable back to one of the criteria defined in section 1.2.

Table 2.1 presents a condensed assessment of these categories, based on their compliance with the above mentioned criteria. Note that in case of the accuracy criterion, most categories have a neutral value. However, this does not mean that all the discussed approaches have the same accuracy for all types of concerns. Many of them in fact exhibit decent accuracies, when it comes to the specific types of concerns they target, but since they assume different concern definitions, the only possibility to compare them was to consider the more general definition, introduced in section 2.1. Also note that none of the categories comply with the expressiveness criterion, which is a fact also reported by Mens et al. (Mens 08a).

Our own concern identification approach fits in the static program analysis category, but given the fact that it is based on the Hierarchic Concern Model, discussed in chapter 3, it complies with the expressiveness criterion. Furthermore, in order to mitigate the lack of scalability, typically characterizing static program analysis techniques, our approach uses a data-oriented abstract representation of the code, which leads to a more compact representation of concern implementations, suitable to support program understanding.

Approach category	Assessment criteria				
	Expr.	Acc.	Prac.	Scal.	Auto.
Manual identification	0	+	+	-	-
Pattern search	0	0	+	0	+
Pattern recognition	-	0	+	+	0
Clustering and FCA	-	0	+	+	+
Clone analysis	-	0	+	0	+
Static program analysis	0	0	+	-	+

Table 2.1: Condensed assessment of concern identification approaches

Chapter 3.

Hierarchic Concern Model

In this chapter we introduce the Hierarchic Concern Model, which is used in our approach to capture functional concerns and establish direct traceability links between them and their corresponding implementations in object-oriented code. The model was designed to allow an accurate representation of the concern space, as defined at the requirements level, supporting concern refinement, concern overlap, and data dependencies between concerns.

Section 3.1 discusses these characteristics, using a typical Persistency concern as an example, while section 3.2 introduces the Hierarchic Concern Model, and provides formal definitions for the main concepts used in the model.

3.1. Anatomy of a Concern

Because concerns are in essence functional requirements, they create a functional decomposition of a system across multiple dimensions. And because this multi-dimensional decomposition space must be mapped to the single-dimensional space supported by object-oriented languages, the implementations of several concerns end up being crosscutting, and thus hindering program understanding.

As pointed out in section 2.4, the implementations of certain crosscutting concerns, specifically homogeneous concerns, are relatively easy to capture using AOP language constructs. But, these constructs introduce an artificial distinction between encapsulated and crosscutting concerns, which only makes program understanding harder.

Our model treats all concerns equally, but because the advantage of having direct traceability links between a concern and its implementation in code is greater in the case of a crosscutting concern, we focused our argument on crosscutting concerns.

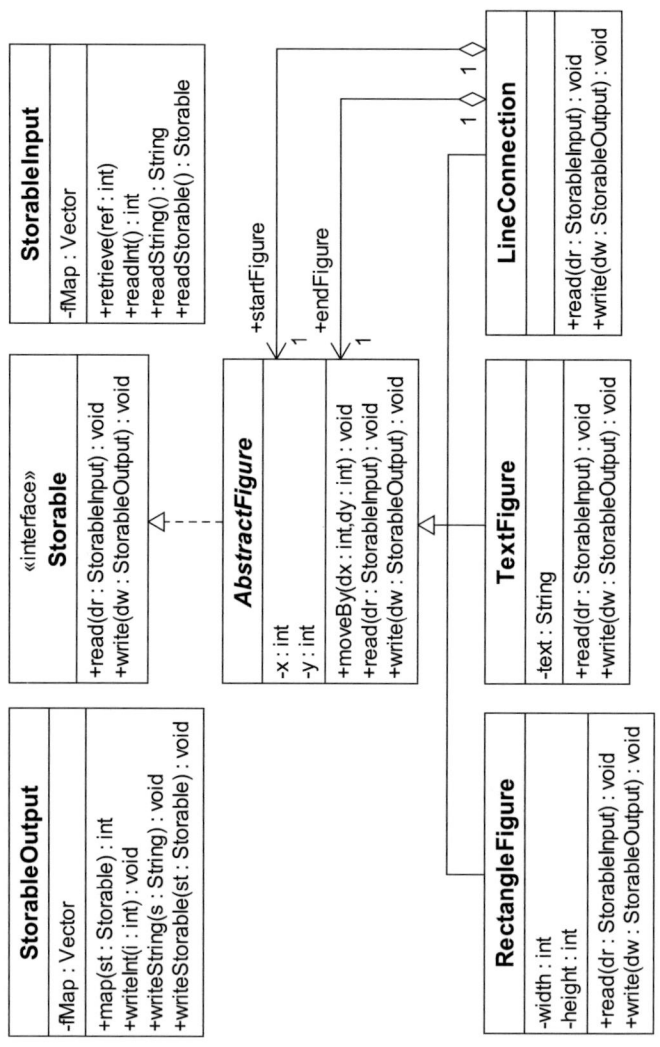

Figure 3.1: Design of typical Persistency concern

3.1.1. A Running Example

Let us consider as an example a **Persistency** concern for a class hierarchy of geometric figures.[1] As suggested by its name, the Persistency concern is responsible for storing and loading `Figure` objects in different persistent formats. The concern is delimited by the persisted data and the persistence media, each of which representing both inputs and outputs of the concern, depending on the considered operation (loading or storing).

Figure 3.1 shows a typical design. The interface `Storable`, residing at the root of the class hierarchy, defines the `read` and `write` operations. The `read` operation is responsible for reading object-specific data from a `StorableInput` object, while the `write` operation is responsible for writing the same object-specific data to a `StorableOutput` object. These operations are implemented by all the classes of the `Figure` class hierarchy as shown in listing 3.1.

Listing 3.1: Implementation of a typical Persistency concern

```
1   public class StorableInput {
2     private Vector fMap;
3     public Storable retrieve(int ref) {
4       return (Storable)fMap.get(ref);
5     }
6     public Storable readStorable() {
7       Storable st;
8       ...
9       st.read(this);
10      if (!fMap.contains(st)) {
11        fMap.add(st);
12      }
13      return st;
14    }
15  }
16  public class StorableOutput {
17    private Vector fMap;
18    public int map(Storable st) {
19      return fMap.indexOf(st);
20    }
21    public void writeStorable(Storable st) {
22      st.write(this);
23      if (!fMap.contains(st)) {
24        fMap.add(st);
```

---

[1] The example was adapted from the *JHotDraw* case study presented in chapter 6.

```
25          }
26      }
27  }
28  public abstract class AbstractFigure implements Storable {
29      private int x,y;
30      public void moveBy(int dx, int dy) {
31          x += dx;
32          y += dy;
33      }
34      public void read(StorableInput dr) {
35          x = dr.readInt();
36          y = dr.readInt();
37      }
38      public void write(StorableOutput dw) {
39          dw.writeInt(x);
40          dw.writeInt(y);
41      }
42  }
43  public class RectangleFigure extends AbstractFigure {
44      private int width, height;
45      public void read(StorableInput dr) {
46          super.read(dr);
47          width = dr.readInt();
48          height = dr.readInt();
49      }
50      public void write(StorableOutput dw) {
51          super.write(dw);
52          dw.writeInt(width);
53          dw.writeInt(height);
54      }
55  }
56  public class TextFigure extends AbstractFigure {
57      private String text;
58      public void read(StorableInput dr) {
59          super.read(dr);
60          text = dr.readString();
61      }
62      public void write(StorableOutput dw) {
63          super.write(dw);
64          dw.writeString(text);
65      }
66  }
67  public class LineConnection extends AbstractFigure {
68      private AbstractFigure startFigure, endFigure;
69      public void read(StorableInput dr) {
70          super.read(dr);
71          startFigure = dr.retrieve(dr.readInt());
72          endFigure = dr.retrieve(dr.readInt());
73      }
74      public void write(StorableOutput dw) {
75          super.write(dw);
76          dw.writeInt(dw.map(startFigure));
```

```
77        dw.writeInt(dw.map(endFigure));
78     }
79   }
```

The actual persistency medium is defined in the StorableInput and StorableOutput classes, and isolated from the Figure class hierarchy by means of type-specific read and write operations. The readInt and writeInt operations implement the de-serialization and serialization of primitive values of type int, while readString and writeString implement the same functionality for values of type java.lang.String.

The implementations of the read and write operations in AbstractFigure, RectangleFigure, and TextFigure are straightforward, because they just use of the above mentioned type-specific operations to read and write their respective attributes.

Somewhat more interesting are the implementations of the read and write operations in LineConnection, because they only read and write the position index values of the objects referenced by startFigure and endFigure in the fMap vectors. The reason for doing so is to avoid the multiple serialization of the same Figure object, when serializing an entire drawing consisting of several figures and connections between these figures. The fMap vectors are used to store the already serialized or de-serialized Figure objects, and the map and retrieve methods are used to translate between Figure objects and their corresponding position index values.

Although rather simple, the example is large enough to exhibit all the characteristics of a complex crosscutting concern.

3.1.2. Concern refinement

The **Persistency** concern can be refined into two disjoint subconcerns: the **Reader** subconcern handling the de-serialization of Storable objects, and the **Writer** subconcern handling the serialization of Storable objects.

These two subconcerns can in turn be refined into even smaller subconcerns, handling the de-serialization and serialization of specific types such as int or java.lang.String. In our example, we have the following subconcerns: **IntReader**, **StringReader**, **IntWriter**, and **StringWriter**, whose implementations are

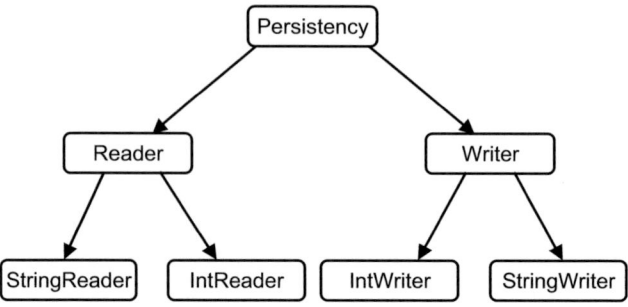

Figure 3.2: Refinement of the Persistency concern

encapsulated in the `readInt`, `readString`, `writeInt`, and `writeString` methods. This refinement of the **Persistency** concern is depicted in figure 3.2, using solid-line arrows pointing at the subconcerns.

For our simple example, this level of refinement may seem excessive, but when we consider alternative persistency media and formats, it no longer seems unreasonable. The refinement process can of course continue even further, until the resulting subconcerns are manageable in terms of size and complexity. The number of levels of this refinement hierarchy is flexible and depends purely on the developer's judgement.

3.1.3. Concern overlap

At first glance the refinement presented above seems reasonable and straightforward, but it is not the only refinement possible. Depending on the specific development or maintenance task, the developer may want to focus on the serialization and de-serialization of references to `Figure` objects, so to capture this functionality, he might define a new subconcern of the **Persistency** concern, which he calls **Reference**.

The implementation of the **Reference** concern contains two `fMap` vectors and uses the position index values of the actual `Figure` objects, designated by `startFigure` and `endFigure`, in these vectors as references for the serialization and de-serialization of `LineConnection` objects.

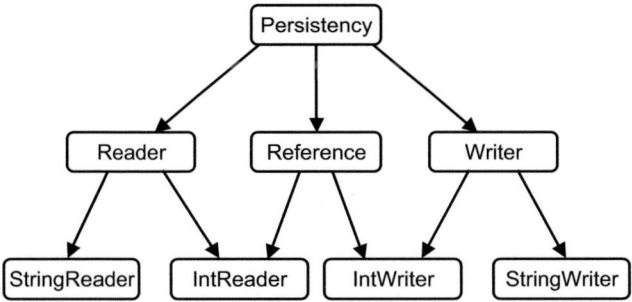

Figure 3.3: Overlapping refinements of the Persistency concern

The **Reference** concern overlaps with both the **Reader** and **Writer** concerns, because it handles the de-serialization and serialization of Figure references. Since these references are in fact primitive values of type int, their de-serialization, represented by the previously mentioned **IntReader** concern, constitutes a shared subconcern of both **Reference** and **Reader**.

Similarly the serialization of primitive values of type int, represented by the previously mentioned **IntWriter** concern, constitutes a shared subconcern of both **Reference** and **Writer**.

Figure 3.3 depicts the two overlapping concern refinements, using solid-line arrows pointing at the subconcerns. Given the fact that a concern can have several overlapping refinements, the concern refinement hierarchy is not a tree, but rather a direct acyclic graph.

3.1.4. Data dependencies between concerns

The actual data persisted by the **Persistency** concern has often nothing to do with the **Persistency** concern itself. Instead, it is defined as part of some other functional concern and is only used in the **Persistency** concern, thus creating a dependency between the defining concern and the **Persistency** concern.

In order to show data dependencies between concerns, we included in our example a part of the implementation of the **FigurePosition** concern, which handles the

Figure 3.4: Data dependencies between concerns

spatial positioning of `Figure` objects in a two-dimensional Cartesian space. The implementation of this concern consists of the `x` and `y` attributes of `Abstract-Figure`, and the `moveBy` method.

The attributes `x` and `y` are passed as arguments to method `writeInt`, thus creating a data dependency between the **FigurePosition** concern and the **IntWriter** concern. Similarly, the return value of method `readInt` is assigned to both attributes, thus creating a data dependency between **IntReader** and **FigurePosition**. These data dependencies are depicted in figure 3.4, using dotted-line arrows.

Note that it is possible to have data dependencies between a concern and its subconcerns. Also, if there is a data dependency between a concern and a subconcern of another concern, then there is a data dependency between the two top-level concerns too.

3.2. Data-Oriented Abstraction

Software systems in general can be described in terms of the inputs they use and the outputs they produce. While the inputs can be optional, the outputs of a system are never optional. A software system with no outputs is completely useless because executing it has no effect on its environment. The same is also true for any part of the system. If we consider the functionality represented by a functional requirement, if it has no outputs it has no influence on the outputs of the system. This means that the functionality is completely useless and so is the functional requirement itself.

Based on the above observation, we can define the functionality represented by any concern based on the outputs it produces. In other words, a concern basically represents the functionality needed to produce its outputs.

The Hierarchic Concern Model follows the typical hierarchic system decomposition (Goos 97), and describes concerns recursively as gray-boxes, in terms of the subconcerns they contain, the inputs they use, and the outputs they produce. A subconcern is also a concern in its own right, exhibiting the same characteristics as any other top-level concern. A top-level concern is a concern, which resides at the top of its refinement hierarchy, meaning that it is not itself a subconcern of some other concern.

In order to define the inputs and outputs of a concern more precisely, first we have to introduce the notion of *observable*.

Definition 1 (Observable). *An observable is defined as a measurable property of the system state, which can be observed directly, independent of other observables.*

Every observable has a value, which, in case of a software system, is either an input of the system itself or the result of an internal computation. Note that copying the value of an observable or transforming its value into a different representation form, creates a new observable, because its value may change independently of the original observable.

Definition 2 (Concern outputs). *The outputs of a concern constitute the subset of the observables produced by the concern, which are either outputs of the software system itself or are used internally by another concern.*

As a result of this definition, the observables produced by a concern and used by one of its subconcerns are also outputs of the concern in question.

Definition 3 (Concern inputs). *The inputs of a concern are observables, which are not produced within the concern but are used to produce its outputs.*

3.2.1. Flow Relations

In order to formally define the notion of concern, first we have to introduce a few basic concepts. Let Σ be a software system and Ω be the set of all observables of Σ.

Definition 4 (Flow relation). *Let $\alpha, \beta \in \Omega$ be two observables. The flow relation $\rightsquigarrow \subset \Omega \times \Omega$ is a binary endorelation over Ω, written $\alpha \rightsquigarrow \beta$ and read "α flows to β", denoting that the value of observable β is derived from the value of observable α.*

The flow relation is transitive, meaning that:

$$\forall \alpha, \beta, \gamma \in \Omega \quad : \quad \alpha \rightsquigarrow \beta \wedge \beta \rightsquigarrow \gamma$$
$$\Rightarrow \quad \alpha \rightsquigarrow \gamma$$

The above definition does not exclude the possibility to derive the value of an observable β from several unrelated observables, meaning that for $\alpha, \beta, \gamma \in \Omega$ the following condition may be satisfied:

$$(\alpha \rightsquigarrow \beta \wedge \gamma \rightsquigarrow \beta) \quad \wedge \quad \neg(\alpha \rightsquigarrow \gamma \vee \gamma \rightsquigarrow \alpha)$$

Note that a flow relation between α and β, does not say anything about how the value of β is derived from α. It just means that if the value of α changed, this would possibly lead to a change in the value of β, or, in other words, the value of α may influences the value of β. Because this influence can be either direct or indirect, we introduce two additional relations to capture direct and indirect flow.

Definition 5 (Direct flow relation)**.** *Let $\alpha, \beta \in \Omega$ be two observables. The direct flow relation $\rightarrow \subset \Omega \times \Omega$ is a binary endorelation over Ω, written $\alpha \rightarrow \beta$ and read "α flows directly to β", meaning that the value of β is derived from the value of α, without the involvement of an intermediate observable.*

Depending on the nature of the influence we distinguish several types of direct flow relations grouped in three categories: dataflow relations, inheritance relations, and direct dependency relations. Each of these types is a subset of the direct flow relation defined above, and will be presented in detail in section 4.2.

The indirect flow relation can be defined in a similar way.

Definition 6 (Indirect flow relation)**.** *Let $\alpha, \beta \in \Omega$ be two observables. The indirect flow relation $--\rightarrow \subset \Omega \times \Omega$ is a binary endorelation over Ω, written $\alpha --\rightarrow \beta$ and read "α flows indirectly to β", meaning that the value of β is derived from the value of α, through at least one intermediate observable.*

This can be written formally as follows:

$$\alpha --\rightarrow \beta \quad \Longleftrightarrow \quad \neg(\alpha \rightarrow \beta)$$
$$\wedge \quad \exists \gamma \in \Omega : \alpha \rightarrow \gamma \wedge \gamma \rightsquigarrow \beta$$

Note that the above formal definition is equivalent to

$$\alpha --\rightarrow \beta \quad \Longleftrightarrow \quad \alpha \rightsquigarrow \beta \wedge \neg(\alpha \rightarrow \beta)$$

which means that the indirect flow relation is in fact the set difference of the flow and the direct flow relations. Formally, this can be written as follows:

$$\dashrightarrow \quad = \quad \rightsquigarrow \; - \; \rightarrow$$

So far, we have shown that the indirect flow relation can be determined based on the flow and direct flow relations. However, as the following lemma shows, the flow and direct flow relations are also not independent of each other.

Lemma 1. *The flow relation* $\rightsquigarrow \subset \Omega \times \Omega$ *is the transitive closure of the direct flow relation* $\rightarrow \subset \Omega \times \Omega$.

Proof. In order to prove this lemma, we need to show that $\rightsquigarrow = \Theta$, where Θ is the transitive closure of $\rightarrow$.

Let $\alpha, \beta \in \Omega$ be two observables, such that $\alpha \rightarrow \beta$. Based on the definitions of the flow and direct flow relations, we also have $\alpha \rightsquigarrow \beta$, meaning that $\rightarrow \subset \rightsquigarrow$. Because Θ is the transitive closure of $\rightarrow$, Θ is also the intersection of all transitive endorelations over Ω, containing $\rightarrow$. This means that any transitive endorelation containing $\rightarrow$, also contains Θ. Given the fact that $\rightarrow \subset \rightsquigarrow$ and $\rightsquigarrow$ is by definition transitive, we have $\Theta \subset \rightsquigarrow$.

Let $\alpha, \beta \in \Omega$ be two observables, such that $\alpha \rightsquigarrow \beta$. This means that $\exists \gamma_1, \gamma_2, ..., \gamma_n \in \Omega, n \geq 2$, so that $\alpha = \gamma_1 \wedge \gamma_n = \beta \wedge \gamma_i \rightarrow \gamma_{i+1}$, for $1 \leq i < n$. Given the fact that $\rightarrow \subset \Theta$, we also have $(\gamma_i, \gamma_{i+1}) \in \Theta$, for $1 \leq i < n$. And because Θ is transitive, we also have $(\alpha, \beta) \in \Theta$. So if $\alpha \rightsquigarrow \beta$, we have $(\alpha, \beta) \in \Theta$, which means that $\rightsquigarrow \subset \Theta$.

If we combine this last result with the fact that $\Theta \subset \rightsquigarrow$, we can conclude that $\rightsquigarrow = \Theta$. □

3.2.2. Concern Definition

As we have already mentioned before, a concern is defined at the requirements level and represents the functionality needed to produce its outputs. Based on the definition of the flow relation, we can now also give a formal definition of a concern.

Let C be the set of all concerns in Σ, $c \in C$ a concern, and Ω_c the set of all observables of c.

Definition 7 (Concern). *A concern c is a tuple $(\ell_c, S_c, \Phi_c, \Psi_c)$, where*

- *ℓ_c is a label denoting the name of the concern,*
- *$S_c \subset C$ is the set of contained subconcerns,*
- *$\Phi_c \subset \Omega_c$ is the set of inputs used by c, and*
- *$\Psi_c \subset \Omega_c$ is the set of outputs produced by c.*

The sets S_c, Φ_c, and Ψ_c must fulfill the following properties:

- **no unnecessary inputs**

$$\forall \alpha \in \Phi_c \quad , \quad \exists \beta \in \Psi_c : \alpha \rightsquigarrow \beta$$

- **subconcerns have no additional inputs**

$$\forall (\ell_c, S_c, \Phi_c, \Psi_c) \in C,$$
$$\forall (\ell_{c'}, S_{c'}, \Phi_{c'}, \Psi_{c'}) \in S_c,$$
$$\forall \beta \in \Phi_{c'} \quad , \quad \exists \alpha \in \Phi_c \cup \Psi_c : \alpha \rightsquigarrow \beta$$

- **subconcern outputs flow to the containing concern outputs**

$$\forall (\ell_c, S_c, \Phi_c, \Psi_c) \in C,$$
$$\forall (\ell_{c'}, S_{c'}, \Phi_{c'}, \Psi_{c'}) \in S_c,$$
$$\forall \alpha \in \Psi_{c'} \quad , \quad \exists \beta \in \Psi_c : \alpha \rightsquigarrow \beta$$

3.2.3. Traceability Function

Because concerns are ultimately defined in terms of their subconcerns, inputs and outputs, defining traceability between a concern c and its implementation in code amounts to defining a mapping between the observables of c and the program elements of its implementation.

Because observables represent quantifiable properties of the system state, whose values can be directly measured, they are represented at the implementation level by variables. The term variable is used here with a broader meaning to denote the following.

Definition 8 (Variable). *A variable is a distinct storage location, used in the implementation of a concern.*

Variables can be either implicitly or explicitly defined in the code, and can be either named or unnamed. They include: fields, local variables, formal parameters, exception parameters, return value variables, object context variables, and object creation variables. An exception parameter is the parameter defined in a catch clause, receiving the caught exception object. A return value variable represents the temporary storage location, holding the return value of a method. An object context variable is a variable defined implicitly within the scope of every instance member, receiving the object on which the member was accessed. This variable is usually accessible using a keyword of the language, such as the reserved name `this` in case of the Java programming language. And finally, an object creation variable is represents a temporary location receiving the result of applying the object creation operator.

Note that the above definition refers to the runtime representation of the implementation. It implies that a non-static field of a class represents several different variables, one for each created instance of that class. The same is also true for all variables defined inside a method. Because these variables are allocated on the stack frame constructed for each method call, they are distinct for every method call.

However, in order to define traceability between concerns and their implementation in source code, we need to map the runtime notion of variable to the static notion of abstract location (Andersen 94).

Definition 9 (Abstract location). *An abstract location is a statically distinguishable storage location, used in the implementation of a concern.*

In the context of the previous definition "statically distinguishable" means that each such storage location has a distinct definition in code. In case of an implicitly defined abstract location, this definition is represented by the definition of its enclosing program element (method or class).

If we compare this definition with that of a variable, we can immediately see that an abstract location represents all the variables defined at a given location in code. For example, this means that a non-static field of a class will be represented by a single abstract location, regardless of the number of created instances of that particular class. The same is true for all variables defined inside a method, whether they are implicitly or explicitly defined. Concretely, we will have a single abstract location representing the same formal parameter in all method calls, a single abstract location representing the return value variables, a single abstract location representing the object context pseudo-variables, and so on. Also, we represent all object instances created at the same location in code with a single abstract location, meaning that we have an abstract location for each distinct appearance of the `new` operator.

Let V be the set of all abstract locations used in the implementation of the software system Σ. Note that V includes all abstract locations directly referenced in the source code, including directly referenced abstract locations defined in library code, but not abstract locations used only internally within the implementation of the library. For example, if a library method is called in the implementation of Σ, the abstract locations corresponding to the object context variable, formal parameter and return value variable of this library method are included in V, but the abstract locations corresponding to the local variables used inside the library method are not.

We can extend the definitions of the flow relations to the set V as given below. The direct flow relation between abstract locations $\rightarrow \subset V \times V$ is a binary endorelation over V, defined based on the direct flow relation between observables, as follows. If there is a direct flow relation between two observables, then there is a direct flow relation between their corresponding abstract locations. The flow relation between abstract locations $\rightsquigarrow \subset V \times V$ and the indirect flow relation between abstract locations $\dashrightarrow \subset V \times V$ are defined in the same way as their counterpart relations between observables. Thus, the flow relation is the transitive closure of the direct flow relation, and the indirect flow relation is the set difference of the flow and the direct flow relations.

Based on these definitions it is trivial to show that if $\alpha, \beta \in \Omega$ are two observables and $u, v \in V$ are their corresponding abstract locations, then we have:

$$
\begin{aligned}
\alpha \rightarrow \beta &\quad \Rightarrow \quad u \rightarrow v \\
\alpha \dashrightarrow \beta &\quad \Rightarrow \quad u \dashrightarrow v \\
\alpha \rightsquigarrow \beta &\quad \Rightarrow \quad u \rightsquigarrow v
\end{aligned}
$$

Note that we did not use the equivalency sign between the above predicates, because a direct flow relation from a source abstract locations to a target abstract location does not mean that there is a direct flow relation from all variables represented by the source abstract location to all variables represented by the target abstract location. As a result, working with abstract locations instead of variables when identifying concern extents may lead to a loss of precision due to mixing different call or object contexts, if appropriate measures are not taken to avoid this. In order to illustrate this situation, let us consider the example in listing 3.2.

Listing 3.2: Abstract locations mixing call contexts

```
1   class Combinatorics {
2     int fact(int n) {
3       if (n <= 1)
4         return 1;
5       else
6         return n * /*(1*/fact(n-1);
7     }
8     int perm(int n, int k) {
9       return /*(2*/fact(n) / /*(3*/fact(n - k);
10    }
11    int comb(int n, int k) {
12      return /*(4*/fact(n) / /*(5*/(fact(k) * /*(6*/fact(n-k));
13    }
14    void main() {
15      int n1 = 5, n2 = 7;
16      int k1 = 3, k2 = 4;
17      int r1 = /*(7*/perm(n1, k1);
18      int r2 = /*(8*/comb(n2, k2);
19    }
20  }
```

Note that because the code in listing 3.2 contains several calls to method fact(int), both the formal parameter and the return value of this method have several corresponding variables, one for each call site. And since the abstract locations representing these variables are unique, we have several direct flow relations to the abstract location representing the formal parameter of method fact() and several direct flow relations from the abstract location representing the return value variable of the same method.

A graphical representation of the direct flow relations between abstract locations in the code is shown in figure 3.5. The convention used to label the abstract locations in the figure will be explained in detail in section 4.1.

Although the code in listing 3.2 clearly contains two separate computations of perm(n,k) and comb(n,k), using two disjoint sets of variables, using abstract locations hides this fact. Based on the direct flow relations depicted in figure 3.5,

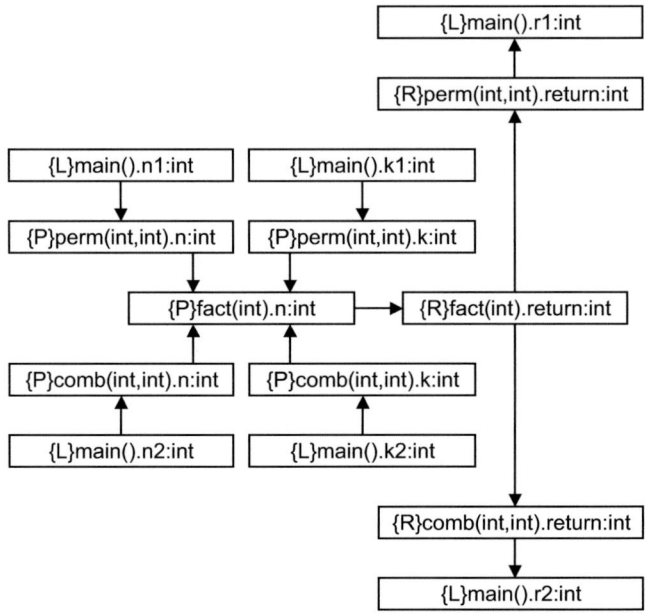

Figure 3.5: Examples of direct flow relations between abstract locations

we can conclude that there is an indirect flow relation between the abstract location representing the local variable n1 and the local variable r2 of method main, when in fact there is no such indirect flow relation between the corresponding variables.

This loss of precision is due to the fact that the abstract locations representing the formal parameter and the return value variable of method fact(int) group together variables corresponding to different call contexts. In order to avoid this loss of precision, the abstract locations involved in a direct flow relation must be qualified with the call and object contexts used for that particular flow relation.

Note that an abstract location qualified by a call or an object context usually represents a smaller number of variables than the original abstract location.

In our example, if we qualify the abstract location representing the formal parameter of method `fact(int)`, with the call context $(_2$ corresponding to the call site prefixed with the comment `/*(2*/` in listing 3.2, we restrict the set of variables represented by the abstract location to the set of formal parameters created as a result of the first call to `fact(int)` from method `perm(int, int)`. In our example, this set contains a single variable, because the method `perm(int, int)` is called only once, but in the general case, the set will contain several different variables.

Note that a qualified abstract location can be further qualified with an additional call or object context, restricting the set of variables represented by it even further.

For example, the abstract location representing the formal parameter of method `fact(int)`, qualified with the call context $(_2$, can be further qualified with the call context $(_7$, to restrict the set of represented variables to a single variable created for a call stack containing the call contexts $(_7$ and $(_2$.

Definition 10 (Access path). *An access path is a sequence of one or more call and object contexts, qualifying an abstract location.*

An abstract location is said to be fully qualified by an access path, when it represents a single variable. In this case, the access path is called an absolute access path. If an abstract location qualified by an access path represents more than one variable, the abstract location is said to be partially qualified, and the access path is called a relative access path.

In our example the formal parameter of method `fact(int)` is fully qualified by the access path $(_7(_2$, meaning that this access path is an absolute access path.

We are now ready to define the traceability function.

Definition 11 (Traceability function). *The traceability function is a function $T : \Omega \rightarrow V$, which associates to every observable of the system its corresponding abstract location in the source code.*

Given the fact that for each abstract location $v \in V$ there is a corresponding observable $\alpha \in \Omega$, we can deduce that the traceability function T is surjective, and thus a graph homomorphism from Ω to V, meaning that:

$$\forall \alpha, \beta \in \Omega \quad , \quad \alpha \rightsquigarrow \beta \Rightarrow T(\alpha) \rightsquigarrow T(\beta)$$

Because the inputs and outputs of a concern $c \in C$ are observables, they each have a corresponding abstract location in V_c, where $V_c \subset V$ is the set of all abstract locations used in the implementation of c.

Definition 12 (Information source). *An information source for the implementation of concern $c = (\ell, S_c, \Phi_c, \Psi_c)$ is an abstract location $u \in V_c$, for which*

$$\exists \alpha \in \Phi_c \quad : \quad u = T(\alpha)$$

An information source is basically an abstract location storing an input value used in the implementation of a concern. Let I_c be the set of all information sources of the implementation of concern c. Then, we have

$$I_c \quad = \quad T(\Phi_c).$$

Definition 13 (Information sink). *An information sink for the implementation of concern $c = (\ell, S_c, \Phi_c, \Psi_c)$ is an abstract location $v \in V_c$, for which*

$$\exists \beta \in \Psi_c \quad : \quad v = T(\beta)$$

In other words, an information sink is an abstract location storing an output value produced by the implementation of a concern. Let O_c be the set of all information sinks of the implementation of concern c. Then, we have

$$O_c \quad = \quad T(\Psi_c).$$

Given the fact that a concern represents the functionality needed to produce its outputs, we can intuitively define the set V_c as the set of all abstract locations flowing to at least one of the information sinks of the concern, without first flowing to an information source of the same concern. A formal definition of V_c will be given in section 5.3.2, after introducing the notion of flow path.

3.2.4. Abstract Representation in Code

Each concern definition from the requirements level can be represented at the implementation level through a concern intent, defining what the concern is supposed to do at the implementation level, and for each such concern intent, there is a corresponding implementation in code, called a concern extent, describing how the intent is implemented.

Originally introduced by Marin et al. (Marin 07), the terms concern intent and concern extent have already been defined informally in section 2.1, but this section provides formal definitions for them, within the context of our Hierarchic Concern Model.

Definition 14 (Concern intent). *The intent of concern $c \in C$ is the tuple $c^{int} = (\ell, S_c, I_c, O_c)$, where*

- *ℓ is a label denoting the name of c,*
- *S_c is the set of subconcerns of c,*
- *I_c is the set of information sources of the implementation of c, and*
- *O_c is the set of information sinks of the implementation of c.*

Note that a concern intent is basically the image of a concern definition in code through the traceability function T, and as a result, the sets I_c, and O_c satisfy the same properties as the sets Φ_c, and Ψ_c in definition 7.

Because current mainstream programming languages do not provide mechanisms to explicitly record concern intents, this information, although available at development time, is lost and has to be recovered over and over again for every software evolution task.

The concern intent specification language presented in section 5.2.1 eliminates this problem, because it allows concern intents to be recorded in a persistent form.

Ideally, concern intents should be specified by their respective developers at development time, but for legacy systems they can also be specified during the software evolution phase by someone trying to discover and understand concern implementations.

The extent of a concern can be defined in several ways, depending on the abstraction level used to describe the implementation of a concern. One alternative is to define it as the list of all program elements used in the implementation of a concern, but this definition sometimes results in very large concern extents, which are hard to follow and understand. Given the fact that our Hierarchic Concern Model is intended to facilitate software understanding, we adopt the following, more abstract definition of a concern extent.

Definition 15 (Concern extent). *The extent of concern $c \in C$ is the tuple $c^{ext} = (V_c, \leadsto_c)$, where*

- *$V_c \subset V$ is the set of all abstract locations used in the implementation of c, and*

- $\leadsto_c$ *is the restriction of the flow relation $\leadsto$ to V_c.*

Note that the identification of a concern extent c^{ext} corresponding to a given concern intent c^{int} amounts to determining the set V_c and the restricted binary relation $\leadsto_c$, starting from the sets I_c and O_c of the concern intent.

Definition 16 (Concern skeleton). *The concern skeleton of a concern $c \in C$ is the tuple (c^{int}, c^{ext}).*

Based on this definition, the concern skeleton is a data-oriented abstract representation of a concern in the code.

Chapter 4.

Concern Graph

This chapter introduces the concern graph, a directed multigraph structure used to represent direct flow relations between abstract locations. The concern graph is primarily used for the automated identification of concern extents, but its graphical representation can also be used as a visual aid in understanding concern implementations as well as the data dependencies between them.

Section 4.1 gives a formal definition of the central notion of concern graph. Section 4.2 discusses the different types of direct flow relations and exemplifies their extraction from Java source code. Section 4.3 deals with concern tangling at the class level and presents a heuristic method to detect and separate superimposed class roles. And, finally, section 4.4 deals with capturing flow relations passing through library code.

4.1. Concern Graph Definition

Before introducing the concern graph, we first need to define some basic concepts.

Let Λ_V be an alphabet consisting of letters (both uppercase and lowercase), digits, and the symbols '_', '(', ')', '{', '}', ',', '.', and ':'. And let L_V be a language over the alphabet Λ_V defined as shown below:

$$L_V \quad = \quad \{\text{'{'} \cdot kind(v) \cdot \text{'}'} \cdot name(v) \cdot \text{':'} \cdot type(v) \mid v \in V\}$$

where

- V is the set of all abstract locations defined in the implementation of software system Σ,

- $kind(v)$ is a letter encoding the kind of the abstract location v, as shown in table 4.1,
- $name(v)$ is the qualified unique name of the abstract location, and
- $type(v)$ is the fully qualified name of the data type of v.

Abstract location kind	Encoding
class field	'F'
formal parameter	'P'
object context	'O'
return value	'R'
local value	'L'
exception parameter	'E'
object creation	'T'

Table 4.1: Encoding of abstract location kinds

The qualified unique name of the abstract location is defined as the simple name of the abstract location prefixed with the qualified unique name of the entity containing it. Class fields are prefixed with the fully qualified name of the containing class, and abstract locations defined inside a method are prefixed with the fully qualified name of the class containing the method, and the signature of the containing method. For unnamed abstract locations representing return values of methods, we use the short name `return`, and for object context abstract locations, we use the short name `this`. For object creation abstract locations we use the short name `new_x`, where x is the order number of the new operator within its containing method or class. Note that in case of the Java programming language, the symbols `return`, `this`, and `new` are reserved keywords, so they cannot serve as names for any named abstract location. As a result, the short names used for the unnamed abstract locations cannot clash with the names of other abstract locations.

The $\cdot$ operator in the definition of L_V is the simple word concatenation operator.

Let $V^o \subset V$ be the set of all abstract locations having a non-primitive data type, and let Λ_A be an alphabet defined as follows:

$$\begin{aligned} \Lambda_A \quad = \quad & \{`e'\} \cup \{`(_i' \mid 1 \le i \le n\} \cup \{`)_i' \mid 1 \le i \le n\} \\ \cup \quad & \{`<_o' \mid o \in V^o\} \cup \{`>_o' \mid o \in V^o\} \end{aligned}$$

where n is the number of call sites found in the implementation of software system Σ.

Definition 17 (Concern graph). *The concern graph is a directed multigraph $G = (V, A, s, t, L_V, L_A, \ell_V, \ell_A)$ with uniquely labelled arcs between each pair of vertices, where*

- *the set of vertices V is the set of all abstract locations defined in a software system Σ,*
- *A is a multiset of ordered pairs of vertices (u, v) called arcs, satisfying the condition $(u, v) \in A \iff u \to v$,*
- *$s, t : A \to V$ are two functions indicating the source and target vertex of an arc,*
- *L_V is the above defined language, whose words are used as labels for the vertices of the concern graph,*
- *L_A is a language over alphabet Λ_A, defined in section 4.1.1, and whose words are used as labels for the arcs of the concern graph,*
- *$\ell_V : V \to L_V$ is a function associating a unique label from L_V to every vertex in G, and*
- *$\ell_A : A \to L_A$ is a function associating a label from L_A to every arc in G.*

In the context of the previous definition "uniquely labelled arcs between each pair of vertices" means that the concern graph may contain several arcs between the same source and target vertices, provided that these arcs are labelled differently, or in formal terms:

$$\forall a_1, a_2 \in A : a_1 \neq a_2 \quad \Rightarrow \quad \ell_A(a_1) \neq \ell_A(a_2)$$

Because we have an exclusively static view on the implementation of the system, we rely on the labels of the arcs in the concern graph to record the call and object contexts of the abstract locations involved in a direct flow relation.

Concern graphs are extracted from source code, and throughout this chapter we present several examples, the first one being shown in figure 4.1. The depicted concern graph corresponds to the code in listing 4.1.

When analyzing source code, it is desirable to do this in a modular fashion (one subsystem at a time) and compose the intermediate results. In our case this means that we need a way to compose concern graphs. Towards this end, we define the union of concern graphs as follows:

Definition   18.   *The   union   of   two   concern   graphs G_1 =
$(V_1, A_1, s_1, t_1, L_{V_1}, L_{A_1}, \ell_{V_1}, \ell_{A_1})$ and $G_2 = (V_2, A_2, s_2, t_2, L_{V_2}, L_{A_2}, \ell_{V_2}, \ell_{A_2})$, with
disjoint multisets of arcs, is the concern graph $G_1 \cup G_2 = (V, A, s, t, L_V, L_A, \ell_V, \ell_A)$,
where:*

$$V = V_1 \cup V_2$$

$$A = A_1 \cup A_2$$

$$s : A \to V, \ s(a) = \begin{cases} s_1(a) & , a \in A_1 \\ s_2(a) & , a \in A_2 \end{cases}$$

$$t : A \to V, \ t(a) = \begin{cases} t_1(a) & , a \in A_1 \\ t_2(a) & , a \in A_2 \end{cases}$$

$$L_V = L_{V_1} \cup L_{V_2}$$

$$L_A = L_{A_1} \cup L_{A_2}$$

$$\ell_V : V \to L_V, \ \ell_V(v) = \begin{cases} \ell_{V_1}(v) & , v \in V_1 \\ \ell_{V_2}(v) & , v \in V_2 - V_1 \end{cases}$$

$$\ell_A : A \to L_A, \ \ell_A(a) = \begin{cases} \ell_{A_1}(a) & , a \in A_1 \\ \ell_{A_2}(a) & , a \in A_2 \end{cases}$$

Note that this union is different from the *disjoint union of graphs*, because the sets
V_1 and V_2 are not treated as disjoint sets, and as a result the occurrence of an abstract
location v in both sets will not result in having two copies of this abstract location
in $G_1 \cup G_2$.

In the above definition we consider only concern graphs with disjoint arc multisets,
because two concern graphs constructed for two disjoint parts of the source code
will always have disjoint arc multisets.

4.1.1. Tracking Call and Object Contexts

As already mentioned briefly in section 4.1, the labels of the arcs in the concern
graph are used to record the call and object contexts of the abstract locations involved in a direct flow relation. These labels represent words in a language L_A over
the alphabet Λ_A, defined in the same section. The alphabet Λ_A contains five types
of symbols, having the following semantic:

- The symbol $($_i$, read "enter call context", shows that the target of a direct flow
  relation is either a formal parameter or an object context abstract location,

and that the direct flow from the source abstract location occurred at call site number i. Should this method call be removed from the code, the direct flow relation would also have to be removed. Note that every call site in the analyzed source code has a unique number, enabling us to perform a context sensitive extraction of concern extents as described in section 5.3.1.

- The symbol $)_i$, read "exit call context", shows that the source of a direct flow relation is a return value abstract location, and that the direct flow to the target abstract location occurred at call site number i. Should this method call be removed from the code, the direct flow relation would also have to be removed.

- The symbol $<_o$, read "enter object context", shows that the target of a direct flow relation is a non-static field, accessed using the object context o. Note that the o used as index in the above symbol is a unique identifier of the abstract location representing the object context. This ensures there is no ambiguity when recording the actual object context. Although in many object-oriented languages, including Java, the non-static fields of an object may be accessed directly from inside a non-static method without an explicit object context, this is just a shorthand for accessing these fields using the object context abstract location `this` of the non-static method. In the concern graph, we record this information explicitly and use the $<_{this}$ symbol in the labels of the corresponding arcs, where *this* is a unique identifier of the abstract location representing the object context.

- The symbol $>_o$, read "exit object context", shows that the source of a direct flow relation is a non-static field, accessed using the object context o, where, as in the case of the "enter object context" symbol, o is a unique identifier of the abstract location representing the object context. In case an implicit object context is used, we record this information using the $>_{this}$ symbol, where *this* is, as explained above, a unique identifier of the abstract location representing the object context.

- The symbol e, read "empty context", can be used for both source and target abstract locations and it shows that the access to the abstract location in question has no call or object context.

The language L_A, used to label the arcs of the concern graph, is the concatenation of the languages L_A^{in} and L_A^{out} defined as follows:

$$L_A^{in} = \{`e'\} \cup \{`(_i' \mid 1 \le i \le n\} \cup \{`<_o' \mid o \in V^o\}^+$$

$$L_A^{out} \quad = \quad \{`e'\} \cup \{`)_i' \mid 1 \le i \le n\} \cup \{`>_o' \mid o \in V^o\}^+$$

$$L_A \quad = \quad L_A^{out} \cdot L_A^{in}$$

where $\cdot$ is the word concatenation operator and $+$ is the Kleene plus operator.

If we take a closer look at the definition of L_A, we notice that each arc label is composed by concatenating two words. The first word captures the call or object context of the source abstract location, while the second word captures the call or object context of the target abstract location. Note that, because the type of captured context information depends on the type of the abstract location involved, the corresponding label either records a call context or an object context. Because the call context information uniquely identifies a call site in the code, and because a single call site always uses the same object context, there is never a need to record both. Note that the object context of an abstract location can actually be a sequence of object context symbols, one for each element of the access path.

The context of the source abstract location can be either the "exit call context" symbol $)_i$ or a sequence of one or more "exit object context" symbols $>_o$, if the direct flow relation "exits" a call or an object context, or the "empty context" e otherwise. Similarly, the context of the target abstract location can be either the "enter call context" symbol $)_i$ or a sequence of one or more "enter object context" symbols $>_o$, if the direct flow relation "enters" a call or an object context, or the "empty context" e otherwise.

Note that in case of a direct flow relation between two fields of the same class or classes of the same hierarchy, it may happen that both the source and the target are accessed using the same object context. In this case instead of recording an "exit object context" and an "enter object context" for the same abstract location representing the accessed object, the arc of the concern graph will be labelled with a double "empty context" ee, meaning that the object context of the source abstract location is the same as the object context of the target abstract location.

4.1.2. Dealing with Reference Types

As we have seen above, a direct flow relation between two abstract locations means that the value of the source abstract location is used directly to derive the value of the target abstract location. If both the source and target abstract locations have simple data types, capturing the direct flow relation between them is straight-forward. If however, the abstract locations involved in a direct flow relation have reference types, capturing this relation requires a special handling, to distinguish between a relation at the reference level and a relation at the referenced object level.

Because in many object-oriented languages such as Java, array types are also reference types, this distinction also applies to direct flow relations between array references and direct flow relations between array elements. And given the fact that when accessing an array element, it is not generally possible, using purely static analysis methods, to precisely identify the referenced element, changing the value of such an element is considered to change the values of all the elements of that particular array, which is why we represent all the elements of an array using a single abstract location, having as its type the base type of the array. This abstract location is then treated as a non-static internal field of the array type, meaning that we rely on the object context tracking, described in section 4.1.1, to avoid mixing multiple array object contexts. The reason for modelling arrays as mentioned above is to enable our approach to cope with situations similar to the one from the example presented in listing 4.1.

Listing 4.1: Examples of direct flow relations between arrays

```
1    int i = 10, val = 20;
2    int[] a = new int[20];
3    int[] b = a;
4    b[i] = val;
5    int res = a[10];
```

The example involves the definition of two array references a and b. The assignment in line 3 has the effect that both a and b refer to the same array object. If we take a closer look at the assignments in lines 4 and 5, we notice that a value is written to the array object using b as array reference, and the same value is read using a as array reference. Note that there is no direct flow from b to a at the array reference level, but because the direct flow relations involving array elements are handled like non-static fields, the indirect flow relation between val and res can be correctly captured as shown by figure 4.1. The figure shows the direct flow relations both at

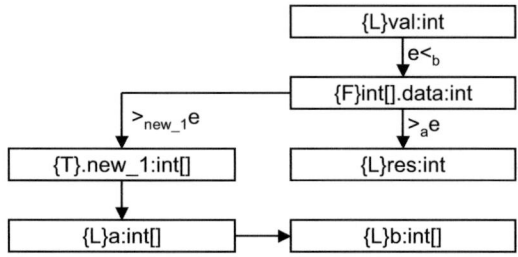

Figure 4.1: Concern graph capturing direct flow relations between arrays

the array reference level and at the level of array elements.

4.2. Direct Flow Relations

As already mentioned above, we consider several types of direct flow relations, depending on the nature of the influence between the source abstract location and the target abstract location. Given the fact that direct flow relations between abstract locations are extracted based on a conservative static analysis of the code, they may in fact represent only potential direct flow relations.

In order to have a uniform structure of the presentation, enabling an easy access to the information, we present each relation type using the following fixed template:

Definition: This paragraph defines the relation type in abstract terms at the intent level, and if necessary provides an intuitive justification for its introduction.

Extraction from code: This paragraph deals with the particularities of extracting this relation type from object-oriented code. In order to keep the presentation succinct, we focus our discussion on the Java language, as a typical object-oriented language, but this does not mean that our approach is only applicable to Java.

Examples: This paragraph shows a typical code example and discusses the corresponding concern subgraph, containing only the relation type in question.

4.2.1. Dataflow Relations

Dataflow relations represent a category of direct flow relation types, used to capture direct value transfer between a source abstract location and a target abstract location. A typical object-oriented language supports the following types of direct value transfer: assigning a value to an abstract location, passing an argument to a method, passing an object context to a method, returning a value from a method, and throwing / catching an exception. For each of these types, a separate dataflow relation has been defined, which we present below using the previously defined fixed template.

In order to illustrate the different types of dataflow relations, let us consider the example in listing 4.2. The example was chosen carefully to contain all dataflow relations, and it will be used during the presentation of each such relation to illustrate its manifestation at the code level.

Listing 4.2: Examples of dataflow relations

```
1   public class Complex {
2     private double r;
3     private double i;
4     public Complex(double rVal, double iVal) {
5       r = rVal;
6       i = iVal;
7     }
8     public Complex div(Complex c) throws DivisionByZeroException {
9       double mod = c.r*c.r + c.i*c.i;
10      if (mod == 0) {
11        throw new DivisionByZeroException();
12      }
13      double rRes = (r*c.r + i*c.i) / mod;
14      double iRes = (i*c.r - r*c.i) / mod;
15      return new Complex(rRes, iRes);
16    }
17    public static void main() {
18      try {
19        Complex a = new Complex(1,2);
20        Complex b = new Complex(3,4);
21        Complex d = a.div(b);
22      } catch (DivisionByZeroException ex) {
23      }
24    }
25  }
```

Simple assignment

Definition: The simple assignment relation represents an assignment between a source abstract location and a target abstract location. The direction of the relation is given by the direction of the value transfer.

Extraction from code: At the code level, the simple assignment relation is a relation between an abstract location referenced in the R-value of an assignment statement and its L-value. If the R-value of an assignment references more than one abstract location, we have several simple assignment relations, one for each of the referenced abstract locations. Because we are only interested to track value transfer between abstract locations, constant literals used in R-values are ignored.

Examples: The assignment statements in lines 5, 6, 9, 13, 14, 19, 20, and 21 of listing 4.2 resulted in the simple assignment relations shown in figure 4.2, which depicts a subgraph of the concern graph. Note that the assignment statements in lines 13 and 14 have complex expressions as R-values, referencing more than one abstract location. As already pointed out, these statements resulted in several simple assignment relations.

Because listing 4.2 contains only a single class definition, in order to improve the readability of the node labels, for abstract locations defined inside methods, we omitted the fully qualified name of the containing class, prefixing their qualified unique names.

The labels of the arcs shown in figure 4.2 contain the object and call contexts of the source and target abstract locations, as defined in section 4.1.1. Because the non-static field `Complex.r` is referenced twice in line 13 of listing 4.2 using two different object contexts, the concern graph contains two differently labelled simple assignment relations between the non-static class field `Complex.r` and the local value abstract location `rRes` defined in method `div(Complex)`. The same is also true for the assignment in line 14, as well as for the non-static class field `Complex.i`, referenced both in lines 13 and 14 of listing 4.2.

Note that the assignment in line 9 of listing 4.2 also references the non-static class field `Complex.r` twice, but using the same object context. As a result, the concern graph contains in this case a single simple assignment relation between the abstract location `Complex.r` and the abstract location `mod` defined in method `div(Complex)`. The same is true for the class field `Complex.i`, which is also referenced in the same assignemnt.

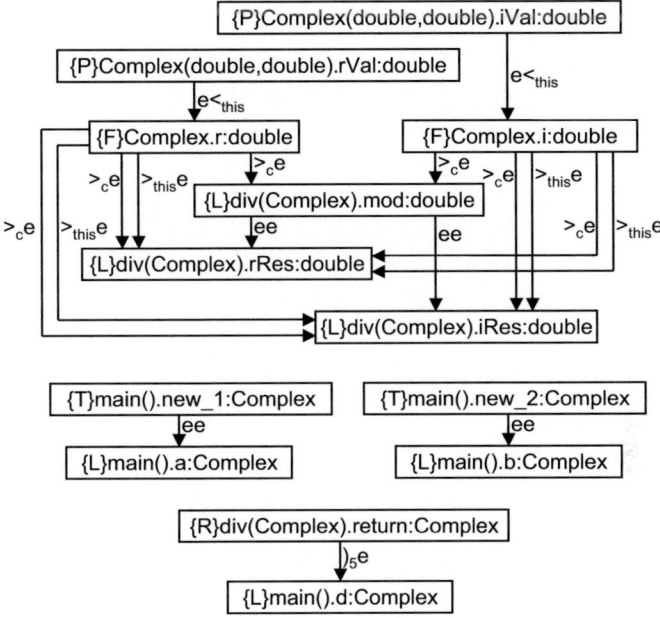

Figure 4.2: Concern subgraph capturing simple assignment relations

Parameter assignment

Definition: The parameter assignment relation represents the passing of an argument to a method, when calling it. It is a relation between an abstract location referenced in the passed argument and the formal parameter of the called method. The direction of the relation is from the argument to the formal parameter.

Extraction from code: At the code level, we extract parameter assignment relations for every argument passed in every method call, if the argument expression references at least one abstract location. As in the case of simple assignment, passing an argument to a method may result in several parameter assignment relations, one for each referenced abstract location. Similarly, constant literals used in the argument expression are ignored.

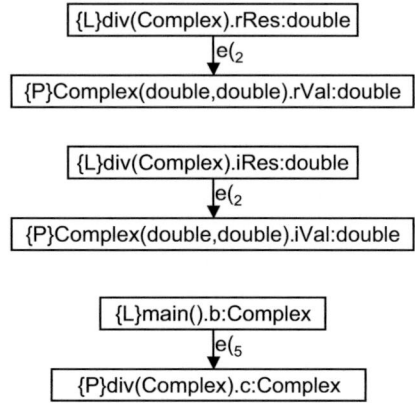

Figure 4.3: Concern subgraph capturing parameter assignment relations

Examples: Listing 4.2 contains three examples of parameter assignment relations, corresponding to the constructor call in line 15 and the method call in line 21. Note that the two constructor calls in lines 19 and 20 produced no parameter assignment relations, because the passed argument expressions contain only literals. Following the same notational conventions as above, the parameter assignment relations are depicted in figure 4.3.

The labels of the arcs shown in figure 4.3 contain the call contexts of the target formal parameters, as defined in section 4.1.1.

Object context assignment

Definition: The object context assignment relation represents the passing of an object context to a method, when calling it. It is a relation between the abstract location representing the object on which the method is invoked, and the implicit object context abstract location of the invoked method. The direction of the relation if from the invocation object to the object context abstract location.

Extraction from code: A call to a non-static method in an OO language can be viewed as a function call in a procedural language, which has as its first argument the invocation object itself. From this perspective, the object context assignment relation is basically a particular case of the parameter assignment relation. In case of Java code, the target of this relation is always the implicitly defined object context abstract location `this` of the called method.

Note that because static methods have no implicitly defined object context abstract locations, the concern graph contains no object context assignment relations for static method calls. Also note that, while constructors are not explicitly invoked on an object, they do have the object context abstract location `this`, which receives the newly created object instance.

Normally, the Java language requires an explicit call to a super constructor or another constructor of the same class as a first statement of each defined constructor. The only exception to this rule is when the called super constructor is actually the default no-args constructor of the super class. In this case, the call may be omitted from the code, because the compiler inserts such a call automatically. When extracting this relation, we follow the same convention as the Java compiler, and extract an implicit object context assignment relation for every constructor, which has no explicit call to another constructor, between its object context abstract location and the object context abstract location of the default no-args constructor.

Furthermore, because the Java language allows direct initialization of non-static class fields at definition, and because these field initializers can also reference an implicitly defined class-level object context abstract location `this`, receiving the value of one of the object context abstract locations of the class constructors, the concern graph contains several additional implicit object context assignment relations, one from each object context abstract location of a constructor to the class-level object context abstract location. We call these relations implicit, because they are not the result of passing an invocation object to a method, but rather the result of the internal class initialization mechanism of the Java language.

Examples: Listing 4.2 contains several examples of this relation, corresponding to the constructor calls in lines 11, 15, 19 and 20, as well as the method call in line 21. These relations are depicted in figure 4.4. Note that the figure also shows two implicit object context assignment relations, one for the class constructor `Complex(double,double)`, and one for the class constructor `DivisionByZeroException()`.

The labels of the arcs shown in figure 4.4 contain the call contexts of the target object context abstract locations of the invoked methods, as defined in section 4.1.1.

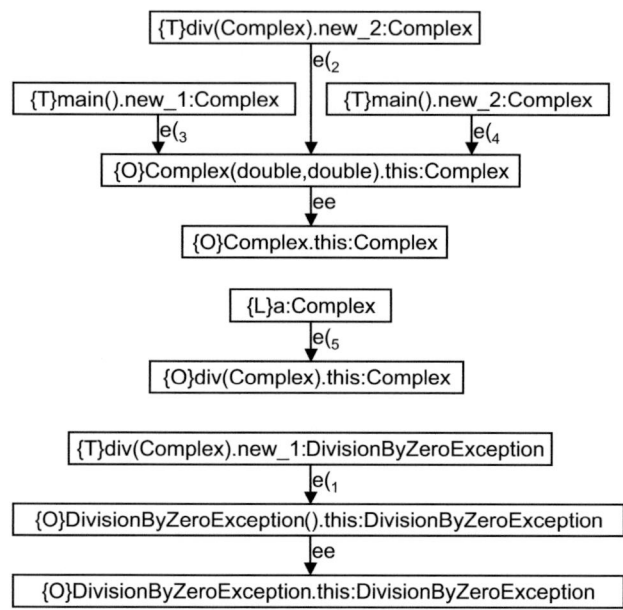

Figure 4.4: Concern subgraph capturing object context assignment relations

Return value assignment

Definition: The return value assignment relation represents the returning of a value from a method. It is a relation between a source abstract location and the return value abstract location of a method. The direction of the relation is from the source abstract location to the return value abstract location.

Extraction from code: At the code level, the return value assignment is a relation between an abstract location referenced in the expression of a return statement and the implicitly defined return value abstract location of a method. As in the case of simple assignment and parameter assignment, constant literals used in the returned expression are ignored. As already pointed out in section 4.1 the return value abstract location in the Java languge is unnamed, but in order to improve the read-

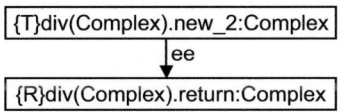

Figure 4.5: Concern subgraph capturing return value assignment relations

ability of the concern graph, we use the short name `return` to refer to it.

Examples: Our example in listing 4.2 contains an example of this relation, corresponding to the return statement in line 15. The corresponding graphical representation of this relation is shown in figure 4.5. Because the return value abstract location of a method is local to the method definition, its context is always the empty context.

Exception assignment

Definition: The exception assignment relation is a relation between an abstract location representing a thrown object and the exception parameter of a catch clause, which can potentially catch this object. The direction of this relation is from the thrown object to the catch parameter.

Extraction from code: At the code level, this relation is not explicit and it is somewhat harder to track, because the actual catch clause, catching an exception object is not identified at the location where the throw occurs. Furthermore, because the catch clause and the throw site may be in different methods, or different classes even, extracting this relation requires a global analysis of the source code.

We extract this relation in two passes. In the first pass, we record for each method the abstract locations representing the locally thrown exception objects, which are not caught within the method itself. In the second pass over the source code, we extract the actual exception assignment relations as follows. For each try statement, we determine all abstract locations representing exception objects thrown inside the try block, including exception objects thrown and not caught in called methods, and match them to the corresponding catch clauses based on type compatibility.

Because an exception may be thrown in an indirectly called method, we traverse the call graph in a depth-first fashion and carry out the above mentioned operations

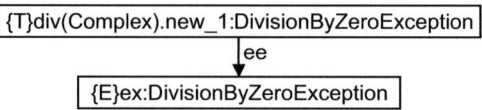

Figure 4.6: Concern subgraph capturing exception assignment relations

recursively for each called method. In order to accelerate the extraction of the exception assignment relations, and to break potential cycles in the call graph due to recursive method calls, we maintain a list of visited methods to avoid visiting the same method multiple times for different calls.

Examples: Listing 4.2 contains an example of this relation, corresponding to the exception throw statement in line 11 and the catch clause in line 22. The relation is graphically depicted in figure 4.6. Because an exception parameter is local to the method definition, its context is always the empty context.

4.2.2. Inheritance Relations

Since the dataflow relations presented in the previous section only take into consideration the declared type of an invocation object and not its actual type, in case of a call to a polymorphic method, they only capture direct value transfer to and from the abstract locations defined in this method. However, because object-oriented languages support dynamic binding, meaning that a call to a polymorphic method may actually result in a call to any of its overriding methods.

If we assume a code base, conforming to the Liskov Substitution Principle (Martin 96b), we can adopt a conservative solution to this problem and consider additional relations to capture the potential value transfers to and from overriding methods.

From a theoretical point of view, the correct solution to this problem is to duplicate each dataflow relation involving value transfer to and from a polymorphic method for every method overriding this polymorphic method. This however, has the disadvantage, that it makes the extraction more complicated and the resulting concern graph rather large.

From a practical point of view, a better solution is to use the following approximation, which keeps the size of the concern graph smaller, while maintaining the integrity of the flow relations between abstract locations. Instead of duplicating dataflow relations, we introduce a number of inheritance relations, which are used to represent potential value transfer relations between the formal parameters, object context abstract location, and return value abstract location of a polymorphic method and the corresponding formal parameters, object context abstract location, and return value abstract location of an overriding method.

Although in the code, there is no actual value transfer between an abstract location of a polymorphic method and the corresponding abstract location of an overriding method, this has no impact on the concern extent identification. This is because we already assume, by using a conservative analysis of polymorphic method calls, that for any value transfer involving an abstract location in a polymorphic method, we also consider all value transfers involving the corresponding abstract locations in all overriding methods.

Inheritance relations are also direct flow relations, and their corresponding arcs in the concern graph are always labelled with a double "empty context" *ee*.

In order to illustrate the different types of inheritance relations, let us consider the example in listing 4.3. The example was chosen carefully to contain all inheritance relations, and it will be used during the presentation of each such relation to illustrate its manifestation at the code level.

Listing 4.3: Examples of inheritance relations

```
1   public abstract class Shape {
2     public abstract void scale(double factor);
3     public abstract double getArea();
4   }
5   public class Circle extends Shape {
6     private double radius;
7     public void scale(double f) {
8       radius = radius * f;
9     }
10    public double getArea() {
11      return Math.PI * radius * radius;
12    }
13  }
14  public class Square extends Shape {
15    private double side;
16    public void scale(double f) {
17      side = side * f;
18    }
```

```
19      public double getArea() {
20          return side * side;
21      }
22  }
```

Parameter inheritance

Definition: The parameter inheritance relation represents a potential value transfer between a formal parameter of a polymorphic method and the corresponding formal parameter of an overriding method. The direction of this relation is from the formal parameter of the polymorphic method to the formal parameter of the overriding method, and the intuitive justification for it is that any argument passed to the polymorphic method may actually end up being passed to one of its overriding methods.

Extraction from code: At the code level, this relation is also not explicit and requires an analysis of the inheritance hierarchies, in order to detect overriding methods. We extract a parameter inheritance relation for every formal parameter of every overriding method of a given polymorphic method. Since constructors are not polymorphic methods, no parameter inheritance relations are extracted for them.

Note that we only extract parameter inheritance relations for direct overriding methods, but because we do this for all methods, including methods defined in libraries, the concern graph will contain in the end all potential flow relations, even though some direct flow relations may only appear as indirect flow relations.

Examples:

The code in listing 4.3 includes two examples of this relation, corresponding to the definitions of the overriding `scale(double)` methods in lines 7 and 16. These relations are shown in figure 4.7, which presents a subgraph of the concern graph.

Note that the arcs in figure 4.7 are all labelled with double empty contexts. This is because the call context of a target abstract location representing a formal parameter is always the same as the call context of the corresponding source formal parameter.

Object context inheritance

Definition: The object context relation is very similar to the parameter inheritance relation, and represents a potential value transfer between an object context ab-

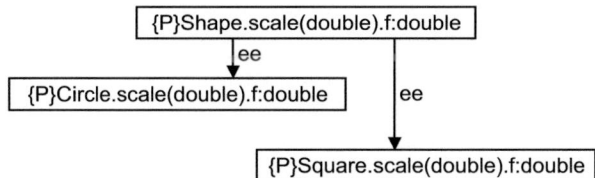

Figure 4.7: Concern subgraph capturing parameter inheritance relations

stract location implicitly defined in a superclass and the corresponding object context abstract location implicitly defined in a subclass. The direction of this relation is from the object context abstract location in the superclass to the object context abstract location in the subclass. Based on the previously discussed observation that the object context abstract location can be regarded as an implicit formal parameter of a method, the intuitive justification for this relation is identical to the one for parameter inheritance.

Extraction from code: As already pointed out in case of the object context assignment relation, object context abstract locations are implicitly defined for all non-static methods of a class. And, for every overriding method of a given polymorphic method, we extract an object context inheritance relation. Since constructors are not polymorphic methods, no object context inheritance relations are extracted for them. We also do not extract any such relations between the class-level object context abstract locations, because the value transfer to these abstract locations is already captured by the object context assignment relations.

Note that we only extract these relations for direct overriding methods, but because we do this for all methods, including methods defined in library code, the concern graph will contain in the end all potential flow relations, even though some direct flow relations may only appear as indirect flow relations.

Examples:

Listing 4.3 contains four examples of this relation, corresponding to the definitions of the overriding methods `scale(double)` and `getArea()` of the `Circle` and `Square` classes found in lines 7, 10, 16, and 19. The relations are depicted in figure 4.8.

Note that the arcs in figure 4.8 are all labelled with double empty contexts. This is because the call context of a target object context abstract location is always the same

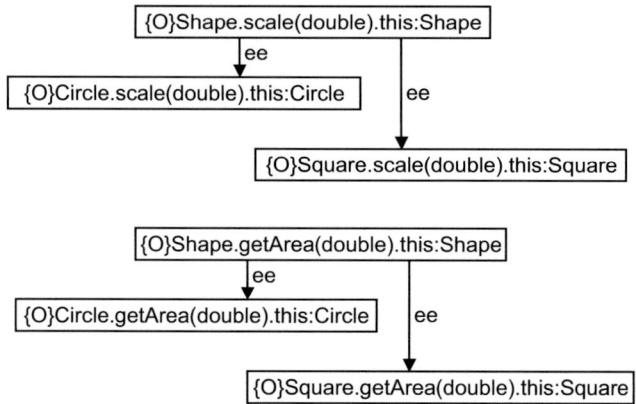

Figure 4.8: Concern subgraph capturing object context inheritance relations

as the call context of the corresponding source object context abstract location.

Return value inheritance

Definition: The return value inheritance relation is intended to capture potential value transfers from the return value abstract locations of an overriding method of a given polymorphic method to the return value abstract location of the polymorphic method. The intuitive justification for this relation is very similar as the one for the previous inheritance relation, with the difference that the direction of the relation is reversed, because returning a value from a polymorphic method may actually result in returning a value from any of its overriding methods.

Extraction from code: At the code level, this relation is also identified through an analysis of the inheritance hierarchies, in order to detect overriding methods. For every overriding method of a given polymorphic method, having a non-void return type, we extract an return value inheritance relation. As in the case of parameter inheritance and object context inheritance, we only extract these relations for direct overriding methods, but also including methods defined in library code.

Examples: The code in listing 4.3 contains two examples of return value inheritance relations, corresponding to the definitions of the overriding getArea() methods

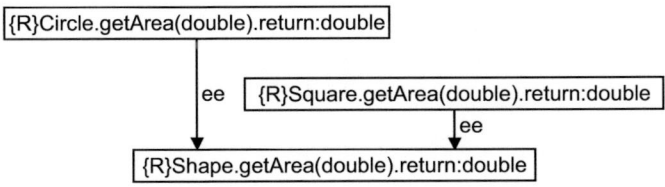

Figure 4.9: Concern subgraph capturing return value inheritance relations

of the `Circle` and `Square` classes from lines 10 and 19. The relations are shown in the subgraph of the concern graph from figure 4.9.

Note that the arcs in figure 4.9 are all labelled with double empty contexts. This is because the call context of a target return value abstract location is always the same as the call context of the corresponding source return value abstract location.

4.2.3. Direct Dependency Relations

The direct dependency relations are also direct flow relations, but they do not represent direct or potential value transfer between abstract locations. These relations are used for any other type of direct influence of a source abstract location on a target abstract location, which is not a direct value transfer. These relations model implicit flow relations such as control-flow induced dependencies, dependencies between an array and its index abstract locations, and dependencies between a non-static field and the abstract location representing its enclosing object.

In order to illustrate the different types of direct dependency relations, let us consider the example in listing 4.4. The example was chosen carefully to contain all direct dependency relations, and it will be used during the presentation of each such relation to illustrate its manifestation at the code level.

Listing 4.4: Examples of direct dependency relations

```
1   public class Vector {
2       private int size;
3       private double[] elems;
```

```
4     public Vector (int size) {
5       this.size = size;
6       elems = new double[size];
7     }
8     public Vector div(double f) {
9       if (f != 0) {
10        Vector res = new Vector(size);
11        double[] tmp = res.elems;
12        for (int i=0; i<size; i++) {
13          tmp[i] = elems[i] / f;
14        }
15        return res;
16      }
17      return null;
18    }
19  }
```

Control-flow dependency

Definition: The control-flow dependency relation is a direct dependency relation between an abstract location used in a condition, whose logical value determines whether a value transfer takes place or not, and the target abstract location of this value transfer. The direction of this relation is from the abstract location used in the condition to the target abstract location of the value transfer. Although there is no actual value transfer between the source abstract location and the target abstract location of this relation, the value of the source abstract location influences the value of the target abstract location, by allowing or disallowing an actual value transfer.

Extraction from code: At the code level, this relation appears between all abstract locations referenced inside the condition part of a conditional branch or a loop statement and all abstract locations, which are assigned to within the body of the conditional branch or the loop statement. Note that in this context "assigned to" actually means that the abstract location in question is the target of any kind of dataflow relation, appearing within the body of the statement containing the condition.

Examples: The code in listing 4.4 contains several examples of this relation type, corresponding to the conditions in lines 9 and 12. These relations are shown in the subgraph of the concern graph from figure 4.10.

Note that the condition part of the loop statement in line 12 references two abstract locations: size and i, and this results in two control-flow dependencies from these

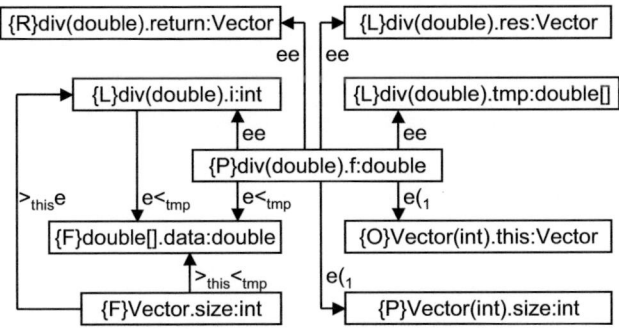

Figure 4.10: Concern subgraph capturing control-flow dependency relations

abstract locations to the internal data field of `double[]`, for the simple assignment in line 13. Furthermore, because the abstract location `i` is a loop counter, its value is incremented within the body of the loop statement, meaning that it is also the target of a control-flow dependency from `size`.

Somewhat less obvious are the control-flow dependencies involving the object context abstract location and the formal parameter of the constructor `Vector(int)`. These abstract locations are also assigned within the body of the conditional statement in line 9.

The labels of the arcs shown in figure 4.10 contain the object and call contexts of the source and target abstract locations, as defined in section 4.1.1. A more interesting case is the label of the arc between the field `size` of class `Vector` and the internal data field of `double[]`, because it captures both the "exit context" of the source abstract location and the "enter context" of the target abstract location.

Collection index dependency

Definition: The collection index dependency relation is a direct dependency relation between an abstract location used to index a collection variable represented by the target abstract location. The direction of the relation is from the index abstract location to the indexed collection, and the intuitive justification behind it is that the value of the index abstract location is used to access the desired element in the collection.

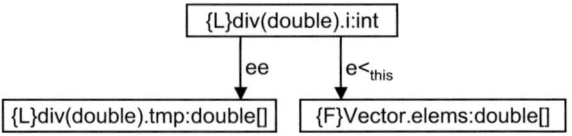

Figure 4.11: Concern subgraph capturing collection index dependency relations

Extraction from code: At the code level, this relation appears between an abstract location and a collection indexed by this abstract location. For each use of the index operator "[]", we extract collection index dependency relations for all abstract locations used in the index expression. Although the Java language allows the use of the index operator only for arrays, other object-oriented languages, such as C++ or C#, support the definition of this operator for other collection types too. Note that this artificial distinction between arrays and other indexable collection types in Java, such as the standard collection classes, can be eliminated by supporting the addition of user-specified relations to the concern graph. A mechanism to do this will be described in section 4.4.

Examples: Listing 4.4 contains two examples of this relation, corresponding to the two uses of the index operator on the two arrays `tmp` and `elems` in line 13, which are shown in figure 4.11. The labels of the arcs in the figure represent the call and object contexts of the source and target abstract locations involved in the relation.

Collection element dependency

Definition: The collection element dependency relation is a direct dependency relation between the internal data field of a collection and the abstract location representing the enclosing collection. The direction of this relation is from the field to the enclosing collection, and the intuitive justification behind it is that changing the value of a collection element represents a change of the entire collection.

Extraction from code: We extract such relations, for each collection type, from its internal data field to every object creation abstract location having the enclosing collection type as data type. Given the fact that our approach treats array types in a similar fashion, and models flow relations involving array elements as flow relations involving an internal data field of the array type, we also extract a collection element

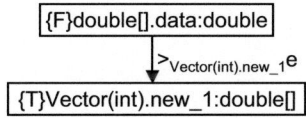

Figure 4.12: Concern subgraph capturing collection element dependency relations

dependency relation, for every array type, from its internal data field to every object creation abstract location having this array type.

Examples: Our example from listing 4.4 contains a collection element relation from the internal data field of `double[]` to the object creation abstract location `new_-1` defined in method `Vector(int)`. This relation is depicted graphically in the subgraph of the concern graph shown in figure 4.12.

4.3. Separation of Superimposed Roles

As defined in section 2.1, a crosscutting concern is a concern whose implementation cannot be encapsulated using object-oriented language constructs, in the context of an existing architecture, design, and set of implementation conventions. The implementation of such a concern is scattered over many locations and tangled with the implementations of other concerns.

Because direct flow relations often cross method or class boundaries, the fact that crosscutting concerns are scattered over many locations does not affect the identification of such concerns. However, in order to cope with the tangling of multiple concerns within the same class, we need a special handling of the abstract locations having such class types. The problem with these abstract locations is that, while holding instances of such classes, they exhibit a superimposition of the different roles fulfilled by the class. The same abstract location may appear in several semantically different contexts, belonging to separate functional concerns, but because the abstract location has a single identity, these roles cannot be properly separated as required by an accurate concern identification approach.

The detection of superimposed class roles is based on the following heuristic rule.

Heuristic rule 1. *Each non-empty interface, implemented or inherited by a class type, represents an additional superimposed role of the class type.*

This heuristic rule is supported by a common object-oriented design principle, known as the Interface Segregation Principle (Martin 96a), stating that "clients should not be forced to depend upon methods that they do not use." A direct consequence of this principle is that interface definitions usually contain a small number of semantically related methods, relevant for a single context, representing a single role.

In many object-oriented languages such as the Java language, the composition of roles at the class interface level is achieved by simultaneously implementing multiple interfaces, either directly or indirectly. This means that if we calculate the transitive closure of the inheritance relation for a given class type and consider only the non-empty interfaces from the set of super types, we end up with the set of superimposed class roles.

In order to achieve the separation of superimposed class roles, we duplicate each abstract location having as type a class fulfilling multiple roles, so that for each distinct role there is a dedicated copy of the abstract location in question. Each class has a main role, given by its type identity and a number of additional superimposed roles, corresponding to the implemented interfaces. For each such role, we create copies of all abstract locations having the given class type and assign them the interface type corresponding to the role in question. Besides allowing us to distinguish the copies of an abstract location in the concern graph, having a different type for each copy is also required in order to select the appropriate copy of an abstract location involved in a direct flow relation, as discussed below.

When extracting a direct flow relation between a source abstract location $u \in V$ and a target abstract location $v \in V$, where the class type of u has several superimposed roles, we select the copy of u corresponding to the superimposed role matching the type of v. If an exact match is not found, the original abstract location u, corresponding to the main role of the class, is selected.

Note that duplicating abstract locations also means that we might need to duplicate direct flow relations. If a direct flow relation involves two abstract locations, which have the same class type and have been duplicated as discussed above, the direct flow relation between these abstract locations also has to be duplicated for each additional superimposed role, resulting in a direct flow relation between the corresponding copies of the two abstract locations.

The situation, where a direct flow relation involves two abstract locations, which have different class type, but both having superimposed roles, was not discussed, because it cannot appear in a typical object-oriented language. The situation is only possible in a language, supporting unrestricted cast operations involving types from outside the type hierarchy of the casted value.

To make things clearer, let us consider the code example in listing 4.5.[1]

Listing 4.5: Example of superimposed class roles

```
1   class Image {
2     public void register(ImageObserver o) {
3     }
4   }
5   class Drawing {
6     public void addListener(DrawingChangeListener l) {
7     }
8   }
9   class DrawingView implements ImageObserver, DrawingChangeListener {
10    private Image image;
11    private Drawing drawing;
12    public void init() {
13       image.register(this);
14       drawing.addListener(this);
15    }
16    public static void main() {
17       DrawingView view = new DrawingView();
18       view.init();
19    }
20  }
```

The class DrawingView implements the interface ImageObserver and fulfils the role of an observer as defined by the Observer design pattern in relation with the class Image. At the same time, it also fulfils the role of a drawing change event listener and implements the interface DrawingChangeListener, with respect to the class Drawing.

The critical piece of code is found in the method init(). This method registers an instance of the class DrawingView both as an observer of the class Image and as an drawing change event listener to the class Drawing. Note that the same object context abstract location this is used for both registrations, which makes it impossible to separate the two superimposed roles, when identifying concern im-

---

[1] The example was adapted from the JHotDraw case study presented in chapter 6.

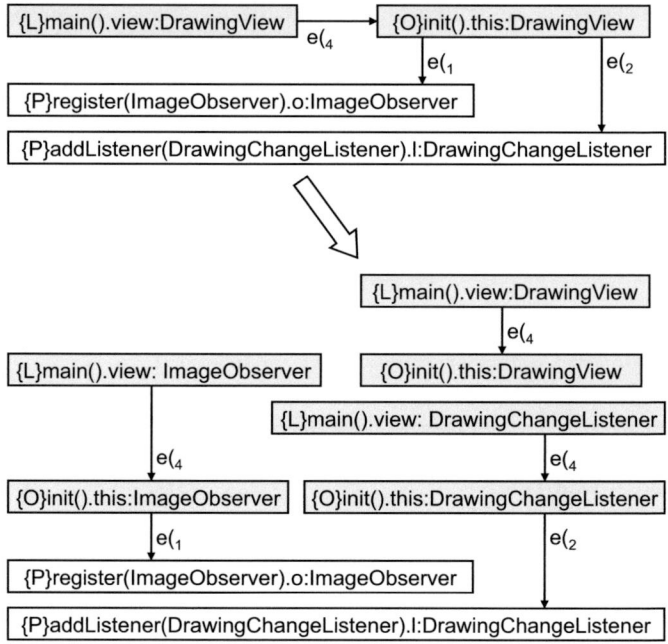

Figure 4.13: Concern graphs showing the separation of superimposed class roles

plementations. And since the two roles in question (`ImageObserver` and `Draw-ingChangeListener`) are completely distinct from a semantic point of view, they represent two different functional concerns.

Figure 4.13 shows the effect of this separation on the concern graph corresponding to our example from listing 4.5. The figure shows only a subgraph of the concern graph, with the affected nodes grayed.

In our concrete example, the object context abstract location `this` of method `init()` in class `DrawingView` is represented in the concern graph by three abstract locations: one for the main role of the class having the type `DrawingView`, one for the observer role having the type `ImageObserver`, and one for the drawing change event listener role having the type `DrawingChangeListener`.

The selection of the actual abstract location is done based on the type of the other abstract location involved in the direct flow relation, which is the formal parameter of the method `register(ImageObserver)` from class `Image` in case of the first call, and the formal parameter of the method `addListener(DrawingChangeListener)` from class `Drawing` in case of the second call. When constructing the concern graph, the parameter assignment relation extracted for the first call uses the copy created for the observer role, whereas the parameter assignment relation extracted for the second call uses the copy created for the drawing change event listener role.

4.4. Dealing with Libraries

In section 4.2 we discussed the particularities of the extraction from source code for all types of direct flow relations. If the entire source code of the analyzed software system is available, we can use this information to construct the entire concern graph.

In real software systems the situation is quite different. Real software systems use libraries, whose source code is sometimes unavailable. In case of Java systems, the situation is even more complicated because many frequently used parts of the Java standard library use native implementations, meaning that for these parts there is no Java source code at all.

Unfortunately, completely ignoring the direct flow relations between abstract locations defined in libraries leads to a loss of precision in the identification of concern implementations, which, depending on the case, might not be tolerable. Note that the direct flow relations to and from library abstract locations directly referenced in the source code of Σ are recorded in the concern graph. But, if we have an indirect flow relation between two abstract locations $u \in V$ and $v \in V$, and this indirect flow passes through at least one intermediate library abstract location $w \notin V$, which is not directly referenced in the source code of Σ, this indirect flow relation will be lost, because the chain of direct flow relations linking u and v, recorded in the concern graph, will be missing the two direct flow relations to and from w.

Even if we assume that we can obtain the complete source code of all the libraries used by a software system, and that we can also extract direct flow relations from the native implementations, because the implementations of libraries tend to be more general in order to fit many usage scenarios, the resulting concern graph will be cluttered with many implementation details of these libraries, making it much larger and much more complex than required for the identification of concern implementations. Furthermore, in some cases it is desirable to treat a separate subsystem of the analyzed system as a library. This would exclude its implementation details from the resulting concern graph, and would allow an effective user control over the scope of the analysis.

Fortunately, there is a middle ground between completely ignoring libraries and analyzing their entire source code. We can compose the concern graph from several smaller concern graphs, using the concern graph union operation defined in section 4.1. The first concern graph is extracted from the source code of Σ, ignoring direct flow relations between library abstract locations, while the remaining concern graphs are actually flow-equivalent concern subgraphs of the libraries used by Σ, containing all library abstract locations referenced in the source code of Σ. The following subsection develops this idea further.

4.4.1. Flow-Equivalent Concern Subgraphs

Definition 19. *A flow-equivalent concern subgraph of a concern graph $G = (V, A, s, t, L_V, L_A, \ell_V, \ell_A)$ is also a concern graph $G^= = (V', A', s', t', L_{V'}, L'_{A'}, \ell_{V'}, \ell_{A'})$ obtained from G by eliminating and short-circuiting some vertices, where $V' \subset V$ and $\forall u, v \in V'$ we have:*

$$(u, v) \in A' \iff (u \to v)$$
$$\vee \quad (u \dashrightarrow v \wedge \nexists w \in V' : w \neq u \wedge w \neq v \wedge u \rightsquigarrow w \wedge w \rightsquigarrow v)$$

In the previous definition, the functions $s', t' : A' \to V'$, the language $L_{V'}$, and the functions $\ell_{V'} : V' \to L_{V'}$ and $\ell_{A'} : A' \to L'_{A'}$ are defined as in definition 17. However, because a flow-equivalent concern subgraph may contain arcs for indirect flow relations, the language $L'_{A'}$, used to label these arcs, must also contain all concatenations of arbitrary length of words from L_A. In formal terms, $L'_{A'}$ is defined as follows:

$$L'_{A'} = L_A \cup \{\ell_1 \cdot \ell_2 \mid \ell_1 \in L_A \wedge \ell_2 \in L'_{A'}\}$$

Note that for a given concern graph, we can construct several flow-equivalent concern subgraphs, depending on the set of eliminated vertices. However, as proven in the following lemma, the results of identifying concern implementations in a software system Σ is independent of the flow-equivalent concern subgraph, provided that this graph contains all abstract locations defined in the library and referenced in the source code of Σ.

Lemma 2. *A flow-equivalent concern subgraph $G_2^=$ for a library Σ_L used by a software system Σ, containing all abstract locations from Σ_L referenced in the source code of Σ, does not affect the precision of concern extent identification for system Σ.*

Proof. Let $G_1 = (V_1, A_1)$ be the concern graph extracted from the source code of Σ, $G_2 = (V_2, A_2)$ the concern graph extracted from the source code of the library Σ_L, and $G_2^= = (V_2', A_2')$ a flow-equivalent concern subgraph for the library Σ_L. Let $\rightarrow_1 \subset (V_1 \cup V_2) \times (V_1 \cup V_2)$ be the direct flow relation defined by the $G_1 \cup G_2$, $\rightarrow_2 \subset (V_1 \cup V_2') \times (V_1 \cup V_2')$ the direct flow relation defined by the $G_1 \cup G_2^=$, $\rightsquigarrow_1 \subset (V_1 \cup V_2) \times (V_1 \cup V_2)$ the transitive closure of $\rightarrow_1$, and $\rightsquigarrow_2 \subset (V_1 \cup V_2') \times (V_1 \cup V_2')$ the transitive closure of $\rightarrow_2$.

In order to prove this lemma, we need to show that the restriction to V_1 of the flow relation $\rightsquigarrow_1$ is equal to the restriction to V_1 of the flow relation $\rightsquigarrow_2$. In other words, we need to show that $\forall u, v \in V_1$, we have $u \rightsquigarrow_1 v \iff u \rightsquigarrow_2 v$.

Let $u, v \in V_1$ be two abstract locations, such that $u \rightsquigarrow_1 v$. Given the fact that $u, v \in V_1$, this means that the two abstract locations are referenced in the implementation of Σ. If $u \rightarrow_1 v$, then we have $(u, v) \in A_1 \cup A_2$. On the one hand, if $(u, v) \in A_1$ then we also have $(u, v) \in A_1 \cup A_2'$. On the other hand, if we have $(u, v) \in A_2$, then we must also have $u, v \in V_2$. And given the fact that u and v are both referenced in the implementation of Σ, we also have by definition of $G_2^=$ that $u, v \in V_2'$. Based on the definition of the flow-equivalent concern subgraph, if $(u, v) \in A_2$ and $u, v \in V_2'$, then we also have $(u, v) \in A_2'$, and therefore $(u, v) \in A_1 \cup A_2'$. We have proven so far that $u \rightarrow_1 v \Rightarrow u \rightarrow_2 v$, which also means $u \rightsquigarrow_2 v$. If, however, $u \dashrightarrow_1 v$, then this means that $\exists w_1, w_2, ..., w_n \in V_1 \cup V_2, n > 2$, so that $u = w_1 \wedge w_n = v \wedge w_i \rightarrow_1 w_{i+1}$, for $1 \le i < n$. If all $w_i \in V_1$, for $1 \le i < n$, then using the same procedure as above, we can prove that $(w_i, w_{i+1}) \in A_1 \cup A_2'$, meaning that $w_i \rightarrow_2 w_{i+1}$, for $1 \le i < n$. Based on this result, we can conclude that $u \dashrightarrow_2 v$, and also that $u \rightsquigarrow_2 v$. We still need to consider the case when $\exists j, k : 1 < j, k < n \wedge j < k \wedge w_j, w_{j+1}, ..., w_k \notin V_1$. Without loosing generality, we can consider that $w_{j-1}, w_{k+1} \in V_1$. Using the same procedure as above we can prove that $u \rightsquigarrow_2 w_{j-1}$ and that $w_{k+1} \rightsquigarrow_2 v$. Because $w_j, w_k \notin V_1$, based on the definitions of G_1, the direct flow relations $(w_{j-1}, w_j), (w_k, w_{k+1}) \notin A_1$, meaning that $(w_{j-1}, w_j), (w_k, w_{k+1}) \in A_2$. Of course this also means that $w_{j-1}, w_{k+1} \in V_2$, and because they are referenced in the implementation of Σ, we also have $w_{j-1}, w_{k+1} \in V_2'$. If $w_i \in V_2'$ for $j - 1 \le i \le k + 1$, then we can conclude that $w_i \rightarrow_2 w_{i+1}$, for $j - 1 \le i < k + 1$, meaning also $w_{j-1} \rightsquigarrow_2 w_{k+1}$. If, however,

$\exists l, m : j - 1 < l, m < k + 1 \ \wedge \ l < m \ \wedge \ w_l, w_{l+1}, ..., w_m \notin V_2'$, based on the definition of the flow-equivalent concern subgraph, we deduce that $(w_{j-1}, w_{k+1}) \in A_2'$, meaning that $w_{j-1} \rightarrow_2 w_{k+1}$, and also that $w_{j-1} \rightsquigarrow_2 w_{k+1}$. Based on this, the fact that $u \rightsquigarrow_2 w_{j-1}$, $w_{k+1} \rightsquigarrow_2 v$, and that the flow relation is transitive, we deduce that $u \rightsquigarrow_2 v$. If we combine all of the above statements, we obtain $u \rightsquigarrow_1 v \Rightarrow u \rightsquigarrow_2 v$.

In order to prove the reverse implication, we will start from the observation that $\rightsquigarrow_2$ is the transitive closure of $\rightarrow_2$. Because $\rightarrow_2$ is defined by the concern graph $G_1 \cup G_2^=$, this means that $\forall u, v \in V_1 \cup V_2'$ we have $u \rightarrow_2 v \iff (u, v) \in A_1 \cup A_2'$. If $(u, v) \in A_1$, this also means that $(u, v) \in A_1 \cup A_2$, meaning that $u \rightarrow_1 v$, and therefore $u \rightsquigarrow_1 v$. If, however $(u, v) \in A_2'$, based on the construction of the flow-equivalent concern subgraph, we deduce that either $(u, v) \in A_2$, meaning that $u \rightarrow_1 v$ and also $u \rightsquigarrow_1 v$, or that $\exists w_1, w_2, ..., w_n \in V_2, n > 2$, so that $u = w_1 \ \wedge \ w_n = v \ \wedge \ (w_i, w_{i+1}) \in A_2$, for $1 \le i < n$. This also means that $w_i \rightarrow_1 w_{i+1}$, for $1 \le i < n$, and therefore $u \rightsquigarrow_1 v$. If we combine the above results, we obtain $u \rightsquigarrow_2 v \Rightarrow u \rightsquigarrow_1 v$. $\qquad \square$

A flow-equivalent concern subgraph can be either defined manually using the notation described in section 4.4.2, or extracted automatically from the source code of a library, if the entire source code is available.

A manually defined flow-equivalent concern subgraph for an entire library is usually smaller, enabling a more efficient concern extent identification, but it also requires a large initial effort for creating it. However, given the fact that such a flow-equivalent concern subgraph is reusable for other software systems too, in case of frequently used libraries, this large initial effort may be justified.

For a less frequently used library, we could rely on automatically extracted flow-equivalent concern subgraphs, if such graphs can be extracted from the source code of the library. The reduced concern graph, defined in section 5.4.1, is an example of an automatically extracted flow-equivalent concern subgraph, which eliminates a large number of abstract locations. Although the reduced concern graph is on average significantly smaller the the original concern graph, as discussed in chapter 6, in some cases it might still be too large or too complex to use directly.

It is also possible to create a flow-equivalent concern subgraph using a combination of manual definition and automatic extraction, if only parts of the source code of the library are used for the analysis, but in this case the effort required to identify and define the missing parts might also be very high.

If the reusability of a flow-equivalent concern subgraph is not an issue, then constructing such a graph for all the libraries used by a given software system Σ is much easier, because it must only contain the flow relations between the library abstract locations directly referenced in the source code of Σ. The list of directly referenced abstract locations can be extracted automatically from the concern graph of Σ, but the flow relations between them must be specified manually.

In some cases, it might even be acceptable to use a flow-equivalent concern subgraph, which covers only parts of a library and captures only a subset of the direct flow relations between the library abstract locations referenced in the source code of Σ, even though this usually affects the precision of the concern extent identification.

It is important to understand that there is a trade-off between the completeness of the flow-equivalent concern subgraphs of the libraries used by Σ, and the size of the concern intent specification, defined in section 5.2.1. A larger and more redundant concern intent specification can compensate to some extent for the loss of precision due to incomplete or even missing flow-equivalent concern subgraphs of the libraries used by Σ.

If we revisit our previous example of an indirect flow relation between two abstract locations u and v used in the implementation of system Σ, passing through an abstract location w defined in a library Σ_L, for which no accurate flow-equivalent concern subgraph is available, the indirect flow relation will be lost and it will affect the precision of the concern extent identification. While it is true that the chain of direct flow relations between u and v will be missing the relations occurring inside the library code, and because of that the flow relation between u and v might be affected, a more redundant concern intent specification can at least accomplish that the two sub-chains of the chain of direct flow relations between u and v to and from the library Σ_L are contained in the same concern extent.

4.4.2. Manual Specification of Concern Graphs

Let $G = (V, A, s, t, L_V, L_A, \ell_V, \ell_A)$ be a concern graph. The manual specification of this graph consists of a list of simple textual representations of all its arcs, each written on a separate line, using the following textual pattern:

$$type(a) \cdot ' - ' \cdot \ell_V(s(a)) \cdot ' - ' \cdot \ell_A(a) \cdot ' - ' \cdot \ell_V(t(a))$$

where $a \in A$ is an arc in G, and $type(a)$ is a string encoding the type of direct flow relation represented by this arc, as shown in table 4.2.

The textual format was created to be human readable and writable, but because of its simplicity, it can also serve as a persistence format for concern graphs. Its main

Direct flow relation type	Encoding
simple assignment	'SA'
parameter assignment	'PA'
object context assignment	'OCA'
return value assignment	'RVA'
exception assignment	'EA'
parameter inheritance	'PI'
object context inheritance	'OCI'
return value inheritance	'RVI'
control-flow dependency	'CFD'
collection index dependency	'CID'
collection element dependency	'CED'

Table 4.2: Encoding of direct flow relation types

advantage is that it allows a user to determine the union of two or more concern graphs, by simply concatenating their respective specifications.

Section A.1 contains a small part of the flow-equivalent concern subgraph specification, created for the library abstract locations directly referenced in our case-studies. Because the specification does not cover the entire standard library, it may lead to a less precise concern extent identification, when used in conjunction with other software systems.

Chapter 5.

Concern Identification Method

This chapter presents our tool-supported concern identification approach, based on context free language reachability in the concern graph. As already mentioned, the approach involves a tool-supported but manual concern intent specification and a fully automated concern extent extraction.

The chapter is structured as follows. Section 5.1 presents a brief overview of the identification process. Section 5.2 is concerned with the manual specification of concern intents, which are used in the automatic extraction of concern skeletons described in section 5.3. Section 5.4 discusses the selection of suitable concern seeds for the specification of concern intents, and finally, section 5.5 introduces three concern maps, particularly useful in supporting program understanding.

5.1. Overview

As already mentioned in section 3.2.4, a concern is represented at the implementation level by a concern skeleton, consisting of a concern intent and a concern extent, and identifying the implementation of a concern amounts to determining the concern extent, which corresponds to a given concern intent.

Beside the label and the set of directly contained subconcerns, a concern intent consists of the sets of information sources and information sinks, collectively known as concern seeds. The concern intent is typically specified manually by the software engineer, but as we will see in section 5.4 the selection of concern seeds can be supported by tools.

These concern seeds act as starting points for the extraction of concern extents, which is based on context free language reachability (Reps 97) in the concern graph. As we will see later in this chapter, this extraction can be reduced to a number of single-source and a number of single-target bounded flow path problems.

However, extracting the concern extents is only part of identifying concern skeletons. It may happen that the extracted concern extents for two concern skeletons overlap, in which case their intersection will form a new concern skeleton, regarded as a shared subconcern skeleton of the two initial concern skeletons. This also means that the concern intents of the two initial concern skeletons must be further refined to reflect this hierarchic decomposition.

Once identified, concern skeletons can be studied in isolation to understand the concern implementations. In order to also support the understanding of the interactions between concern skeletons, we define several abstract representations of the system called concern maps, highlighting specific aspects of these interactions such as: the hierarchic decomposition of concern skeletons, the data dependencies between concern skeletons, or the dispersion of concern skeletons within the class structure.

5.2. Specification of Concern Intents

Given the fact that the Hierarchic Concern Model was created to establish direct traceability links between concerns and their corresponding implementations in code, the model requires a persistent notation for the specification of concern intents. And in order to achieve this, we have defined a simple language, which we describe in the following subsection.

Because our model explicitly separates the concern intent from its extent, and because the extent of a concern is determined using an automated tool, changes to the implementation, which do not affect the intent of the concern, such as most code refactorings, require no manual update of the traceability links. This allows the reuse of an existing intent specification for subsequent versions of the source code, provided that the specified concerns did not change.

The situation is analogous to the separation between interface and implementation in object-oriented programming, allowing clients of the interface to be oblivious to changes in the implementation. In our case, the concern intent is equivalent to the interface, and its extent is equivalent to the implementation.

5.2.1. The CoDEx Language

The concern intent specification language was primarily designed to be readable by humans, but also to be easily parsed by our automated concern skeleton identification tool CoDEx, described in section 6.1.

⟨specification⟩ → ⟨header⟩ ⟨concerns⟩
⟨header⟩ → **namespace** ⟨name⟩ **;**
⟨concerns⟩ → ⟨concern⟩ | ⟨concern⟩ ⟨concerns⟩
⟨concern⟩ → **concern** ⟨identifier⟩ **{** ⟨declarations⟩ **}**
⟨declarations⟩ → ⟨declaration⟩ | ⟨declaration⟩ ⟨declarations⟩
⟨declaration⟩ → ⟨subconcern⟩ | ⟨source⟩ | ⟨sink⟩
⟨subconcern⟩ → **subconcern** ⟨name⟩ **;**
⟨source⟩ → **source** **[exclude]** ⟨name⟩ ⟨bounds_declaration⟩
⟨sink⟩ → **sink** **[exclude]** ⟨name⟩ ⟨bounds_declaration⟩
⟨bounds_declaration⟩ → **;** | **{** ⟨bounds⟩ **}**
⟨bounds⟩ → ⟨bound⟩ | ⟨bound⟩ ⟨bounds⟩
⟨bound⟩ → **cut** ⟨name⟩ **;**
⟨name⟩ → *IDENTIFIER*

Figure 5.1: Grammar of the concern intent specification language

Figure 5.1 shows the grammar of the CODEX language in EBNF (Extended Backus-Naur Form) notation. The token *IDENTIFIER* should be replaced with a sequence of alphanumeric characters, consisting of letters (both uppercase and lowercase), digits, and the symbols '_', '(', ')', ',', and '.', where the first character is either a letter or the '_' symbol.

A closer look at the grammar suggests that a concern intent specification consists of a set of **concern** declarations, each corresponding to a separate concern intent. Concern declarations must have globally unique names, which is why they are defined within the namespace declared in the header section of the specification, using the **namespace** keyword. If defined in the same namespace, subconcerns may be referenced directly by their short name, or otherwise by their fully qualified name, consisting of the namespace name concatenated with the symbol '.', and the simple name of the concern.

For each concern intent, the language allows the software engineer to declare subconcerns, using the **subconcern** keyword, information sources, using the **source** keyword, and information sinks, using the **sink** keyword. The **source** and **sink** keywords use the *qualified unique names* of the abstract locations, defined in section 4.1.

For each information source or sink, using the **cut** keyword, the language supports the declaration of an optional set of bounds to be used in the determination of the corresponding flow sets, as discussed in section 5.3.2.

Given the fact that a complete concern intent specification can be rather large, the CoDEx language supports the following shorthand rules.

- If several information sinks of a concern c flow directly to the same abstract location $v \notin V_c$ and v has no other incoming direct flows, instead of the information sinks, the abstract location v can be declared as an excluded information sink of c. An excluded information sink is specified using the **exclude** keyword, and is just a shorthand for the following set

$$\{u \in O_c \mid u \rightarrow v \land \nexists w \in V - O_c : w \rightarrow v\}$$

- Similarly, if the same abstract location u flows directly to several information sources of a concern c and u has no other outgoing direct flows, instead of these information sources, the abstract location u can be declared as an excluded information source of c. An excluded information source is specified using the same **exclude** keyword, and is just a shorthand for the following set

$$\{v \in I_c \mid u \rightsquigarrow v \land \nexists w \in V - I_c : u \rightarrow w\}$$

- An information sink $v \in O_c$ with no outgoing direct flows, for which there is an information source $u \in I_c$, such that $u \rightsquigarrow v$, is redundant and can be left out from the specification, provided that this information source u or an excluded information source flowing to u is included in the specification.

- An information source $u \in I_c$ with no incoming direct flows is redundant and can be left out from the specification, provided that the concern intent specification includes an information sink v, either excluded or not, such that $u \rightsquigarrow v$.

Note that in the last shorthand rule, the existence of an information sink $v \in O_c$ for every $u \in I_c$, such that $u \rightsquigarrow v$ is guaranteed by the definition of the concern notion.

5.2.2. Specification Example

Listing 5.1 shows the concern intent specification of the concerns from our running example. As discussed in the previous section, the excluded information sources and information sinks are used as shorthands to reduce the size of the specification.

Listing 5.1: Specification of concern intents in the Persistency example

```
1    namespace codex.examples.persistency;
2
3    concern Persistency {
4      subconcern Reader;
5      subconcern Writer;
6      subconcern Reference;
7    }
8    concern Reader {
9      subconcern IntReader;
10     subconcern StringReader;
11     source StorableInput.readStorable().this;
12     source Storable.read(StorableInput).this;
13     sink StorableInput.readStorable().return;
14   }
15   concern IntReader {
16     source StorableInput.readInt().this;
17     sink StorableInput.readInt().return;
18   }
19   concern StringReader {
20     source StorableInput.readString().this;
21     sink StorableInput.readString().return;
22   }
23   concern Writer {
24     subconcern IntWriter;
25     subconcern StringWriter;
26     source StorableOutput.writeStorable(Storable).this;
27     source StorableOutput.writeStorable(Storable).st;
28   }
29   concern IntWriter {
30     source StorableOutput.writeInt(int).this;
31     source StorableOutput.writeInt(int).i;
32   }
33   concern StringWriter {
34     source StorableOutput.writeString(String).this;
35     source StorableOutput.writeString(String).s;
36   }
37   concern Reference {
38     subconcern IntReader;
39     subconcern IntWriter;
40     source StorableInput.retrieve(int).this;
41     sink StorableInput.retrieve(int).return;
42     sink StorableInput.retrieve(int).ref;
43     sink StorableInput.fMap {
44       cut StorableInput.readStorable().st;
45     }
46     source StorableOutput.map(Storable).this;
47     source StorableOutput.map(Storable).return;
48     source StorableOutput.map(Storable).st;
49     sink StorableOutput.fMap {
```

```
50        cut StorableOutput.writeStorable(Storable).st;
51    }
52  }
```

5.3. Identification of Concern Skeletons

As already mentioned before, a concern is represented at the implementation level by a concern skeleton, consisting of a manually specified concern intent and a concern extent. The identification of concern skeletons is a fully automated process, which uses the a concern intent specification as input, extracts the corresponding concern extents, and refines the hierarchic decomposition of concern skeletons based on the discovered overlaps between the identified concern extents.

The algorithm used to extract concern extents is based on CFL reachability in the concern graph and is presented in detail in the following subsections.

5.3.1. CFL Reachability Formulation

As already pointed out in section 2.2, CFL-reachability is a generalization of graph reachability, and it can be applied to a graph G, whose edges are labelled with the symbols of a given alphabet Σ. According to CFL-reachability in a labelled graph G, a target node is considered reachable from a source node, when there is a path inside G from source to target, such that the word obtained by concatenating in sequence the labels of the edges along this path belongs to a context-free language L, defined over Σ.

The context free language of balanced parentheses, introduced by Reps (Reps 97; Reps 98), can be used to compute precise context-sensitive solutions to a number of static program analyses. In the above mentioned work, Reps also showed that an insensitive solution to any of the above mentioned program analysis problems can also be obtained using ordinary graph reachability. Note that ordinary graph reachability can be defined as a special case of CFL reachability, if the context free language is defined to be Σ^*, where Σ is the alphabet used to label the arcs of the graph.

Although context-sensitivity improves the precision of static program analyses, it is not enough for precisely analyzing object-oriented languages. This requires both

⟨path⟩ → ⟨prefix⟩ ⟨field⟩ ⟨path⟩ | ⟨suffix⟩
⟨prefix⟩ → ⟨prefix⟩ ⟨prefix⟩ |)$_i$ | >$_o$ | e | ϵ
⟨suffix⟩ → ⟨suffix⟩ ⟨suffix⟩ | ($_i$ | <$_o$ | e | ϵ
⟨field⟩ → ⟨realizable⟩ ⟨field⟩ | ⟨aliased⟩ | ϵ
⟨aliased⟩ → <$_o$ ⟨aliased⟩ >$_{o'}$ | e | ϵ
⟨realizable⟩ → ⟨matched⟩ ⟨realizable⟩ | ($_i$ ⟨realizable⟩ | ϵ
⟨matched⟩ → ⟨matched⟩ ⟨matched⟩ | ($_i$ ⟨matched⟩)$_i$ | e | ϵ

Figure 5.2: The grammar of the context free language L

context-sensitivity and object-sensitivity. Our extraction of concern extents is both context-sensitive and object-sensitive, and it can be formulated as a CFL reachability problem as follows.

Let $G = (V, A, s, t, L_V, L_A, \ell_V, \ell_A)$ be a concern graph. As already discussed in chapter 4, the arcs in the concern graph encode in their labels the call and object contexts of the two abstract locations involved in a direct flow relation. The labels represent words in the language L_A over the alphabet Λ_A, both defined in section 4.1.1.

A path p inside G is a sequence of vertices $p = (v_0, v_1, ..., v_n), n \geq 0$ such that $(v_i, v_{i+1}) \in A$ for $0 \leq i < n$. Given the fact that the arcs of the concern graph are labelled using words from L_A, by concatenating in order the labels of the arcs in p, we obtain a word in L_A^*.

Let $L \subset \Lambda_A^*$ be a context free language over the same alphabet Λ_A, defined by the context free grammar shown in figure 5.2. The language L is an extension of the balanced parentheses language defined in (Reps 97; Reps 98), similar to the one presented in (Liu 08; Liu 09), which adds object-sensitivity to the already existing context-sensitivity.

Note that the abstract locations o and o', representing the object contexts of the "enter object context" and "exist object context" symbols in the production of the non-terminal ⟨aliased⟩ are qualified abstract locations in a must-alias relation, meaning that they must point to the same set of objects. For a given path p inside G, the above mentioned abstract location o is qualified by the access path consisting of the already encountered "enter context" symbols. The access path qualifying o' is unknown, but given the fact that the two qualified abstract locations must be in a must-alias relation, this access path can be determined as shown in section 5.3.3.

Using the definition of the above language L, we can now define the notion of flow path.

Definition 20 (Flow path). *A flow path inside a concern graph G is a path, whose corresponding word belongs to the context free language L.*

It is clear from the above definition that the notion of flow path depends on the concrete definition of the language L, which is why a flow path is sometimes referred to as an L-path (Reps 97).

Because the language L ensures a context-sensitive and object-sensitive analysis of the concern graph, the existence of a flow path from a source abstract location $u \in V$ to a target abstract location $v \in V$ also means that there is a flow relation between the source observable corresponding to u and the target observable corresponding to v.

Note that using the above context free language definition, we can also simulate a context-sensitive analysis, if we relax the condition that o and o' must be in a must-alias relation.

Let $\mathscr{F}_L$ be the set of all flow paths in a concern graph G for the given context-free language L.

Given the above definition of a flow path, a set $V_{cut} \subset V$, and an abstract location $u \in V - V_{cut}$, we formulate the single-source bounded flow path problem as the problem of identifying the set of all vertices $v \in V$, such that exists a flow path from u to v, containing none of the vertices in V_{cut}. The solution to this problem is the *closed forward flow* set, written $f_L^{\bullet}(u, V_{cut})$, and defined as follows:

$$f_L^{\bullet}(u, V_{cut}) \quad = \quad \{v \in V \mid \exists(v_0, v_1, ..., v_n) \in \mathscr{F}_L, n \geq 0 : u = v_0 \wedge v = v_n$$
$$\wedge \quad v_i \notin V_{cut}, 0 < i < n\}$$

Intuitively, the closed forward flow set represents the set of all abstract locations reachable through a flow relation from a given source abstract location u, for which there is at least one flow path from u, which contains no other abstract locations from V_{cut}.

Note that in the general case $f_{L_A^*}^{\bullet}(u, V_{cut})$ is not equivalent to the set

$$V_f(u, V_{cut}) = \{v \in V \mid u \rightsquigarrow v \wedge \nexists w \in V_{cut} : u \rightsquigarrow w \wedge w \rightsquigarrow v\}$$

as one might expect, because the above set requires all paths from u to v to contain no other abstract locations from V_{cut} and not just one of them.

The simplest example, for which $f_{L_A^*}^\bullet(u, V_{cut})$ and $V_f(u, V_{cut})$ are different, is a concern graph containing a cycle between an abstract location $v_1 \in f_{L_A^*}^\bullet(u, V_{cut})$ and an abstract location $v_2 \in V_{cut}$. If such a cycle exists, we have

$$v_1 \rightsquigarrow v_2 \quad \wedge \quad v_2 \rightsquigarrow v_1$$

Since $v_1 \in f_{L_A^*}^\bullet(u, V_{cut})$, we have $u \rightsquigarrow v_1$, and because $v_2 \in V_{cut}$ and $v_2 \rightsquigarrow v_1$, we conclude that $v_1 \notin V_f(u, V_{cut})$.

In a similar fashion, we formulate the single-target bounded flow path problem as the problem of identifying the set of all vertices $v \in V$, such that exists a flow path from v to u, containing none of the vertices in V_{cut}. The solution to this problem is the *closed backward flow* set, written $b_L^\bullet(u, V_{cut})$, and defined as follows:

$$
\begin{aligned}
b_L^\bullet(u, V_{cut}) \quad = \quad & \{v \in V \mid \exists (v_0, v_1, ..., v_n) \in \mathscr{F}_L, n \geq 0 : u = v_n \wedge v = v_0 \\
\wedge \quad & v_i \notin V_{cut}, 0 < i < n\}
\end{aligned}
$$

Intuitively, the closed backward flow set represents the set of all abstract locations flowing to a given target abstract location u, for which there is at least one flow path to u, which contains no other abstract locations in V_{cut}.

Note that in the general case $b_{L_A^*}^\bullet(u, V_{cut})$ is not equivalent to the set

$$V_b(u, V_{cut}) = \{v \in V \mid v \rightsquigarrow u \wedge \nexists w \in V_{cut} : v \rightsquigarrow w \wedge w \rightsquigarrow u\}$$

as one might expect, because the above set requires all paths from v to u to contain no other abstract locations from V_{cut} and not just one of them. The proof of this statement is based on the same reasoning as the one used in the previous statement.

Note that because $u \notin V_{cut}$ and because a flow path may also consist of a single node, both the closed forward flow and closed backward flow sets contain the abstract location u. As we will see in the following section, it is sometimes useful to have the forward flow and backward flow sets without the abstract location u, for which case we introduce the additional *open forward flow* set, written $f_L^\circ(u, V_{cut})$, and the additional *open backward flow* set, written $b_L^\circ(u, V_{cut})$. These sets are defined as follows:

$$f_L^\circ(u, V_{cut}) \quad = \quad f_L^\bullet(u, V_{cut}) - \{u\}$$

$$b_L^\circ(u, V_{cut}) \quad = \quad b_L^\bullet(u, V_{cut}) - \{u\}$$

A particular case of the closed backward flow set is the so called *closed object context flow set*, written $x_L^\bullet(u, V_{cut})$. This set is defined in the same way as the closed backward flow set, but using a subgraph G' of the original concern graph G, obtained from G by eliminating all data dependency relations. Given the fact that G' is a subgraph of G, the closed object context flow set $x_L^\bullet(u, V_{cut})$ is a subset of the closed backward flow set $b_L^\bullet(u, V_{cut})$.

Intuitively, the closed object context flow set represents the set of all abstract locations whose values are assigned directly or indirectly to a given target abstract location u, for which there is at least one flow path to u in G', which contains no other abstract locations in V_{cut}.

The *open object context flow* set $x_L^\circ(u, V_{cut})$ is defined in a similar fashion as the open backward flow set:

$$x_L^\circ(u, V_{cut}) \quad = \quad x_L^\bullet(u, V_{cut}) - \{u\}$$

Armed with these definitions, we are now ready to give a formal delimitation for concern extents.

5.3.2. Concern Extent Delimitation

In section 3.2.4, we defined a concern extent as a data-oriented abstraction of the concern implementation, consisting of a set of abstract locations V_c and the restriction of the flow relation $\rightsquigarrow$ to this set. However, we did not provide a formal criterion to delimit the set V_c, but we do so in the following.

Let $c^{int} = (\ell, S_c^{int}, I_c, O_c)$ be a concern intent, and $c^{ext} = (V_c, \rightsquigarrow_c)$ its corresponding concern extent. By definition, the set V_c consists of all the abstract locations used in the implementation of concern c. And since a concern represents the functionality needed to produce its outputs, as pointed out in section 3.2, the set V_c was defined intuitively in section 3.2.4 as the set of all abstract locations flowing to at least one of the information sinks of c, without first flowing to an information source. In formal terms, this translates to the following:

$$V_c = \bigcup_{u \in O_c} b_L^\bullet(u, I_c)$$

Intuitively, this means that a concern extent consists of all the abstract locations of all the bounded flow paths to all information sinks of a concern intent c^{int}, and that these paths are bounded by the set of information sources of c^{int}.

Lemma 3. *Given a concern intent $c^{int} = (\ell, S_c^{int}, I_c, O_c)$ and its corresponding extent $c^{ext} = (V_c, \rightsquigarrow c)$, the following property holds*

$$\bigcup_{u \in I_c} f_L^\bullet(u, O_c) \subset V_c.$$

Proof. In order to prove this lemma, we need to show that $\forall (v_0, v_1, ..., v_n) \in \mathscr{F}_L, n \geq 0 : v_0 \in I_c \wedge v_i \notin O_c, 0 < i < n$, we have $v_n \in V_c$.

Because the concern intent c^{int} is the image of a concern c through the traceability function T, the sets I_c, and O_c satisfy the same properties as the sets Φ_c, and Ψ_c from the definition of the concern notion, including the property that $\forall u \in I_c, \exists v \in O_c : u \rightsquigarrow v$. This means that $\exists (v_0, v_1, ..., v_n) \in \mathscr{F}_L, n \geq 0 : v_0 = u \wedge v_n = v$, or in other words $u \in b_L^\bullet(v, I_c)$. If we combine this result with the formal definition of V_c, we conclude that $u \in I_c \Rightarrow u \in V_c$.

Let $(v_0, v_1, ..., v_n) \in \mathscr{F}_L, n \geq 0$ be a flow path such that $v_0 \in I_c \wedge v_i \notin O_c, 0 < i < n$. If we use our previous result, we also have $v_0 \in V_c$. If $n = 0$, this means that $v_n \in V_c$. The case where $n > 0$ will be proven by reducing it to the absurd.

For $n > 0$, we consider $v_n \notin V_c$. But since $v_0 \in V_c$, without loosing generality, we can assume that $\exists k : 0 \leq k < n$ such that $v_0, v_1, ..., v_k \in V_c$ and $v_{k+1}, v_{k+2}, ..., v_n \notin V_c$. Because $v_{k+1} \notin V_c$, this means that v_{k+1} belongs to a different concern implementation. Given the fact that $v_k \in V_c \wedge v_k \rightarrow v_{k+1}$, based on the definitions of concern output and information sink, we conclude that v_k is an information sink. This means that $v_k \in O_c$, which contradicts our hypothesis that $v_n \notin V_c$.

If we combine all the statements from above, we get $\forall (v_0, v_1, ..., v_n) \in \mathscr{F}_L, n \geq 0 : v_0 \in I_c \wedge v_i \notin O_c, 0 < i < n \Rightarrow v_n \in V_c$. $\square$

The formal definition of V_c assumes the sets I_c and O_c to be specified by the user, as part of the concern intent specification. However, as pointed out in section 5.2.1, such a specification can be rather large, which is why the concern intent specification language defined in the same section supports a number of shorthands. As a consequence of these shorthands, the specification does not define for each concern intent the complete sets I_c and O_c. Instead, it defines only subsets of I_c and O_c, for which we use the notations I_c^i and O_c^i respectively. In addition to these sets, a concern intent specification may also define for each concern intent, a set of excluded information sources I_c^x and a set of excluded information sinks O_c^x.

Furthermore, for each abstract location u representing an information source or a sink, the CODEX language supports the definition of an optional set of bounds to be used in the determination of the corresponding flow sets. To represent these sets, we use the notations O_{cut}^u for the set of bounds specified for the information source u, and I_{cut}^u for the set of bounds specified for the information sink u.

Because the previous lemma guarantees, that a forward flow set, originating in an information source $u \in I_c$, is always a subset of V_c, if its specified set of bounds contains all abstract locations $v \in O_c$ reachable from u, using the the above sets I_c^i, O_c^i, I_c^x, O_c^x, I_{cut}^u, and O_{cut}^u we can now redefine the set V_c as follows:

$$
\begin{aligned}
V_c \;=\; & \Big(\bigcup_{u \in O_c^i} b_L^{\bullet}(u, I_c^i \cup I_c^x \cup I_{cut}^u) \;\cup\; \bigcup_{u \in O_c^x} b_L^{\circ}(u, I_c^i \cup I_c^x \cup I_{cut}^u) \\
& \cup\; \bigcup_{u \in I_c^i} f_L^{\bullet}(u, O_c^i \cup O_c^x \cup O_{cut}^u) \;\cup\; \bigcup_{u \in I_c^x} f_L^{\circ}(u, O_c^i \cup O_c^x \cup O_{cut}^u) \Big)
\end{aligned}
$$

This last definition of V_c is used for the automatic extraction of concern extents.

5.3.3. Concern Extent Extraction Algorithm

As shown in the previous section, the set of abstract locations of a concern extent V_c is essentially a union of forward and backward flow sets, which can be calculated using the algorithm described below. The presentation of the algorithm focuses only on the extraction of forward flow sets, because the extraction of backward flow sets exhibits only minor differences, which we discuss at the end of this section.

The algorithm to extract a forward flow set $f_L^{\bullet}(u, V_{cut})$ is based on a context-sensitive and object-sensitive depth-first traversal of the concern graph, starting from the abstract location u. The abstract locations from V_{cut} act as cutting points for this traversal, meaning that the depth-first traversal of the currently visited flow path stops, when one of these abstract locations is encountered.

The algorithm maintains a call context stack, in order to match the encountered "enter call context" to corresponding "exit call context" symbols, and thus achieve context-sensitivity. This is shown by the production of the non-terminal ⟨matched⟩ in the grammar of the context free language L depicted in figure 5.2. Note that the definition of the language L requires that an "exist call context" always matches and empty call context stack, as shown by the production of the non-terminal ⟨prefix⟩ in the same grammar.

The handling of object contexts is somewhat more complicated. As already suggested, an "enter object context" symbol is matched by a corresponding "exit object context" symbol, if their corresponding abstract locations o and o', from the production of the non-terminal ⟨aliased⟩ in the above mentioned grammar, point to the same set of objects. A closer look at the grammar in figure 5.2 also suggests, that the call context stack must be emptied, when an "enter object context" symbol is encountered, in order to allow the propagation of the side-effects of a setter method to a corresponding getter method.

The set of objects an abstract location points to is called the points-to set of the abstract location, and calculating it is not a trivial problem. In the general case it cannot be solved using purely static program analysis methods, but it can be approximated reasonably well.

Given the fact that pointer analysis can also be reduced to a CFL reachability problem, we can use the same flow set extraction algorithm, to determine the set of assignment roots for the abstract location o, defined as below:

$$R(o) \quad = \quad \{u \in x_L^\bullet(o, \emptyset) \mid \forall v \in x_L^\bullet(o, \emptyset) : u \rightsquigarrow v\}$$

Note that in the definition of $R(o)$, we use the object context flow set $x_L^\bullet(o, \emptyset)$, which means that our flow set extraction algorithm must be parameterized to support the exclusion of direct dependency relations from the depth-first traversal of the concern graph. This slightly modified algorithm for extracting object context flow sets is briefly discussed at the end of this section.

Also note that because the abstract location o is qualified by the access path consisting of the already encountered call and object context symbols of the visited flow path, we start the object context flow extraction algorithm with an initial call context stack containing the matching "exit call context" symbols for the "enter call context" symbols found on the stack when the abstract location o was reached. This way, we can make sure that the algorithm will determine only the set of valid assignment roots $R_v(o)$ for the qualified abstract location o.

Intuitively, the set $R_v(o)$ contains the abstract locations, representing the objects whose values are potentially assigned directly or indirectly to the qualified abstract location o, and thus approximates the points-to set of the qualified abstract location o.

Let $\mathscr{F}_L(o)$ be the set of visited flow paths corresponding to the above defined set $R_v(o)$. Each of these flow paths corresponds to a valid access path for o, and because our algorithm considers all valid access paths for o, the above mentioned flow paths are also the only valid ones. This means that all other flow paths from the assignment roots $R_v(o)$ to o are invalid. Such invalid flow paths may indeed exist, because between any given two abstract locations in the concern graph, there might be several alternative flow paths, corresponding to different access paths.

Once determined, the set of valid assignment roots $R_v(o)$ for the qualified abstract location o is also used to determine all flow paths from these assignment roots to the abstract location o'. For each visited flow path from an assignment root, when the depth-first traversal reaches the vertex o', the sequence of already encountered call and object context symbols represent a valid access path, qualifying o'. Given the fact that our algorithm considers all valid access paths for o', their corresponding flow paths are also the only valid ones, and all other flow paths from the assignment roots $R_v(o)$ to o' are invalid. We use the notation $\mathscr{F}_L(o')$ to refer to the set of valid flow paths to o'.

The above defined sets of valid flow paths $\mathscr{F}_L(o)$ and $\mathscr{F}_L(o')$ can be used to determine a set of invalid "call context" and "object context" symbols for the pair of object context abstract locations o and o', called filtered contexts, and defined as the union of the set of all "context" symbols from all incoming flow paths from the assignment roots to o not contained in $\mathscr{F}_L(o)$, and the set of all "context" symbols from all incoming flow paths to o' not contained in $\mathscr{F}_L(o')$. Let $Q_f(o, o')$ be the set of filtered contexts. In formal terms this set can be defined as follows:

$$
\begin{aligned}
Q_f(o, o') \;=\; & \{\ell \in \Lambda_A \mid \exists (v_0, v_1, ..., v_n) \in \mathscr{F}_L - \mathscr{F}_L(o), n \geq 0 : o = v_n \\
\wedge\; & \exists 0 \leq i < n, \exists \ell_1, \ell_2 \in L_A^* : \ell_A((v_i, v_{i+1})) = \ell_1 \cdot \ell \cdot \ell_2\} \\
\cup\; & \{\ell \in \Lambda_A \mid \exists (v_0, v_1, ..., v_n) \in \mathscr{F}_{L_A^*} - \mathscr{F}_L(o'), n \geq 0 : o' = v_n \\
\wedge\; & \exists 0 \leq i < n, \exists \ell_1, \ell_2 \in L_A^* : \ell_A((v_i, v_{i+1})) = \ell_1 \cdot \ell \cdot \ell_2\}
\end{aligned}
$$

The set $Q_f(o, o')$ is then used in the extraction of the forward flow set $f_L^{\bullet}(u, V_{cut})$ to filter all arcs, whose labels contain a "context" symbol matching any of the contained "context" symbols. This filtering ensures that the depth-first traversal will visit only the flow paths, for which the qualified abstract locations o and o' are in a must-alias relation.

In order to better explain the handling of object contexts, let us consider the example in listing 5.2. Furthermore, let us assume we are interested in the forward flow set $f_L^{\bullet}(q1, \emptyset)$.

Listing 5.2: Object context handling example

```
1   class Product {
2     private String name;
3     private double price;
4     public Product(String n, double p) {
5       name = n;
6       price = p;
7     }
8     public double getPrice() {
9       return price;
10    }
11  }
12  class ProductInventory {
13    private Product product;
14    private int quantity;
15    public ProductInventory(Product prod, int q) {
16      product = prod;
17      quantity = q;
18    }
19    public double getStockValue() {
20      return quantity * product.getPrice();
21    }
22    public static void main() {
23      double p1 = 0.15, p2 = 0.20;
24      int q1 = 5, q2 = 7;
25      Product prod1 = new Product("apple", p1);
26      Product prod2 = new Product("orange", p2);
27      double v1 = new ProductInventory(prod1, q1) .getStockValue();
28      double v2 = new ProductInventory(prod2, q2) .getStockValue();
29    }
30  }
```

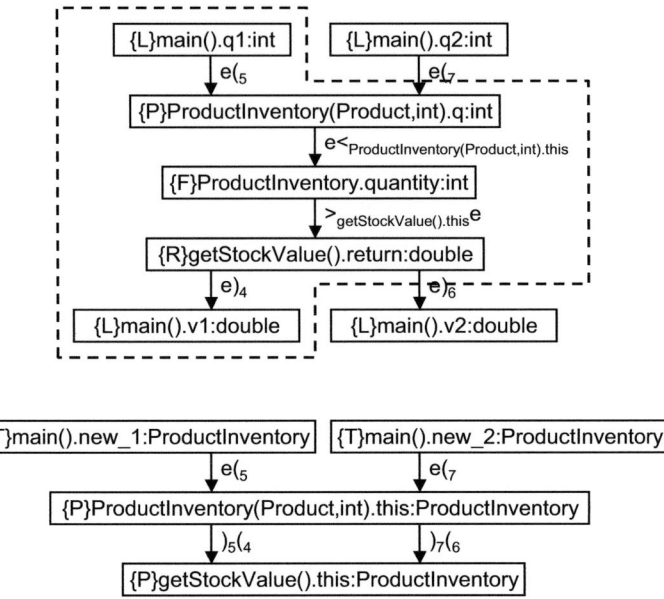

Figure 5.3: Object context handling example

Figure 5.3 shows the section of the extracted concern graph relevant for our example. The dotted-line encloses the vertices of the desired forward flow set $f_L^\bullet(\texttt{main()}.\texttt{q1}, \emptyset)$.

A careful analysis of the example reveals that the local value abstract location `main().q1` flows to the non-static field `quantity` of class `ProductInventory`. This field is accessed using the object context abstract location `ProductInventory(Product,int).this` for writing and using the object context abstract location `getStockValue().this` for reading. Furthermore, the above mentioned field flows to both local abstract locations `main().v1` and `main().v2`, but given the fact that the object context abstract location `ProductInventory(Product,int).this` is qualified by the access path $(_5$, our algorithm will correctly determine the set of valid assignment roots

R_v(ProductInventory(Product,int).this) for this qualified abstract location to contain only the object creation abstract location main().new_1. This will result in the following Q_f set:

$$Q_f(\text{ProductInventory(Product,int).this,}$$
$$\text{getStockValue().this)} \quad = \quad \{(_7,)_7,(_6\}$$

This ensures that the arc from getStockValue().return to main().v2 will be filtered, because its label contains the "exit call context" $)_6$ matching the "enter call context" $(_6$ contained in Q_f, and thus only the correct local value abstract location main().v1 will be included in the forward flow set.

Note that, in the general case, the concern graph may contain cycles between abstract locations, either as a result of loops or as a result of recursive method calls, in which case a simple depth-first traversal would never terminate. In order to cope with such situations, our algorithm allows an arc to be visited multiple times only if the last encountered "enter call context" symbol of the currently investigated flow path is distinct. This basically means that a cycle in the concern graph will be visited at most once and thus avoid an endless loop in the depth-first traversal.

Algorithm 1 shows a pseudocode listing of the forward flow set extraction algorithm, described above.

Algorithm 1: Extraction of the forward flow set

function FORWARDFLOWSET(u, V_{cut})
    return FORWARDFLOWPATHS(u,"e",V_{cut},$\emptyset$,*False*)
end function

function FORWARDPATHS(v,$ctxt$,V_{cut},Q_f,contextPath)
    $path \leftarrow \{v\}$
    for all $(v, w) \in A$ **do**
        if contextPath $\wedge (v, w)$ has data dependency type **then**
            skip (v, w)
        else if (v, w) was not visited for $ctxt$ **then**
            mark (v, w) as visited for $ctxt$
            if $w \notin V_{cut}$ **then**
                $label \leftarrow \ell_A(v, w)$
                $i \leftarrow 0$
                while $label$ has more symbols **do**
                    $symbol \leftarrow label[i]$

```
                        i ← i + 1
                        if symbol does not match any of the symbols in Q_f then
                            if symbol is enter call context then
                                push label on callContextStack
                                path ← path∪ FORWARDPATHS(w,label,V_cut,Q_f,contextPath)
                            else if symbol is exit call context then
                                if symbol matches top of callContextStack then
                                    remove top of callContextStack
                                    ctxt ← "e"
                                    if callContextStack is not empty then
                                        ctxt ← top of callContextStack
                                    end if
                                    path ← path∪ FORWARDPATHS(w,ctxt,V_cut,Q_f,contextPath)
                                end if
                            else if symbol is enter object context then
                                o ← object context encoded in symbol
                                visitedPath ← VISITEDFLOWPATHS(o,callContextStack)
                                R_v ← ASSIGNMENTROOTS(o,visitedPath)
                                push o on objectContextStack
                                push contextPath on contextPathsStack
                                push R_v on rootsStack
                                clear callContextStack
                                path ← path∪ FORWARDPATHS(w,ctxt,V_cut,Q_f,contextPath)
                            else if symbol is exit object context then
                                o' ← object context encoded in symbol
                                pop o from objectContextStack
                                pop contextPath from contextPathsStack
                                pop R_v from rootsStack
                                Q_f ← FILTERCONTEXTS(o,o',contextPath,R_v)
                                path ← path∪ FORWARDPATHS(w,ctxt,V_cut,Q_f,contextPath)
                            else
                                path ← path∪ FORWARDPATHS(w,ctxt,V_cut,Q_f,contextPath)
                            end if
                        end if
                    end while
                end if
                mark (v, w) as not visited for ctxt
            end if
        end for
        return path
    end function

    function VISITEDFLOWPATHS(o,cStack)
        initialize callContextStack with matching call contexts of the ones in cStack
        ctxt ← "e"
        if callContextStack is not empty then
            ctxt ← top of callContextStack
        end if
        path ← BACKWARDPATHS(o,ctxt,∅,∅,True)
        return path
    end function
```

```
function ASSIGNMENTROOTS(o, visitedPath)
    roots ← visitedPath
    for all u ∈ visitedPath do
        for all v ∈ visitedPath − {u} do
            if ¬(u ⤳ v) then
                roots ← roots − {u}
            end if
        end for
    end for
    return roots
end function

function FILTERCONTEXTS(o, o′, visitedPath, R_v)
    rootPaths ← ∅
    for all u ∈ R_v do
        rootPaths ← rootPaths ∪ FORWARDPATHS(u, "e", ∅, ∅, True)
    end for
    path ← rootPaths ∩ BACKWARDPATHS(o, "e", ∅, ∅, True)
    path ← path − visitedPath
    tmpPath ← BACKWARDPATHS(o′, "e", ∅, ∅, True)
    tmpPath ← tmpPath − rootPaths
    path ← path ∪ tmpPath
    filteredContexts ← ∅
    for all (u, v) ∈ A : u, v ∈ path do
        label ← ℓ_A(u, v)
        i ← 0
        while label has more symbols do
            symbol ← label[i]
            i ← i + 1
            if symbol is not "e" then
                filteredContexts ← filteredContexts ∪ {symbol}
            end if
        end while
    end for
    return filteredContexts
end function
```

Note that because our algorithm calculates points-to information on demand, it is able to calculate context-sensitive and object-sensitive points-to information. This makes our algorithm very expensive. Its complexity is basically exponential, because processing any "object context" symbol triggers the recursive extraction of its corresponding object context flow set. Because of this, the algorithm as presented is unlikely to scale well for large software systems, which is why we modified it to calculate an approximation of the desired flow set. The modification, inspired by the object-sensitivity parameterization introduced by Milanova et al.

(Milanova 02; Milanova 05), is based on the observation that if we ignore all "object context" symbols, we end up with a context-sensitive algorithm.

The precision of this approximation can be tuned by the user by specifying a precision factor, representing the maximum allowed depth of recursion when extracting object context flow sets. A precision factor of 0 results in a pure context-sensitive algorithm, while a depth of $\frac{n}{2}$, where n is the number of arcs containing "object context" symbols, results in a full context and object-sensitive algorithm. All other values in between result in increasingly accurate approximations of the desired flow set. Of particular interest is the precision factor 1, because it results in a context and object-sensitive flow set extraction, that uses context-sensitive points-to information, whose complexity is polynomial. Note that the precision factor essentially controls the complexity of the flow set extraction algorithm.

As already mentioned, the algorithm used to extract a backward flow set is very similar to the one used to extract a forward flow set. The only differences are that it traverses the arcs of the concern graph in opposite direction (from target to source) and reverses the handling of "enter context" and "exit context" symbols. Note that this reverse handling of "enter context" and "exit context" symbols also means that the context free language L, defined in section 5.3.1, must have its "enter context" and "exit context" symbols reversed.

And finally, the algorithm for extracting object context flow sets is virtually identical to the one for extracting backward flow sets, but it only traverses arcs corresponding to dataflow and inheritance relations between abstract locations.

5.3.4. Hierarchic Concern Decomposition

The extraction of concern extents, described in the previous section, does not guarantee that two concern extents, corresponding to different concern intents, are always disjoint. It may in fact happen that two such concern extents overlap, meaning that they share a subset of their respective abstract locations.

The Hierarchic Concern Model, introduced in chapter 3, was explicitly designed to deal with such overlaps by regarding the intersection of two concern extents as a separate concern extent representing a common shared subconcern of the overlapping concerns. And given the fact that a concern skeleton is an abstract representation of a concern at the implementation level, consisting of a concern intent and the corresponding concern extent, the extraction of a common shared subconcern requires a refinement of the concern intents of the overlapping concern skeletons.

Fortunately, this refinement can be largely automated, using the iterative algorithm described below, and results in a hierarchic decomposition of the concern skeletons. Human intervention is only required for understanding the extracted subconcerns within the given domain context and for assigning meaningful names to them.

The algorithm takes as input a list of possibly non-disjoint concern skeletons and produces a list of disjoint concern skeletons. The algorithm starts with an empty output list and populates it in n iterations, where n is the number of concern skeletons in the input list. In each iteration, a concern skeleton from the input list is taken and its concern extent intersected in turn with the concern extents of every concern skeleton already in the output list. For every non-empty intersection set V_c, a new concern skeleton (c^{int}, c^{ext}) is created having this intersection set as the set of abstract locations used in its implementation. The sets I_c and O_c in the concern intent of the newly created concern skeleton are determined based on the sets of abstract locations V_{c_1} and V_{c_2} of the overlapping concern extents as follows:

$$I_c \ = \ \{v \in V_c \mid \exists u \in (V_{c_1} \cup V_{c_2}) - V_c : u \rightarrow v\}$$

$$O_c \ = \ \{v \in V_c \mid \exists w \in (V_{c_1} \cup V_{c_2}) - V_c : v \rightarrow w\}$$

The intersection set V_c is then subtracted from both V_{c_1} and V_{c_2}, while the newly created concern skeleton is added to the list of subconcerns of the overlapping concern skeletons. After all the intersections for a given input concern skeleton have been processed as described above, the updated input concern skeleton is also added to the output list.

Listing 5.3: Overlapping concern extents example: initial concern intent specification

```
1   concern AppleStockValue {
2       sink ProductInventory.main().v1;
3   }
4   concern OrangeStockValue {
5       sink ProductInventory.main().v2;
6   }
```

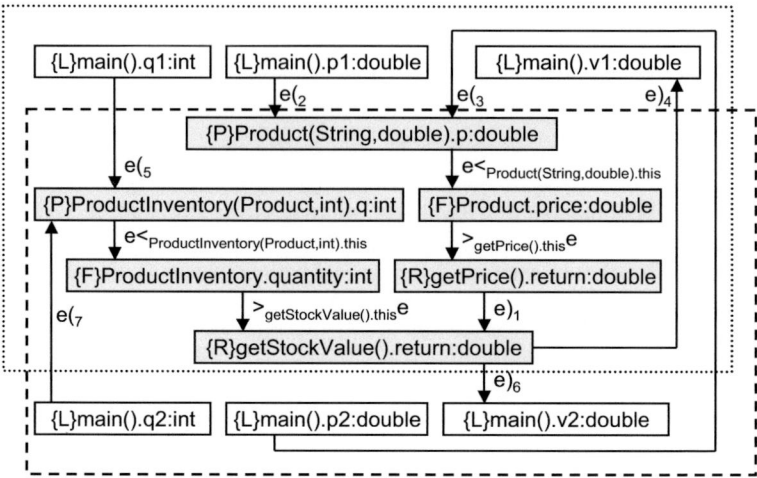

Figure 5.4: Overlapping concern extents

Note that because the concern skeletons in the output list are disjoint the intersection sets determined for a given input concern skeleton are also guaranteed to be disjoint, meaning that after each iteration the output list is guaranteed to contain only disjoint concern skeletons.

Let us consider our previous example from listing 5.2, and use the initial concern intent specification shown in listing 5.3.

After running the concern extent extraction algorithm, described in the previous section, we end up with two overlapping concern extents, as shown in figure 5.4. The grayed vertices in the figure represent the abstract locations shared by the two overlapping concern extents.

By applying the above described iterative algorithm, we obtain a hierarchic decomposition of the concern skeletons, reflected by the concern intents shown in listing 5.4.

Listing 5.4: Overlapping concern extents example: hierarchic decomposition of the identified concern skeletons

```
1   concern AppleStockValue {
2     subconcern StockValueCalculation;
3     sink ProductInventory.main().v1;
4   }
5   concern OrangeStockValue {
6     subconcern StockValueCalculation;
7     sink ProductInventory.main().v2;
8   }
9   concern StockValueCalculation {
10    source Product.Product(String,double).p;
11    source ProductInventory.ProductInventory(Product,int).q;
12    sink ProductInventory.getStockValue().return;
13  }
```

Note that the name of the `StockValueCalculation` subconcern was assigned by hand rather than being derived automatically. However, given the fact that names in general incorporate semantic knowledge, it is neither possible nor desirable to generate them automatically. Our approach is to generate temporary names (placeholders), which the user can change afterwards.

5.4. Selection of Concern Seeds

As shown in section 2.1, a concern seed is defined in the literature as a well-chosen program element, used as a starting point for concern identification, In the case of the Hierarchic Concern Model, defined in chapter 3, this definition translates to an abstract location, representing either an information source or an information sink of the corresponding concern intent.

In section 5.2 we discussed the manual specification of concern intents using the CoDEx language, but we did not discuss any selection criteria for concern seeds. Although in theory any arbitrary set of abstract locations can serve as concern seeds for the identification of a concern skeleton, this is not the case in practice, because a concern represents a self-contained collection of functional requirements. The concern seeds of a concern are semantically related and as a result not entirely independent, which means that it is possible to define heuristic rules to filter unlikely candidate seeds.

The selection of suitable concern seeds is not a trivial task and it involves semantic knowledge about what the system does, but not about how it does it. Given the fact that semantics is involved, we do not believe that this activity can be fully automated, but it can be greatly supported by appropriate filtering techniques.

As we have seen in chapter 2, there are many techniques for identifying candidate concern seeds, based on a very broad spectrum of heuristic rules, ranging from lexical and type-based similarity to various software metrics. The following subsections discuss two additional techniques, especially designed to exploit the particularities of the Hierarchic Concern Model, which can be used to significantly reduce the search space for suitable concern seeds.

The first technique focuses on the concern graph as a whole and tries to filter out unlikely concern seed candidates, whereas the second technique is used to iteratively refine and augment an initial set of concern seeds.

5.4.1. Reduced Concern Graph

The reduced concern graph is a flow-equivalent subgraph of the original concern graph, which filters out a large number of abstract locations, considered unlikely concern seed candidates based on a set of heuristics we present below. As seen in section 4.4.1, when constructing a flow-equivalent concern graph, eliminating a vertex from the original concern graph is equivalent to short-circuiting the vertex. This means that the integrity of the flow relation between abstract locations is preserved, thus allowing software engineers to explore the flow paths and understand the dependencies between abstract locations. The filtering of abstract locations is done using the four filters presented below.

In order to achieve an even greater filtering effect, several filters can be chained together, but it is important to understand that the order, in which the filters are chained, may impact the outcome of the filtering. As a result, in order to avoid any unintended interference between them, the chaining order must be the order in which they are presented below.

The first filter, called the *isolation filter*, eliminates isolated abstract locations, that is abstract locations with no incident arcs in the concern graph. Although rare, isolated abstract locations can occur in the concern graph, if they are only assigned constant values (literal values) and their value is never used in the analyzed source code. Such cases can be safely ignored, because they provide no interesting candidate concern seeds.

The isolation filter must be applied first, because applying the other filters may result in additional isolated abstract locations, which would then be erroneously filtered by this filter.

The second filter, called the *polymorphism filter*, is intended to filter the formal parameters, return value and object context abstract locations of all overriding methods, which are not called directly in the code. The polymorphism filter is based on the following heuristic rule:

Heuristic rule 2. *An abstract location representing a formal parameter, return value or object context of an overriding method belongs to the same functional concern as the corresponding abstract location of the overridden method.*

The heuristic rule can be justified using the Liskov Substitution Principle (Martin 96b), stating that: "subtypes must be substitutable for their base type", or, in other words, subtypes should fulfil the same roles as the substituted base type. If we consider a single method hierarchy, this principle states that all overriding methods should be substitutable for their corresponding overridden method, or, in other words, they should fulfil the same roles as the substituted overridden method.

In the above definition of the polymorphism filter, we explicitly stated that an abstract location can be eliminated by this filter, only if the defining method is not called directly. The condition is necessary in order to guarantee that for all flow paths from the original concern graph, containing a formal parameter, return value or object context defined in a given method hierarchy, there is a corresponding flow path in the reduced concern graph, containing at least one of the above mentioned abstract locations of the method hierarchy in question.

If the source code of a given software system was developed following the principle "program to an interface" (Gamma 95), there should be no direct calls to overriding methods, meaning that the reduced concern graph will contain only the formal parameters, return value and object context abstract locations of the root methods of a method hierarchy.[1]

The third filter is the *local scope filter*. Its purpose is to short-circuit and eliminate abstract locations with local scope, having both incoming and outgoing arcs. This filter only affects local value abstract location and is based on the following heuristic rule:

Heuristic rule 3. *Local value abstract locations with both incoming and outgoing arcs represent unlikely concern seed candidates.*

---

[1] Due to multiple interface inheritance, in the general case the shape of the method hierarchy is not a tree, but a direct acyclic graph, having several different root nodes.

The above rule can be justified by the fact that information sources and sinks store the important input values and results of a concern, and as a result must be easily accessible. Given the fact that local value abstract locations are allocated on the stack frame of the called method, they are created when the control-flow enters the method at the earliest, and are destroyed when the control-flow returns from the method at the latest. They are meant to store short-lived intermediate values. Because local value abstract locations have local scope, they cannot be assigned a value from outside the method and their values are inevitably lost when the execution of the method ends, unless transfered in time to other abstract locations with a wider scope and longer life span.

Note that object creation abstract locations also have local scope, but they have no incoming arcs, which is why they are not eliminated by this filter. Formal parameters and object context abstract locations have local scope when it comes to read operations, but a broader scope depending on the visibility of the method when it comes to write operations, meaning that their value can be written from call sites outside the method. In a similar fashion, return value abstract locations have local scope when it comes to write operations, but a broader scope depending on the visibility of the method when it comes to read operations, meaning that their value can be read from call sites outside the method. Exception parameters are similar to formal parameters, but their scope with respect to write operations is not determined by the visibility of the method containing them, but rather is limited to the a set of methods called directly or indirectly by the containing method. And finally, class fields always have at least class scope for both read and write operations, meaning that their value can be read and written at least from anywhere inside that particular class.

Because the polymorphism and the local scope filters target different types of abstract locations, the two filters are confluent, meaning that they can be applied in any order without changing their combined outcome.

The last filter, called the *post-dominance filter*, has a rather aggressive filtering strategy and can only be used when looking for information sinks. The filter essentially eliminates all post-dominated vertices of the concern graph. Post-dominance analysis is a well-known technique from compiler construction, primarily used in the implementation of various compiler optimizations. The analysis computes the post-dominance relation between the vertices of a flow-graph, which in the case of our concern graph is defined as follows:

Definition 21. *Let $G = (V, A, s, t, L_V, L_A, \ell_V, \ell_A)$ be a concern graph, and $u, v \in V$ two abstract locations. The abstract location u is said to be post-dominated by the* *abstract location v, iff*

$$u \rightsquigarrow v \quad \wedge \quad \not\exists w \in V : u \rightsquigarrow w \wedge \neg(w \rightsquigarrow v)$$

The post-dominance filter is based on the following heuristic rule:

Heuristic rule 4. *Post-dominated abstract locations represent unlikely information sink candidates.*

The justification for the above rule resides in the fact that an information sink usually stores an important result of the concern, which usually represents an output of the system or a widely used intermediate value.

In order to show the combined effect of the above defined filters, let us consider the example in listing 5.5.

Listing 5.5: Reduced concern graph example

```java
1   public class Employee {
2     protected double baseSalary;
3     public double getSalary() {
4       return baseSalary;
5     }
6   }
7   public class Broker extends Employee {
8     public static double MaxPercent = 0.02;
9     private double percentage;
10    private double[] sales;
11    public double getSalary() {
12      double amount = baseSalary;
13      for (int i=0; i<sales.length; i++) {
14        amount += sales[i] * percentage;
15      }
16      return amount;
17    }
18  }
```

Figure 5.5 shows both the initial concern graph for the example in listing 5.5, as well as its corresponding reduced concern graph. The grayed boxes in the figure represent the filtered abstract location. The isolation filter eliminated the static field

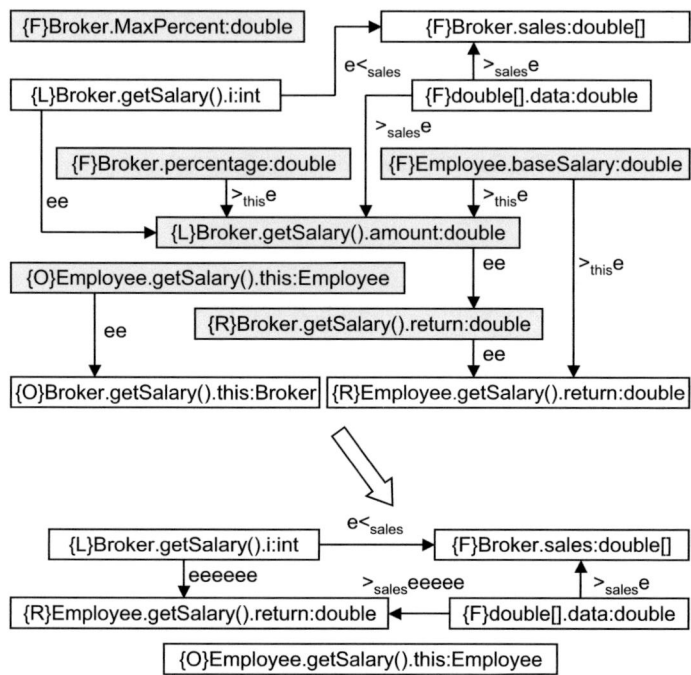

Figure 5.5: Reduced concern graph example

`Broker.MaxPercent`, while the polymorphism filter eliminated the object context and the return value abstract locations from method `Broker.getSalary()`. The local scope filter eliminated the local value abstract location `amount` from the same method, and finally, the post-dominance filter eliminated the fields `Broker.percentage` and `Employee.baseSalary`.

Given the fact that the reduced concern graph is a flow-equivalent concern subgraph, the label of an arc, representing an indirect flow relation in the original concern graph, is obtained by concatenating in order the labels of the arcs in the corresponding path of the original concern graph. The reduced concern graph from our example contains two such arcs, both having as target the return value abstract location of method `Employee.getSalary()`.

It is important to note that all the filters described above are based on heuristic rules, which means that they may accidentally filter some of the potential concern seeds. However, if the filters are chained in the order mentioned above, the resulting reduced concern graph will contain at least one abstract location, for each filtered concern seed, such that the filtered concern seed belongs to either the forward flow set or the backward flow set of that abstract location.

This observation is significant because it means that we can use the reduced concern graph to identify initial sets of concern seeds for each concern, and then refine and augment these sets using the technique, described in the following section.

5.4.2. Growing Flow Sets

The growing flow sets technique is used to iteratively refine and augment an initial set of concern seeds, typically identified directly in the reduced concern graph. It is not meant to replace the reduced concern graph, but rather to complement it.

Being based on the flow set extraction algorithm, presented in section 5.3.3, the growing flow sets algorithm uses a set of concern seeds V_s of the same type (either information sources or information sinks), called the current seed set. In each iteration, it extracts flow sets for each concern seed in this set, and replaces the current seed set with the set of abstract locations terminating the extracted flow paths. Concretely, if the current seed set contains information sinks, it extracts backward flow sets for each of these seeds and replaces the current seed set with the following set:

$$V_s' \; = \; \{u \in \bigcup_{v \in V_s} b_L^\bullet(v, V_{src}) \mid \forall w \in \bigcup_{v \in V_s} b_L^\bullet(v, V_{src}) : u \rightsquigarrow w\}$$

where V_{src} is the set of already discovered candidate information sources.

If, however, the current seed set contains information sources, it extracts forward flow sets for each of these seeds and replaces the current seed set with the following set:

$$V_s'' \; = \; \{u \in \bigcup_{v \in V_s} f_L^\bullet(v, V_{snk}) \mid \forall w \in \bigcup_{v \in V_s} f_L^\bullet(v, V_{snk}) : w \rightsquigarrow u\}$$

125

where V_{snk} is the set of already discovered candidate information sinks.

The newly discovered concern seeds are added to their corresponding set V_{src} or V_{snk}, and the process continues with the next iteration, until no new candidate concern seeds are discovered.

Initially, the sets V_{src} and V_{snk} contain respectively the information sources and information sinks from the initial set of concern seeds. Because the initial set of concern seeds must contain at least a concern seed, V_{src} and V_{snk} cannot be both empty at the same time, so the non-empty one can be used to initialize the current seed set. If both V_{src} and V_{snk} are not empty, we need to apply the above described algorithm twice, using each of these sets as initial current seed set.

The algorithm maintains a list of all abstract locations from all visited flow paths, which allows the software engineer to focus on a subset of the concern graph, represented by all the flow paths from the candidate information sources to the candidate information sinks, and enhance the initial set of concern seeds.

5.5. Concern Maps

As we have seen so far, using the approach described in this work and starting from an initial manual specification of concern intents, we can automatically identify the corresponding concern skeletons. And given the fact that the concern intent part of a concern skeleton explicitly defines the information sources and sinks, representing the inputs and the outputs of the corresponding concern, each concern skeleton can be studied in isolation to understand its implementation.

The separate investigation of concern skeletons is very important because it allows a systematic and modular understanding of the system, but it is not enough for the understanding of the system as a whole. Concerns often exhibit interdependencies between them, which is why a global overview of the entire system, highlighting a particular aspect of these interdependencies, can significantly improve program understanding at the system level.

Given our abstract data-oriented definition of the concern skeleton, we define the following three kinds of system overviews, called *concern maps*, each highlighting a different aspect of the interdependencies between concerns.

The *concern aggregation map* provides a graphical representation of the hierarchic decompositions of concern skeletons. This map is always defined relative to a set of

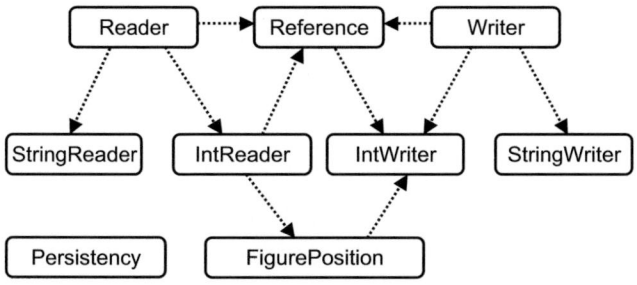

Figure 5.6: Concern interaction map

concern skeletons, which can also be only a subset of the identified concern skeletons. It can be generated automatically from the hierarchic decompositions, obtained using the algorithm described in section 5.3.4.

If we consider our running example from section 3.1.1, and the set of concern skeletons identified based on the concern intent specification shown in listing 5.1, the concern aggregation map will contain only the refinement of the Persistency concern, and is actually shown in figure 3.3. Note that figure 3.2 also depicts a concern aggregation map, but this map corresponds to a subset of the concern skeleton, not containing the Reference concern skeleton.

The *concern interaction map* provides a graphical representation of the data dependencies between a specified set of concern skeletons. This map is also defined relative to a set of concern skeletons and can be generated automatically based on the concern extents of these concern skeletons and the direct flow relations contained in the concern graph. The map contains single nodes for each of the represented concern skeletons (including subconcern skeletons) and edges corresponding to each direct flow relation between two abstract locations contained in different concern skeletons.

Figure 3.4 shows a simple concern interaction map, depicting three of the concern skeletons discussed in our running example from section 3.1.1. A more complete concern interaction map, containing all the concern skeletons discussed in our example, is shown in figure 5.6.

Because both concern aggregation and concern interaction maps use concern skeletons as nodes, in order to differentiate between them, we used different line styles. Refinement relationships between concern skeletons are depicted, by convention, using solid lines, whereas data dependencies are depicted using dotted lines. Given these conventions, it is possible to depict both concern refinement and data dependencies in a single combined concern map, called the concern aggregation and interaction map, but such a representation is usually more difficult to follow.

The last concern map, considered in this work, is the so called *concern dispersion map*. It is defined relative to a set of classes and a set of concern skeletons, and its purpose is to highlight the scattering and tangling of concern skeletons with respect to classes.

The concern dispersion map depicts a set of classes with the inheritance relations between them, and inside each class the set of defined abstract locations. Classes are depicted using the UML class diagram notation, but instead of the lists of fields and methods, the class nodes in a concern dispersion map contain several sequences of coloured squares, one for each method of the class, and an additional one to represent the abstract locations defined directly inside the class, such as fields. Each sequence, representing a method, is organized using a horizontal layout, and contains one square for each of the abstract locations defined inside the method.

All sequences of abstract locations are ordered by the location of their definition in the source code. The first element of a the sequence representing a method corresponds to the return value abstract location, followed by the object context abstract location, formal parameters and the remaining abstract locations defined inside the method.

Abstract locations belonging to a single concern (subconcern) have the same colour, and the colours used are listed in a legend.

Figure 5.7 shows the dispersion map corresponding to the classes and concern skeletons defined in our running example from section 3.1.1. To improve the readability of the figure, a method having no return value is represented in the figure by a sequence, having a missing square on its first position. A static method is represented by a sequence, having a missing square on its second position, while a method with no formal parameters is represented by a sequence, having a missing square on its third position.

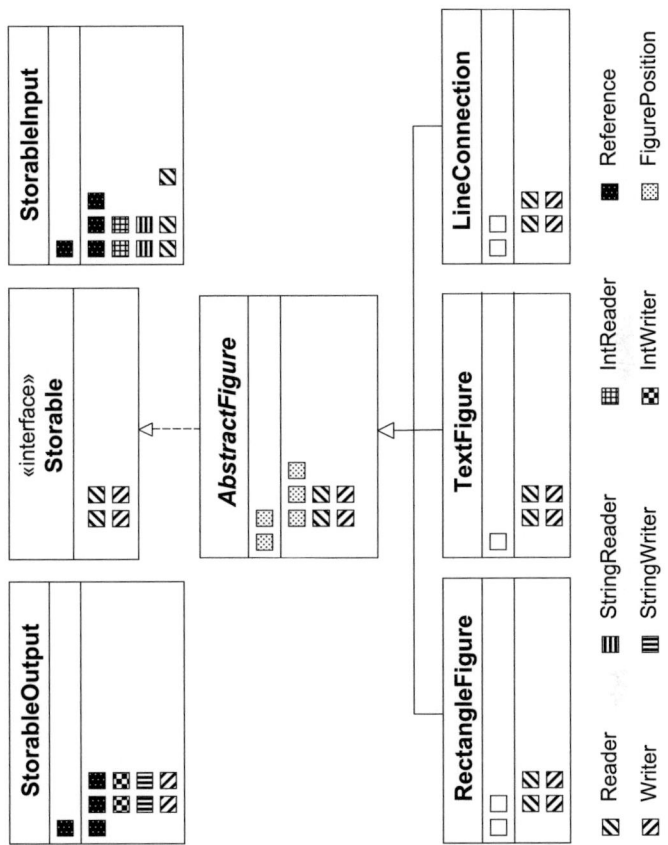

Figure 5.7: Concern dispersion map

Chapter 6.

Evaluation

The purpose of this chapter is to validate the concern identification approach described in the previous chapters, by evaluating its ability to accurately identify functional concern implementations in real software systems. The validation takes the shape of an experiment, carried out using our prototype tool CoDEx on two consecutive versions of the JHotDraw framework as case study.

Section 6.1 gives an overview of the implemented tool support, briefly discussing its architecture and the major implementation decisions. Section 6.2 presents the evaluation goals, the experimental objectives, and the corresponding evaluation approach, while section 6.3 presents and discusses the results of the experiment.

6.1. Tool Support

The Concern Detection and Exploration (CoDEx) tool is an experimental platform, which implements our approach for automatic identification of concern skeletons, described in the previous chapters. The tool uses as input an initial concern intent specification, such as the one shown in section 5.2.2, and produces a set of concern skeletons, corresponding to the implementations of the specified functional concerns.

6.1.1. Architectural Overview

As shown in figure 6.1, the architecture of the CoDEx tool is a hybrid architecture, derived from the *Repository* architectural styles. It uses a layered central repository, consisting of three repository components, depicted in the figure using ellipses. This repository is constructed, updated, and accessed by a number of specialised action

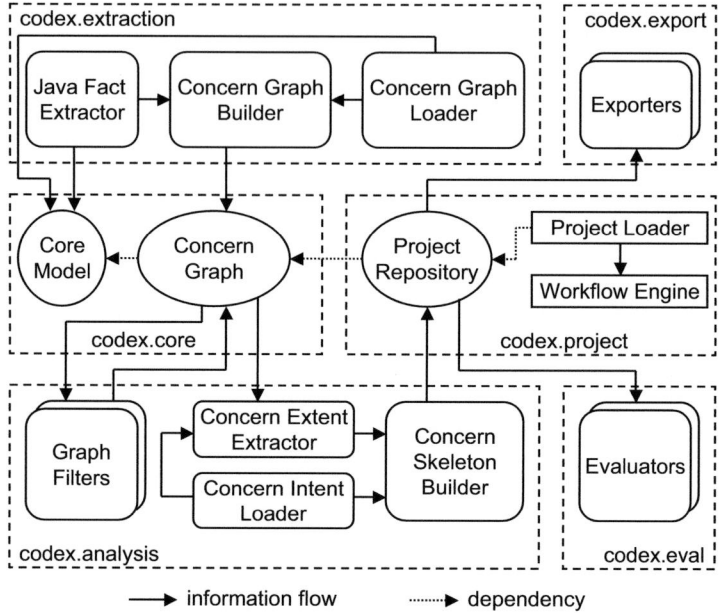

Figure 6.1: Architectural overview of the CODEX tool

components, depicted using round rectangles. Other components, which are neither action nor repository components are depicted using normal rectangles. Information flow between action components or between an action component and the central repository is depicted in the figure using solid arrows, whereas simple dependency between components using dotted arrows.

The CODEX tool was designed to operate in batch mode and as a result it has no interactive user interface. Instead, it is controlled by a single project file, which defines and configures its entire workflow: from parsing the source code to exporting the results of the identification. The tool is divided into several subsystems, depicted in the figure using the dotted rectangles, and each subsystem contains several components. The remainder of this section briefly presents each subsystem and its corresponding components.

The `codex.core` subsystem houses the lower layers of the central repository, consisting of the `Core Model` and the `Concern Graph` components. The first component stores an abstract Document Object Model (DOM) of the analyzed object-oriented code. Its meta-model was designed to support typical object-oriented languages such as Java, and it contains first-class entities for all the major language constructs such as classes, methods and different kinds of abstract locations. Beside the basic primitives for DOM manipulation, the component also implements a set of advanced queries, such as finding all the overriding methods of a given method, or finding all the methods called either directly or indirectly by a given method, both needed during the extraction of the different direct flow relations.

As suggested by its name, the `Concern Graph` component stores the homonymous directed multigraph structure described in chapter 4. The component references the abstract locations in the `Core Model`, hence the dependency in figure 6.1, and provides primitive graph manipulation operations such as adding and removing direct flow relations between abstract locations, or collapsing a subgraph to a single composite node.

The `codex.project` subsystem contains the top layer of the central repository, represented by the `Project Repository` component, as well as the components needed to load and execute CoDEx project files. The `Project Repository` component represents a single access point for the central repository, and is responsible for bootstrapping and facilitating direct access to the lower layers of the repository, as well as for storing the identified concern skeletons.

The CoDEx project file is an XML file containing the entire workflow for a concern identification run. The project file is read by the `Project Loader` component, which is also responsible for instantiating and configuring the corresponding action components, as well as the `Project Repository`. Each action component is implemented by a corresponding action class, or a group of classes hidden behind a common façade acting as an action class. As shown in the sample project file from section A.3, the workflow is defined as a sequence of `Action` elements, each specifying the fully qualified name of the corresponding action class. Action components may be instantiated multiple times.

Once a workflow has been instantiated and configured, it is passed to the `Workflow Engine` component, which is responsible to execute the specified workflow. The component also provides logging and time measurement services.

The `codex.extraction` subsystem is concerned with and constructing the lower layers of the repository, and it consists of the `Java Fact Extractor`, `Concern Graph Builder`, and `Concern Graph Loader` components. The first component is the only programming language-specific component of the entire tool, and is responsible for parsing Java code and for triggering the construction of the lower levels of the repository. The parsing is done in two passes: the first one to extract the static structure of the code and to construct the `Core Model`, and the second one to extract the direct flow relations.

The `Java Fact Extractor` component communicates through an abstract factory interface with the `Concern Graph Builder` component, which is responsible for constructing the `Concern Graph`. As pointed out in section 4.4, the concern graph may be composed from several concern subgraphs, some of which being specified manually using the notation defined in section 4.4.2. The `Concern Graph Builder` component is also responsible for correctly assembling these subgraphs.

As suggested by its name, the `Concern Graph Loader` component is responsible for loading the above-mentioned manual concern subgraph specifications, and for triggering the construction of the corresponding parts of the repository. In order to do so, it communicates with the `Concern Graph Builder` component through the above-mentioned abstract factory interface. Note that a manual concern graph specification may contain abstract locations not referenced in the analyzed source code, for which there are no corresponding objects in the DOM. For these abstract locations, the `Concern Graph Loader` component is also responsible for constructing dummy objects in the `Core Model`, which may then be referenced in the `Concern Graph`.

The `codex.analysis` subsystem in concerned with the actual identification of concern skeletons. The main component is the `Concern Extent Extractor` component, which implements the concern extent extraction algorithm, described in section 5.3.3. The component can be configured to perform an insensitive, context-sensitive, or context and object-sensitive flow analysis of the concern graph, and it determines for each specified concern intent its corresponding concern extent.

The initial set of concern intents is specified manually, using the language defined in section 5.2.1. This specification is read by the `Concern Intent Loader` component, which is responsible for parsing the CoDEx language and creating an internal representation of the read concern intents.

Both the initial set of concern intents as well as their corresponding concern extents are passed to the `Concern Skeleton Builder`, which is responsible for determining the hierarchic decomposition of concern skeletons, as discussed in section 5.3.4. The final set of concern skeletons is stored in the `Project Repository`.

The `codex.analysis` subsystem also contains four `Graph Filter` action components, used to compute the reduced concern graph, as discussed in section 5.4.1.

The `codex.export` subsystem contains several action components, designed to export parts of the central repository in various human or machine readable formats. Of particular interest are the `GML Graph Exporter` and the `GML Concern Exporter` components, used to export the concern graph and the identified concern skeletons, respectively, in the GML portable graph file format (Himsolt 97). The format is supported by many third-party graph visualization and manipulation tools, such as the freely available YED graph editor (yWorks 00).

And finally, the `codex.eval` subsystem contains components for automated evaluation of the identified concern skeletons, such as the `Accuracy Evaluator` component, used to determine the identification accuracy by comparing the identified concern skeletons with a set of manually extracted reference concern skeletons. More details about evaluating the identification accuracy are given in section 6.2.3.

6.1.2. Implementation Details

The CODEX tool is implemented in Java as a standalone tool, using several third-party libraries and frameworks. It uses RECODER (Ludwig 02; Ludwig 01) for parsing and cross-referencing the java source code, and JGRAPHT (Naveh 03) for constructing and manipulating the concern graph.

RECODER is an open-source framework for Java source code meta-programming, used by many source code analysis and transformation tools. It features a very fast Java frontend with integrated type analysis and cross-reference resolution, supporting the full Java language specification (Gosling 05), including all Java 5 language features.

JGRAPHT is an open-source graph library, providing mathematical graph-theory objects and algorithms for a wide range of both directed and undirected graphs, multigraphs, and pseudographs, supporting weighted, unweighted, and labelled edges.

The CODEX tool was designed to be able to analyze syntactically correct, although potentially incomplete code bases, so in case of large systems, it can be used in a modular fashion to analyze different subsystems separately.

6.2. Evaluation Approach

In order to evaluate the practical applicability of our concern identification approach, we designed an experiment based on two consecutive versions of a real-world software system and using the previously described CODEX tool. The reason for choosing two consecutive versions of the same system was to assess the reusability of the user-defined concern intent specifications.

6.2.1. Evaluation Goals and Experimental Objectives

Since the ultimate purpose of this evaluation is to validate the fulfilment of the criteria defined in section 1.2, we formulate the following evaluation goals and concrete experimental objectives:

- **G1:** The first evaluation goal, meant to validate the fulfilment of the *Expresiveness* criterion from section 1.2, is to validate the **suitability of the Hierarchic Concern Model**, which separates the concern intent from its corresponding concern extent, to express functional concerns in object-oriented code. For this evaluation goal, we define the following experimental objectives:
    - **O1:** Validate the hypothesis that a concern can be outlined by a small set of concern seeds (information sources and sinks).
    - **O2:** Validate the hypothesis that the manual selection of concern seeds is feasible.
    - **O3:** Validate the hypothesis that concern intent specifications can be reused for subsequent versions of the analyzed code base, provided that the corresponding concerns remain unchanged.
- **G2:** The second evaluation goal, meant to validate the fulfilment of the *Accuracy* and *Scalability* criteria, is to assess the **effectiveness of the automated identification of concern skeletons**, based on the analysis of flow relations in the concern graph. For this evaluation goal, we define the following experimental objectives:
    - **O4:** Measure the accuracy of the identified concern skeletons for different types of flow analysis (insensitive, context-sensitive, and context and object-sensitive).
    - **O5:** Measure the execution time of the automated concern skeleton identification for different types of flow analysis (insensitive, context-sensitive, and context and object-sensitive).

– **O6:** Measure the impact of the superimposed roles separation on both the accuracy and the execution time of the automated concern skeleton identification.

Note that the formulated evaluation goals and experimental objectives only cover three out of the five criteria defined in section 1.2, but as we will discuss in section 6.4, the remaining two criteria are fulfilled in case of our approach by construction.

The following two subsections discuss the details of the evaluation approach.

6.2.2. Suitability of the Hierarchic Concern Model

In order to validate the suitability of the Hierarchic Concern Model to express functional concerns in object-oriented code, we use as case-study two consecutive releases of a real middle-sized object-oriented system, where the second release contains a significant number of new features and not just a few minor bugfixes.

For the first release of the two, we define a number of concerns, whose implementations we want to identify in the source code. Each concern is defined based on a typical software maintenance scenario and specified in the Hierarchic Concern Model through its concern intent. For the selection of information sources and sinks, we use the reduced concern graph and the growing flow sets techniques, presented in section 5.4.

Once created, the manual concern intent specification is used as input for the automated concern skeleton identification, which we apply to both releases of the case-study. We compare the identified concern skeletons with the corresponding set of reference concern skeletons, created manually for each release of the case study by a human expert.

Note that because this comparison is also influenced by the accuracy of the concern skeleton identification, a mismatch between reference and identified concern skeletons is not necessarily an indication that the Hierarchic Concern Model is not suitable to express functional concerns in object-oriented code. A match, however, is a good indication of both the suitability of the Hierarchic Concern Model and the accuracy of the concern skeleton identification.

The experimental objective O1 is achieved if we are able to concisely specify suitable concern intents for the chosen functional concerns, and these concern intents lead to accurate concern skeletons after the automated identification process. The accuracy of identified concern skeletons is measured using standard information retrieval metrics, as discussed in section 6.2.3.

The second experimental objective is achieved if the reduced concern graph and the growing flow sets techniques are successful in reducing the search space for concern seeds. The reduction of the search space is measured as the number of filtered abstract locations relative to the total number of abstract locations in the concern graph.

If $G = (V, A, s, t, L_V, L_A, \ell_V, \ell_A)$ is the concern graph of the analyzed software system and $G_r^= = (V', A', s', t', L_{V'}, L'_{A'}, \ell_{V'}, \ell_{A'})$ is its corresponding reduced concern graph, the reduction of the search space is defined as follows:

$$Reduction \quad = \quad \frac{|V| - |V'|}{|V|}$$

where $|\cdot|$ is the cardinality operator.

And finally, the experimental objective O3 is achieved if the concern intent specification created for the first release of the analyzed system can be reused without modifications for the second release to produce comparable concern skeletons for all unchanged concerns. This comparison is done both using the accuracy metrics defined in the following section and through manual investigation.

6.2.3. Effectiveness of the Identification Approach

As mentioned before, the second evaluation goal is to assess the effectiveness of the concern skeleton identification approach, by measuring its accuracy and execution time for each of the different types of flow analysis (insensitive, context-sensitive, and context and object-sensitive). The measurements are collected for both releases of the considered case-study.

In order to measure the accuracy of the identified concern skeletons, we use the standard information retrieval metrics: *Recall*, *Precision*, and the commonly used aggregate metric F_β (van Rijsbergen 79). Note that to compute these metrics, we need two sets of reference concern skeletons, one for each release of the case-study, created by a human expert, based on a detailed analysis of the design documents and source code of both releases of the analyzed system.

Let $c \in C$ be a concern, $V_c \subset V$ the set of all abstract locations contained in the identified concern skeleton, and $V_r \subset V$ the set of all abstract locations contained in the corresponding reference concern skeleton. Using these notations, we define the previously mentioned metrics as follows:

$$Recall(c) \quad = \quad \frac{|V_c \cap V_r|}{|V_r|}$$

$$Precision(c) \quad = \quad \frac{|V_c \cap V_r|}{|V_c|}$$

$$F_\beta(c) \quad = \quad \frac{(1 + \beta^2) * Recall(c) * Precision(c)}{\beta^2 * Precision(c) + Recall(c)}$$

where β is a non-negative real factor, used to vary the relative importance of Precision over Recall.

Because we consider *Recall* and *Precision* equally important in measuring the accuracy of the identified concern skeletons, we calculate the value of F_β for $\beta = 1$, which is in fact the harmonic mean of *Recall* and *Precision*.

$$F_1(c) \quad = \quad \frac{2 * Recall(c) * Precision(c)}{Precision(c) + Recall(c)}$$

Note that the above metrics are defined solely based on the sets V_c and V_r, which are contained exclusively in the concern extent parts of the corresponding concern skeletons, thus apparently ignoring the concern intent parts altogether. This is, however, not entirely true, because when we calculate these metrics for a given concern, we consider all abstract locations contained in the concern skeleton, including those contained in the concern skeletons of its subconcerns. And because we also compute the metrics for each subconcern separately, we actually test the accuracy of the identified concern skeleton hierarchy. The sets of information sources I_c and information sinks O_c are manually specified by the user, so there is no point in testing their accuracy.

In order to measure the execution time of the automated concern skeleton identification, we use the basic time functionality built into the Java standard library. Note that the Java implementation measures the actual wall clock time and not the time spent executing the identification thread, but we chose to use it anyway, because the wall clock time is also the time perceived by a software engineer using our CoDEx tool.

And finally, in order to measure the impact of the separation of superimposed class roles, we run all the above-mentioned measurements twice: once with superimposed class roles separation turned on, and once with superimposed class roles separation turned off.

6.3. The JHotDraw Case Study

JHotDraw is a framework for the creation of drawing editors, ranging from simple graphical editors to more complex domain-specific diagram editors, supporting behavioural constraints on how their elements can be used and altered.

We chose JHotDraw as case-study mainly because of its size and complexity, which are large enough to make it a relevant and at the same time small enough to allow a manual investigation of the results. Furthermore, JHotDraw has been used several times to assess different concern identification approaches and even as benchmark for comparing different approaches (Ceccato 05), which is why many of its functional concerns are widely-known and well-documented in the literature.

Note that for this case-study, we did not actually use the full context and object-sensitive flow analysis, but rather its approximation with a precision factor of 1, as discussed in section 5.3.3. Nevertheless, we refer to it as context and object-sensitive flow analysis, because the extraction of the flow sets is both context and object-sensitive, even though the points-to information used in the analysis is only context-sensitive. As pointed out in section 5.3.3, this approximation basically trades accuracy for speed, meaning that the accuracy of the full context and object-sensitive flow analysis is by construction at least as high as the accuracy of the approximation.

6.3.1. Overview

As mentioned before, for our evaluation we used two consecutive releases of JHotDraw, namely release versions 5.3 and 5.4b1. Note that JHotDraw 5.4b1 is more or less identical to JHotDraw 6.0b1, with the notable difference that it uses the old "CH.ifa.draw" package prefix, also used in release 5.3, instead of the new "org.jhotdraw" package prefix used in release 6.0b1. For both releases, the analyzed code base also included the standard example applications accompanying the framework.

As shown by the data in table 6.1, which summarizes the most important size measurements for both releases of JHotDraw, the second release contains a significant number of new features, representing an addition of over 40% to the code base of the first release.

	JHD 5.3	JHD 5.4
Lines of code	27628	39565
Number of files	195	281
Number of classes	273	389
Number of methods	2283	3205

Table 6.1: Code base size measurements for JHotDraw

6.3.2. Experimental Setup

In order to collect the experimental data required for objectives O4, O5 and O6, we ran the CODEX tool on both releases of the case study six times, each time with a different combination of configurations parameters: analysis sensitivity (insensitive, context-sensitive, and context and object-sensitive) and handling of superimposed class roles (with and without the separation of superimposed class roles). A sample CODEX project file is shown in section A.3.

For all runs of the tool, we used a manually specified flow-equivalent concern graph of the standard library, covering only the parts of the standard library used in both releases of the case-study. Because this manual specification is rather large, we only show a portion of it in section A.1.

Furthermore, all runs of the CODEX tool used the concern intent specification shown in section A.2. A closer look at the intent specification reveals that it contains 17 concern and subconcern intents, outlined by 106 concern seeds, yielding an average of around 6 concern seeds per concern intent. And although some concern intents are more complex, requiring more concern seeds, none of them requires more than 12 concern seeds.

Of course, we cannot exclude the possibility that some concerns may be more difficult to outline using information sources and sinks, but given the fact that the functional concerns, defined in the above mentioned concern intent specification and discussed in detail in the following section, cover a wide range of different types of functionality, we conclude that an average concern can be outlined by a small set of concern seeds (**O1**).

All concern seeds were selected by a human expert, based on a detailed analysis of the available design documents and source code of the two releases, from the set of abstract locations obtained using the reduced concern graph and the growing flow sets techniques. Table 6.2 summarizes the reduction of the search space for abstract

	JHD 5.3		JHD 5.4	
Number of	**CG**	**RCG**	**CG**	**RCG**
class fields	496	225	665	289
formal parameters	2449	782	3501	1132
exception parameters	20	0	40	0
local value locations	1219	0	1610	0
return value locations	1127	398	1653	629
object context locations	2784	1277	3956	1794
object creation locations	1014	0	1268	0
class role instances	1251	52	1524	84
abstract locations	10360	2734	14217	3928
Reduction	**73.61%**		**72.37%**	

Table 6.2: Search space reduction achieved using the reduced concern graph for JHotDraw

locations, achieved using the reduced concern graph. Note that this reduction was achieved by applying in sequence all four filters described in section 5.4.1.

The table clearly shows that the reduced concern graph technique is very effective in reducing the search space, achieving a reduction of over 70% for each of the two releases of our case-study. Furthermore, if we calculate the relative number of abstract locations found in the reduced concern graph per 1000 lines of code (1 kLOC), we end up with just under 100 abstract locations / kLOC. And if we consider that the reduced concern graph also contains the flow relations between abstract locations, making it easier to track their interdependencies, the manual investigation of the reduced concern graph becomes feasible for systems having the size of a typical subsystem (**O2**).

Although we did not measure the time used for this manual investigation precisely, we estimate that using the Reduced Concern Graph and the Growing Flow Sets techniques, the selection of all 106 concern seeds, from the concern intent specification shown in section A.2, took a single experienced software engineer about 12 hours. However, given the fact that the selection of concerns seeds for the specified concerns can be parallelized, this time can be reduced significantly.

Concern Name	JHD 5.4		JHD 5.4	
	Ref. Size	Coverage	Ref. Size	Coverage
Clipboard	10	0.10%	10	0.07%
DrawRendering	85	0.82%	164	1.15%
DrawingTitle	46	0.44%	47	0.33%
FigureChange	140	1.35%	160	1.13%
FigureChange.Events	64	0.62%	75	0.53%
FigureZOrder	11	0.11%	11	0.08%
Mouse.Click	44	0.42%	63	0.44%
Mouse.Move	31	0.30%	44	0.31%
Persistency.Reader	83	0.80%	115	0.81%
Persistency.Reference	22	0.21%	18	0.13%
Persistency.Writer	75	0.72%	98	0.69%
StorageFormatManager	35	0.34%	34	0.24%
ToolActivation	81	0.78%	76	0.53%
ToolActivation.Actions	18	0.17%	18	0.13%
Undo	359	3.47%	375	2.64%
Undo.Actions	154	1.49%	156	1.10%
Undo.Activities	81	0.78%	87	0.61%
Total	**1,022**	**9.86%**	**1,215**	**8.55%**

Table 6.3: Coverage of the reference concern extents for JHotDraw

6.3.3. Functional Concern Examples

This section discusses in more detail the functional concerns, outlined by the concern intent specification from section A.2, and identified in both releases of JHotDraw. Among these concerns we included both examples already documented in the literature, such as the **Persistency** and the **Undo** concerns (Ceccato 05; Marin 07), and also several new concerns.

Table 6.3 shows and overview of the specified functional concerns, together with the percentages covered by their respective reference concern extents, for both releases of the JHotDraw case-study. The table also lists the total coverage achieved by all concern extents, which in our case clearly shows that the two code bases must also contain additional concern implementations, not captured in our concern intent specification.

The **Clipboard** concern implements a basic clipboard functionality, allowing the storage and retrieval of a single `Object`, using the well-known *copy and paste* mechanism present in most graphical applications. The implementation of this concern is completely encapsulated in the `CH.ifa.draw.util.Clipboard` class and consists of the actual store and retrieve functionality, as well as the management of a singleton `Clipboard` instance.

The **DrawRendering** concern handles the rendering of graphical objects such as `Figure` objects on a given graphics context. Its implementation is scattered across the `Figure` and `DrawingView` hierarchies, and consists of various methods, having names starting with `draw` and `paint`.

As its name suggests, the **Drawing title** concern is responsible for managing the titles of `Drawing` instances. Its implementation is scattered across several locations from the `DrawApplication` class, as well as the `Drawing` and `StorageFormat` hierarchies. The reason for this scattering is that drawing titles are used for several purposes. The title of the active drawing is displayed in the application frame of the graphical editor application, accompanying the JHotDraw framework, and it is also used as filename when saving the drawing to the disk. Furthermore, when saving a drawing under a different name, or when loading a saved drawing, the title is updated automatically in the corresponding `Drawing` instance, and also reflected in the application frame. Figure 6.2 depicts the concern extent identified for the **DrawingTitle** concern[1].

The **FigureChange** concern implements an Observer-type notification mechanism for figure change events. It handles the registration and unregistration of `FigureChangeListener` objects as well as the firing, dispatch and handling of the various figure change events. In order to divide this concern into smaller, more manageable pieces, the dispatch and handling of **FigureChangeEvent** objects was specified separately in the **FigureChnage.Events** subconcern. The implementation of the **FigureChange** concern is scattered across the `Figure` hierarchy and in overrides of the methods defined in `FigureChangeListener`.

The **FigureZOrder** is a rather small concern, which handles the ordering of figures on the Z axis. Its implementation is centered around the `_nZ` field from the `AbstractFigure` class and its accessor methods defined in the `Figure` interface and implemented in the `AbstractFigure` class.

The **Mouse.Click** and **Mouse.Move** concerns are two subconcerns of a **Mouse** concern, responsible for dispatching and handling mouse events. As suggested by their names, the first subconcerns handles button events (press and release), while

---

[1] The figure was generated using the yEd graph editor (yWorks 00)

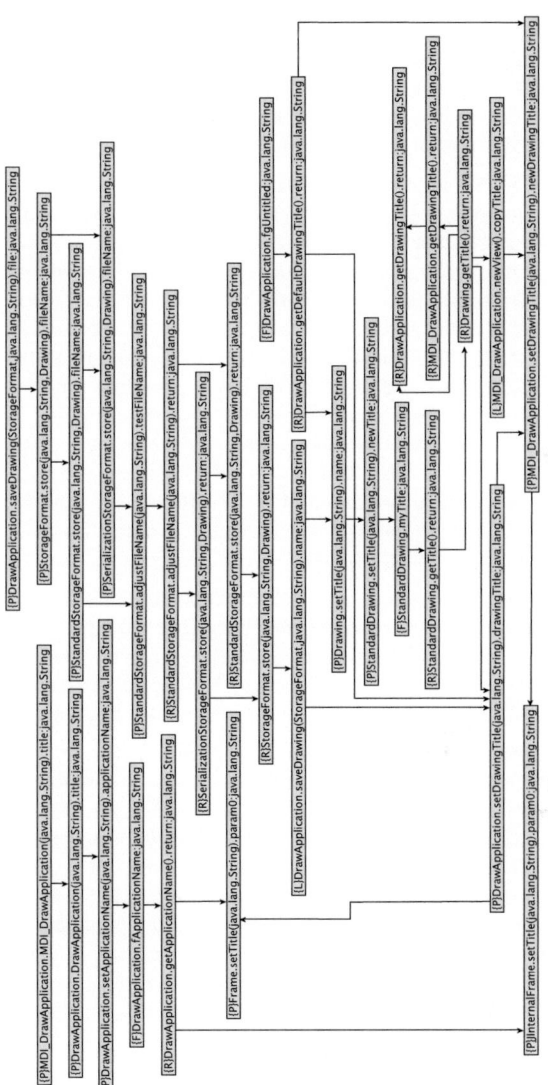

Figure 6.2: Concern extent of the DrawingTitle concern

the second subconcerns handles movement events (move and drag). The implementations of these concerns is scattered across the `MouseListener` and `MouseMotionListener` hierarchies. Although both subconcerns use the same `MouseEvent` library class, their implementations are completely separated, with no single dispatch point for movement and button events.

As suggested by its name, the **Persistency** concern is responsible for the serialization and deserailization of the `Storable` hierarchy, which also includes the `Figure` and `Drawing` subhierarchies. This concern has already been discussed in several different forms in the literature (Ceccato 05; Marin 07), which is why we also chose to base the running example from section 3.1.1 on it. Because this running example represents in essence a simplified version of the **Persistency** concern presented here, we used the same concern refinement for both, containing two disjoint subconcerns: **Persistency.Writer** responsible for the serialization of `Storable` objects and **Persistency.Reader** responsible for the deserialization of the same objects, as well as a third **Persistency.Reference** subconcern, overlapping with the previous subconcerns, and responsible for storing and restoring references to `Storable` objects. The implementation of this concern is mainly concentrated in the `read` and `write` methods of the `Storable` hierarchy, and the methods of the `StorableInput` and `StorableOutput` classes.

The **StorageFormatManager** concern is responsible for managing a registry of available storage formats for `Drawing` objects, including the registration of a new storage format or the lookup of the proper `StorageFormat` class based on the user-selected extension. Its implementation is located in the `StorageFormatManager`, `DrawApplication` and the `StorageFormat` hierarchy.

The **ToolActivation** concern deals with the activation of different tools and the corresponding notification mechanism for `ToolListener` objects. In order to divide this concern into smaller, more manageable pieces, the dispatch and handling of these notifications was separated in the **ToolActivation.Activities** subconcern. The implementation of this concern is scattered across the `Tool` and `ToolListener` hierarchies. What is truly remarkable about this concern is that it captures the semantic relationships between the states of being enabled, usable and active for `Tool` objects. These states are neither exclusive, nor synonymous. They simply represent overlapping concepts. As suggested by the partial concern extent shown in figure 6.3, a tool is considered active if it is enabled and it is usable in a given context.

And finally, the **Undo** concern, which was also presented in the literature (Ceccato 05; Marin 07), deals with the *undo and redo* mechanism built into the

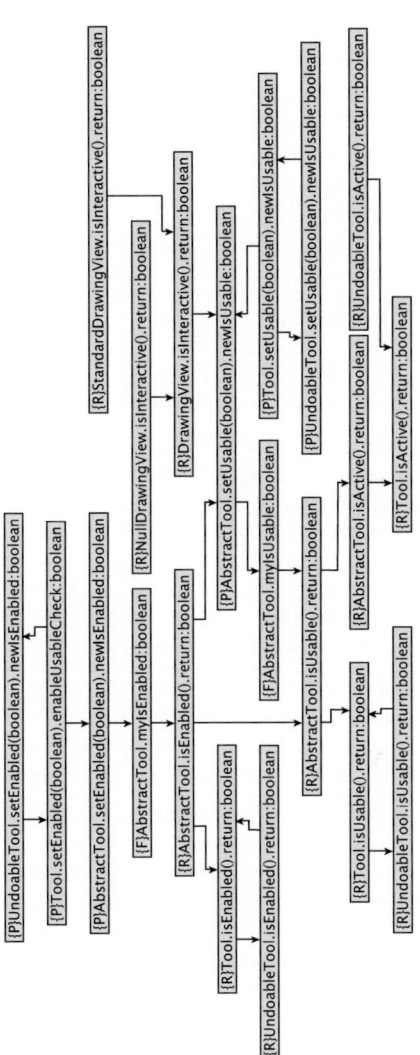

Figure 6.3: Partial concern extent of the ToolActivation concern

`Tool`, `Handle`, and `Command` hierarchies. The concern has two subconcerns: **Undo.Actions** responsible for the actual execution of the `undo` and `redo` operations, and **Undo.Activities** responsible for the creation of `Undoable` objects and their registration with the appropriate `UndoableTool`, `UndoableHandle` or `UndoableCommand`. The implementation of this concern is mainly concentrated in the `UndoActivity` inner classes and the `createUndoActivity` methods, both defined in the above mentioned hierarchies, as well as in the `UndoManager` class, responsible for managing the undo and redo stacks.

6.3.4. Accuracy Measurements

This section discusses the accuracy of the identified concern skeletons, which, as already mentioned in section 6.2.3, is measured by the F_1 aggregate metric.

Figure 6.4 shows a comparison of the F_1 metric values obtained for all considered functional concerns, when using different types of flow analysis (insensitive, context-sensitive, context and object-sensitive) in combination with the separation of superimposed class roles on version 5.3 of the JHotDraw case-study. For each of the considered concerns, the exact values of the F_1 metric for each type of flow analysis, as well as the values of *Recall* and *Precision* used to calculate them are listed in table A.2, together with the respective sizes of the identified concern extents, and the size of the reference concern extent.

A closer look at the figure reveals that for the context and object-sensitive analysis, all F_1 values are within the upper quarter of the value range of the metric or very close to it. As a result, we conclude that the context and object-sensitive flow analysis with role separation produces highly accurate results (**O4**).

Furthermore, the figure also reveals that the results produced by the insensitive and the context-sensitive analyses are virtually identical. This should come as no surprise, given the nature of object-oriented code, which typically uses object fields as primary storage for its data and encourages a tight bundling of data and behaviour in a single class. Because of that, methods in object-oriented code usually operate on data originating in object fields, which also represent typical destinations for their results. And since a context-sensitive flow analysis is not able to differentiate between different object contexts, it usually ends up mixing them.

The above observation is also confirmed by the F_1 metric values obtained in case of the second release of the JHotDraw case-study we considered in our experiment. Figure 6.5 shows these results.

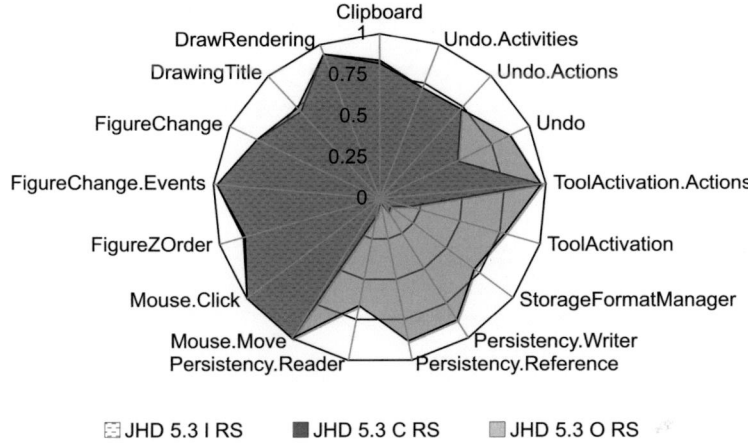

Figure 6.4: Accuracy of the identified concern skeletons, when using insensitive (I), context-sensitive (C), and context and object-sensitive (O) flow analysis with superimposed roles separation (RS) for JHotDraw 5.3

An interesting fact about this figure is that, in case of the **Persistency.Reader**, **Persistency.Writer**, **Persistency.Reference**, **StorageFormatManager**, and **ToolActivation** concerns, it shows very low values of the F_1 metric. If we take a closer look at the corresponding *Recall* and *Precision* values in table A.4, we notice that in all five cases, this is due to a low *Precision* value, which also correlates with the significantly larger sizes of the identified concern extents relative to the corresponding reference concern extents. This can only mean that in all of these cases the automatic concern extraction was missing some cutting points for the concern graph traversal, either in the form of additional concern seeds or additional flow set bounds specified in their respective concern intents. The above interpretation of the metric values was also confirmed by a manual investigation of the identified concern extents.

If we dig a little deeper in order to find the cause of this unexpected results, we actually reach the conclusion that the results are not at all unexpected. They can be explained by the fact that the second version of the JHotDraw case-study contains significant additions to the `Figure`, `StorageFormat`, and `Tool` hierarchies, for which no appropriate cutting points were defined in the concern intent specifica-

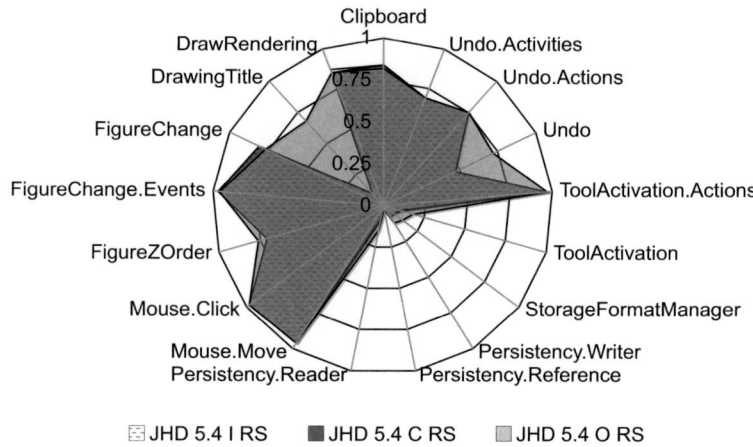

Figure 6.5: Accuracy of the identified concern skeletons, when using insensitive (I), context-sensitive (C), and context and object-sensitive (O) flow analysis with superimposed roles separation (RS) for JHotDraw 5.4

tion, created exclusively for the first version of the case-study. As a result of these changes, in all of the above mentioned cases the concern definitions changed, thus invalidating their respective concern intents. Furthermore, judging by the high F_1 values obtained for the remaining 12 out of 17 concerns, defined in our concern intent specification, and despite the changes in their implementations suggested by the different concern extent sizes, we conclude that concern intents can be reused for subsequent versions of the analyzed code base, if and only if their corresponding concerns remain unchanged (**O3**).

All the accuracy measurements presented so far have been obtained using the separation of superimposed class roles. In order to investigate the effect of this separation on the accuracy of the identified concern skeletons, we turned the role separation off and repeated all the measurements again. The exact values of the obtained results are shown in tables A.1 and A.3.

Figure 6.6 shows a comparison of the F_1 metric values obtained for all considered functional concerns using context and object-sensitive flow analysis with and without role separation on version 5.3 of the JHotDraw case-study. The figure shows

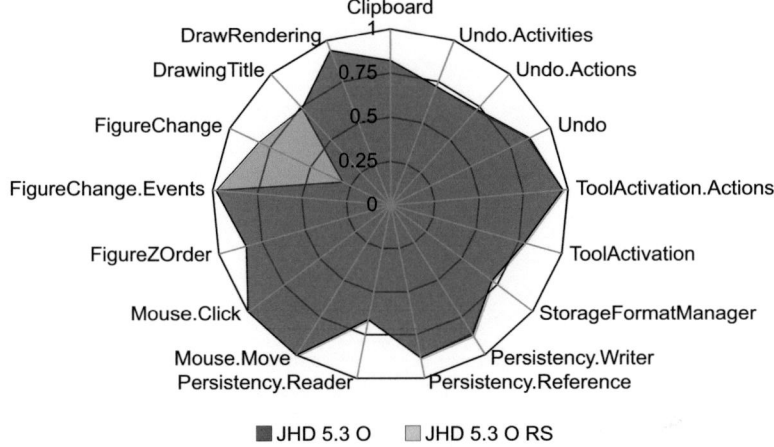

Figure 6.6: Impact of superimposed class roles separation on the accuracy of the identified concern skeletons for JHotDraw 5.3

that in case of the **FigureChange** concern, using the separation of superimposed class roles significantly improved the accuracy of the concern skeleton identification, while in case of the other 16 concerns the results were identical.

The same comparison carried out on the F_1 metric values obtained for JHotDraw 5.4 shows similar results, which we summarize in figure 6.7. The figure shows an improvement in the identification accuracy for the **Undo** concern, when using the role reparation, while the other 16 concerns exhibit identical results for both cases.

Given the fact that the separation of superimposed roles is based on a heuristic rule, it cannot be guaranteed that it will never have a negative effect on the identification accuracy, even if our measurements suggest this. All we can say at this point is that this heuristic rule seems to be very effective (**O6**).

6.3.5. Execution Time Measurements

The execution times of the automated identification of concern skeletons for the JHotDraw case-study are shown in table 6.4. The table lists all runs of the CoDEx

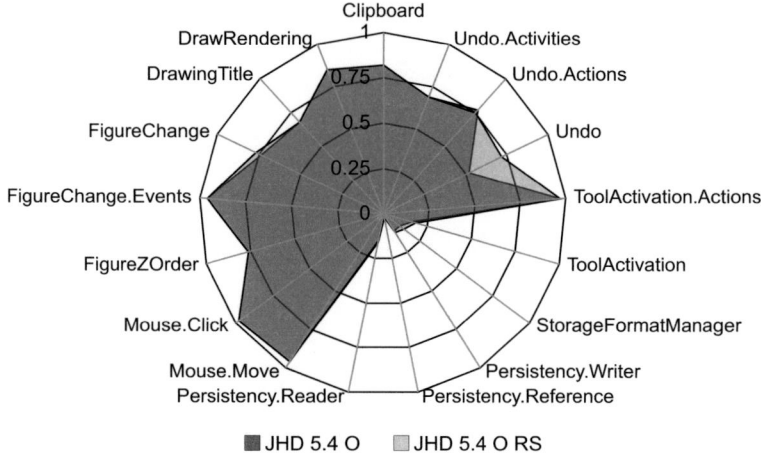

Figure 6.7: Impact of superimposed class roles separation on the accuracy of the identified concern skeletons for JHotDraw 5.4

tool using: insensitive (I), context-sensitive (C), and context and object-sensitive (O) flow analysis, with and without superimposed roles separation (RS) for both versions of the case-study. The execution times are expressed in seconds, and except for the two runs using context and object-sensitive flow analysis for JHotDraw 5.4, they are well within acceptable limits.

The table also shows that the execution times of the above-mentioned two runs are at least one order of magnitude higher the the rest, which made us suspect that something went wrong during these runs. As a result we analyzed the execution times for the identification of the individual concern skeletons and noticed that, in both cases, over 90% of the total execution time was spend in the identification of the same five concerns, for which we obtained low accuracy measurements. The exact identification times for the individual concern skeletons together with the percentages these times represent from the total execution time are shown in table 6.5.

Note that in the case of these five concerns the sizes of the identified concern extents, as shown in tables A.3 and A.4, are also one order of magnitude higher than the corresponding reference concern extents, and thus explain the very high execu-

	no RS (sec)	RS (sec)
JHD 5.3 I	496	169
JHD 5.3 C	3,369	1,168
JHD 5.3 O	5,511	2,136
JHD 5.4 I	1,819	1,300
JHD 5.4 C	6,081	3,832
JHD 5.4 O	191,665	103,135

Table 6.4: Identification times of the concern skeletons for JHotDraw

Concern Name	no RS (sec)		RS (sec)	
	Time (sec)	Percent.	Time (sec)	Percent.
Clipboard	0.16	0.00%	0.25	0.00%
DrawRendering	0.63	0.00%	0.65	0.00%
DrawingTitle	565.73	0.30%	485.93	0.47%
FigureChange	2,646.89	1.38%	2,050.80	1.99%
FigureChange.Events	0.04	0.00%	0.04	0.00%
FigureZOrder	324.38	0.17%	377.14	0.37%
Mouse.Click	0.13	0.00%	0.15	0.00%
Mouse.Move	0.04	0.00%	0.05	0.00%
Persistency.Reader	46,318.02	24.17%	15,832.13	15.35%
Persistency.Reference	29,480.80	15.38%	7,610.64	7.38%
Persistency.Writer	87,241.19	45.52%	68,224.95	66.15%
StorageFormatManager	769.94	0.40%	402.55	0.39%
ToolActivation	7,798.95	4.07%	5,954.14	5.77%
ToolActivation.Actions	0.30	0.00%	0.31	0.00%
Undo	16,515.51	8.62%	2,192.69	2.13%
Undo.Actions	0.52	0.00%	0.52	0.00%
Undo.Activities	0.37	0.00%	0.43	0.00%

Table 6.5: Identification times of the individual concern skeletons, when using context and object-sensitive flow analysis for JHotDraw 5.4

tion times. Based on this observation, we can conclude that the execution time of the automated concern skeleton identification is within acceptable limits, provided that the concern intent specification is accurate (**O5**).

Another interesting fact revealed by the data shown in tables 6.4 and 6.5 is that using the separation of superimposed class roles significantly reduces the execution time of the automated concern skeleton identification in all runs of the CODEX tool, and in some cases it even cuts this time in half, thus indicating again the effectiveness of this heuristic rule (**O6**).

6.4. Assessment of the Approach

As already pointed out in section 6.2.1, the purpose this evaluation was to validate the fulfilment of the criteria defined in section 1.2. In the following we revisit these criteria and show that our tool-supported concern identification approach indeed fulfils them.

- **Expressiveness:** According to this criterion, a concern identification approach should be able to express functional concerns and the typical relationships between them, such as concern overlaps and refinements. In order to express functional concerns in object-orineted code, the Hierarchic Concern Model uses a data-oriented abstraction, called a concern skeleton, which separates the definition of a concern at the implementation level into a user-specified concern intent and an automatically identified concern extent. As pointed out in section 6.3.2, the CODEX language, especially designed for the specification of concern intents, was successfully used to manually define in a very concise form 17 concerns and subconcerns, spanning a wide functionality spectrum, and exhibiting both concern overlap and refinement.

- **Accuracy:** According to this criterion, an automated concern identification approach and a human expert should produce similar results. In section 6.2.3 we defined the F_1 aggregate metric based on a set of reference concern skeletons created by a human expert, and used it in section 6.3.4 to measure the accuracy of the identified concern skeletons. The measurements clearly show that for accurate concern intent specifications, even using an approximation of the context and object-sensitive flow analysis produces highly accurate concern skeletons for both versions of the case-study. Moreover, the measurements also suggest that the separation of superimposed class roles improves this accuracy even further.

- **Practicability:** This criterion requires that a concern identification approach support the typical languages features found in most object-oriented languages, such as structured data types, object aliasing, exception handling, dynamic dispatch, and polymorphism. As shown in chapter 4, in the case of our approach, this criterion is fulfilled by construction, but also additionally proven by the successful analysis of two consecutive releases of a middle-sized open source software systems.

- **Scalability:** According to this criterion, a concern identification approach should be applicable for realistic software systems, having at least the size of a typical subsystem (around 200 classes). As discussed in section 5.3.3 the full context and object-sensitive analysis has an exponential complexity, which clearly does not scale for middle-sized software systems. However, the complexity of its approximation for a precision factor of 1, which we used in our evaluation, is polynomial. And although the implementation of the CoDEx tool is not optimized for speed, the execution time measurements from section 6.3.5 show that the approach is applicable even for object-oriented systems having double the size of a typical subsystem. Furthermore, the measurements also suggest that the separation of superimposed class roles significantly reduces these execution times.

- **Automation:** And finally, this criterion requires a high degree of automation of the concern identification process. In the case of our approach, this is guaranteed by construction, because it handles the identification of concern skeletons in a fully automated fashion. And although the initial concern intent specification is largely manual, as discussed in section 6.3.4, this specification can be reused in subsequent versions of the code base, provided that the specified concerns remain unchanged.

Chapter 7.

Conclusions

Section 7.1 of this chapter gives a brief summary of our tool-supported concern identification approach and of the main contributions of this thesis. Then, the assumption and limitations of the proposed approach are discussed in section 7.2. Finally we conclude by giving some perspectives on future work in section 7.3.

7.1. Summary

The goal of this work was to support program understanding of object-oriented code during software evolution, by creating and maintaining direct traceability links between functional concerns defined at the requirements level, and their respective implementations in code. Towards that end, we defined the **Hierarchic Concern Model**, which represents functional concerns using data-oriented abstractions called concern skeletons, and is capable of expressing both concern refinement and overlap relationships.

A concern skeleton consists of a concern intent, specifying the inputs (information sources) and outputs (information sinks) of the concern, as well as its contained subconcerns, and a corresponding concern extent, containing all abstract locations used in the implementation of the concern. The concern intent is initially defined by the software engineer, using the **CoDEx language**, and later refined automatically, based on the intersections of its corresponding concern extent with the other concern extents, identified in the same software system.

A concern intent captures a small subset of the traceability links between a functional concern and its implementation in code, namely the traceability links between the inputs and outputs of a concern on the one hand, and the information sources and sinks used in its implementation on the other.

The information sources and sinks are then used as concern seeds in the **automated identification of concern skeletons**, consisting of the extraction of concern extents and the previously mentioned automatic refinement of concern intents. This extraction of concern extents is based on context-free language reachability and a demand-driven flow analysis of a directed multigraph structure, called the concern graph, which captures the direct flow relations between abstract locations. The method supports different flow analysis techniques (insensitive, context-sensitive, and context and object-sensitive), and, in case of the context and object-sensitive flow analysis, a tunable precision factor, which essentially controls the complexity of the extraction algorithm.

In order to improve the accuracy of the extracted concern extents, we introduced a technique for **detecting and separating superimposed class roles**, which creates dedicated copies of each abstract location for every superimposed role implemented by its class type.

The manual selection of the concern seeds in the concern intent specification is supported by the **Reduced Concern Graph** and the **Growing Flow Sets** techniques, which, when used together, are very effective in focusing the search by significantly reducing the manually investigated search space.

The entire method is supported by an **extensible tool (CoDEx)**, created for the analysis of software systems implemented in the Java programming language. Its main advantage is that it makes no assumptions about the forward engineering process used for these systems and allows software engineers to specify and maintain direct traceability links between functional concerns and their implementation in code. And because the manually specified traceability links represent only a small subset of the much larger set of automatically identified links, the approach significantly reduces the effort needed to maintain these links.

7.2. Assumptions and Limitations

In section 6.4, we showed that our tool-supported concern identification approach indeed fulfills all criteria defined in section 1.2, but we have not discussed the assumptions we made regarding the analyzed software systems, and the limitations resulted therefrom. And because understanding these assumptions and limitations is essential for the successful application of our method, a list of the most important ones is given below.

- **Static interaction**. The interaction between objects is assumed to be static and realized using synchronous blocking calls.

Note that this assumption does not limit the use of virtual calls, which we handle conservatively as discussed in section 4.2.2, but rather it limits the use of our approach when either the target of an interaction is dynamically selected based on a lookup mechanism such as the Java Reflection API, or the target of an interaction is not identified at all, as it is for example the case of event-based systems with a bus architecture.

- **Explicit flow relations**. The flow relations between abstract locations are assumed to be explicitly specified in the source code. This assumption may lead to a lower accuracy of our approach for systems using a dependency injection framework such as the Spring Framework (Johnson 02).

Note that this is not an inherent theoretical limitation of the method, but rather a limitation of the current implementation, which only extracts flow relations from source code. In principle however, it is possible to extract the missing direct flow relations from other sources such as the XML-based metadata descriptors, commonly used by such frameworks.

- **Good object-oriented design**. The analyzed code is assumed to conform to good object-oriented design principles and best practices, and in particular to the Interface Segregation Principle (Martin 96a) and the Liskov Substitution Principle (Martin 96b). This assumption is needed to ensure the applicability of the heuristic rules used for detecting superimposed class roles, for handling virtual calls conservatively, and for filtering abstract locations in the reduced concern graph.

Note that this assumption does not limit the use of our approach on a system exhibiting a bad object-oriented design, but in such cases the obtained results are likely to be less accurate.

- **No renaming of concern seeds**. As we have seen in section 6.3, the manually created concern intent specification can be reused for subsequent versions of the code base, provided that the concerns defined in it, and not their implementations, remain unchanged. Of course, this is only true under the assumption that the qualified unique names of the specified concern seeds also remain unchanged, which in turn means that the concern seeds themselves and the language constructs containing them must not be renamed or moved.

As a result the concern intent specification created for a software system cannot be reused without adaptation after a major refactoring of that system.

7.3. Perspectives on future work

This section provides a perspective on possible future extensions and improvements of the work presented in this thesis.

A first possible improvement of the proposed approach is the selection of concern seeds, which, although supported by tools, is still largely a manual effort. As already pointed out in chapter 2, there are already a number of approaches proposed in the literature, relying on various heuristic rules to automatically identify candidate concern seeds, which could be coupled with our approach to reduce the manual effort even further.

Furthermore, although some of these heuristics are quite promising, we believe there is much room for improving them by incorporating knowledge about the system architecture.

Directly related to this improvement is the automatic detection of flow set bounds, which could potentially make our concern identification more resistant to additions to the implementation of a concern, as the ones reported in section 6.3.4 for the second version of the JHotDraw case-study.

Another area, that we believe to be well-worth exploring, is the coupling of our concern identification approach with a formal requirements modelling language, in order to automatically derive the concern hierarchies, currently defined manually in the concern intent specification.

Particularly promising is the coupling of our concern identification approach with the Feature-Architecture Mapping (FArM) approach (Sochos 06; Sochos 07), used for the domain engineering of software product lines.

FArM defines a methodology for architectural design, based on the iterative refinement of an initial set of features (functional concerns), which strives to ensure a one-to-one mapping between features and architectural components. The approach already creates traceability links between the functional concerns and the architectural design, and combining it with our approach could extend these links all the way to the concern implementations in code.

Further improvements could target the CODEX tool, which could be extended to support the extraction of direct flow relations from other sources than the existing code base. And given the last limitation discussed in section 7.2, the direct specification of a concern seed by its qualified unique name could be replaced with a unique annotation, attached to the definition of the concern seed in code. This alternative specification of concern seeds has the advantage that concern intent specifications remain unaffected by a refactoring of the system, even if this refactoring renames or moves concern seeds.

And finally, an empirical study could be performed, to obtain a quantitative measure of the amount of program understanding effort saved, as a result of applying our functional concern identification method. Since our method allows the specification of traceability links between functional concerns and their respective implementations in code in a persistent form, the study should measure the saved efforts for functional concerns both with and without available specifications of such traceability links.

There are many ways to perform such a study, but one potential approach is to set up an experiment, in which a number of subjects are asked to independently perform a series of program understanding tasks in an unfamiliar software system. Each program understanding task involves locating the code fragments, that need to be changed in order to implement a given change request. The change requests will be chosen to address both new and recurring functional concerns, in order to cover both of the above mentioned situations.

Before receiving the tasks, the subjects are divided into two groups, one using our concern identification method and the other not using it. Each group will consist of an equivalent mix of experienced and unexperienced subjects. The division into groups is done based on the results of an initial calibration test, in which each subject is asked to perform a single program understanding task manually, without any support from our method.

The effort required to complete a program understanding task can be assessed in several ways. One way would be to measure the time the subjects require to complete each task. In general, this metric is not very objective, because more experienced subjects tend to complete the tasks faster, but if we use the previously mentioned calibration test, it can be objectified to some extent.

A much better way would be to measure the amount of code investigated by a subject in order to complete a program understanding task. This metric can be easily calculated from recorded investigation transcripts, such as the ones described by Robillard and Murphy (Robillard 03).

Another interesting result of the study could be to assess the percentage of program understanding effort saved for recurring functional concerns, as a result of reusing the persistent specifications of traceability links between these concerns and their respective implementations in code.

Appendix A.

JHotDraw Experiment Details

This appendix presents additional detailed information about the experiment carried out on the JHotDraw case-study, which was discussed in section 6.3. The information covers parts of the flow-equivalent concern subgraph specification for the standard library, the concern intent specification used as input for the identification of concern skeletons, a sample CoDEx project file, and the collected accuracy measurements.

A.1. Specification of the Java Standard Library

As already suggested in section 4.4.2, the flow-equivalent concern subgraph specification used in our experiment was created to contain the library abstract locations referenced in the source code of the case study. But because we used two different versions of JHotDraw, the specification contains all library abstract locations, referenced in at least one of the two versions. The complete specification contain 356 relations, which is why listing A.1 only shows a small part of it, covering widely used classes from the `java.lang` package and some of the standard Java collection classes.

Listing A.1: Flow-equivaent concern subgraph specification of the Java standard library

```
1   RVA -{F}java.lang.Boolean.data
         ->{O}java.lang.Boolean.booleanValue().this
         -{R}java.lang.Boolean.booleanValue().return
2   SA  -{P}java.lang.Boolean.Boolean(boolean).param0
         -<{O}java.lang.Boolean.Boolean(boolean).this
         -{F}java.lang.Boolean.data
```

```
3    RVA  -{F}java.lang.Double.data
              ->{O}java.lang.Double.doubleValue().this
              -{R}java.lang.Double.doubleValue().return
4    SA   -{P}java.lang.Double.Double(double).param0
              -<{O}java.lang.Double.Double(double).this
              -{F}java.lang.Double.data
5    RVA  -{F}java.lang.Float.data   ->{O}java.lang.Float.floatValue().this
              -{R}java.lang.Float.floatValue().return
6    SA   -{P}java.lang.Float.Float(float).param0
              -<{O}java.lang.Float.Float(float).this  -{F}java.lang.Float.data
7    RVA  -{F}java.lang.Integer.data
              ->{O}java.lang.Integer.intValue().this
              -{R}java.lang.Integer.intValue().return
8    SA   -{P}java.lang.Integer.Integer(int).param0
              -<{O}java.lang.Integer.Integer(int).this
              -{F}java.lang.Integer.data
9    RVA  -{P}java.lang.Math.abs(double).param0
              --{R}java.lang.Math.abs(double).return
10   RVA  -{P}java.lang.Math.ceil(double).param0
              --{R}java.lang.Math.ceil(double).return
11   RVA  -{P}java.lang.Math.cos(double).param0
              --{R}java.lang.Math.cos(double).return
12   RVA  -{P}java.lang.Math.floor(double).param0
              --{R}java.lang.Math.floor(double).return
13   RVA  -{P}java.lang.Math.max(double,double).param0
              --{R}java.lang.Math.max(double,double).return
14   RVA  -{P}java.lang.Math.max(double,double).param1
              --{R}java.lang.Math.max(double,double).return
15   RVA  -{P}java.lang.Math.min(double,double).param0
              --{R}java.lang.Math.min(double,double).return
16   RVA  -{P}java.lang.Math.min(double,double).param1
              --{R}java.lang.Math.min(double,double).return
17   RVA  -{P}java.lang.Math.sin(double).param0
              --{R}java.lang.Math.sin(double).return
18   RVA  -{P}java.lang.Math.sqrt(double).param0
              --{R}java.lang.Math.sqrt(double).return
19   SA   -{F}java.lang.String.data
              ->{P}java.lang.String.String(java.lang.String).param0
              <{O}java.lang.String.String(java.lang.String).this
              -{F}java.lang.String.data
20   SA   -{F}java.lang.String.data
              ->{O}java.lang.String.replace(char,char).this
              <{R}java.lang.String.replace(char,char).return
              -{F}java.lang.String.data
21   SA   -{F}java.lang.String.data
              ->{O}java.lang.String.substring(int,int).this
              <{R}java.lang.String.substring(int,int).return
              -{F}java.lang.String.data
22   SA   -{F}java.lang.String.data
              ->{O}java.lang.String.toLowerCase().this
              <{R}java.lang.String.toLowerCase().return
              -{F}java.lang.String.data
```

23 SA −{P}java.lang.String.replace(char,char).param1
        −<{O}java.lang.String.replace(char,char).this
        −{F}java.lang.String.data
24 RVA −{F}java.lang.String.data ->{O}java.lang.String.charAt(int).this
        −{R}java.lang.String.charAt(int).return
25 CID −{P}java.lang.String.charAt(int).param0
        −−{O}java.lang.String.charAt(int).this
26 CID −{P}java.lang.String.substring(int,int).param0
        −−{O}java.lang.String.substring(int,int).this
27 CID −{P}java.lang.String.substring(int,int).param1
        −−{O}java.lang.String.substring(int,int).this
28 SA −{P}java.util.Collection.add(java.lang.Object).param0
        −<{O}java.util.Collection.add(java.lang.Object).this
        −{F}java.util.Collection.data
29 RVA −{F}java.util.Collection.data
        ->{O}java.util.ArrayList.get(int).this
        −{R}java.util.ArrayList.get(int).return
30 SA −{P}java.util.ArrayList.add(java.lang.Object).param0
        −<{O}java.util.ArrayList.add(java.lang.Object).this
        −{F}java.util.Collection.data
31 SA −{F}java.util.Collection.data
        ->{P}java.util.ArrayList
        .ArrayList(java.util.Collection).param0
        <{O}java.util.ArrayList .ArrayList(java.util.Collection).this
        −{F}java.util.Collection.data
32 SA −{F}java.util.Collection.data   ->{P}java.util.HashSet
        .HashSet(java.util.Collection).param0 <{O}java.util.HashSet
        .HashSet(java.util.Collection).this
        −{F}java.util.Collection.data
33 CID −{P}java.util.List.add(int,java.lang.Object).param0
        −−{O}java.util.List.add(int,java.lang.Object).this
34 CID −{P}java.util.List.get(int).param0
        −−{O}java.util.List.get(int).this
35 CID −{P}java.util.List.remove(int).param0
        −−{O}java.util.List.remove(int).this
36 CID −{P}java.util.List.set(int,java.lang.Object).param0
        −−{O}java.util.List.set(int,java.lang.Object).this
37 RVA −{F}java.util.Collection.data ->{O}java.util.List.get(int).this
        −{R}java.util.List.get(int).return
38 RVA −{F}java.util.Collection.data
        ->{O}java.util.List.remove(int).this
        −{R}java.util.List.remove(int).return
39 SA −{P}java.util.List.add(int,java.lang.Object).param1
        −<{O}java.util.List.add(int,java.lang.Object).this
        −{F}java.util.Collection.data
40 SA −{P}java.util.List.add(java.lang.Object).param0
        −<{O}java.util.List.add(java.lang.Object).this
        −{F}java.util.Collection.data
41 SA −{P}java.util.List.set(int,java.lang.Object).param1
        −<{O}java.util.List.set(int,java.lang.Object).this
        −{F}java.util.Collection.data

```
42   SA  -{F}java.util.Collection.data                   ->{P}java.util.List
          .addAll(java.util.Collection).param0
          <{O}java.util.List.addAll(java.util.Collection).this
          -{F}java.util.Collection.data
43   SA  -{P}java.util.Set.add(java.lang.Object).param0
          -<{O}java.util.Set.add(java.lang.Object).this
          -{F}java.util.Collection.data
44   CID -{P}java.util.AbstractList.listIterator(int).param0
          --{O}java.util.AbstractList.listIterator(int).this
45   RVA -{F}java.util.Iterator.data ->{O}java.util.Iterator.next().this
          -{R}java.util.Iterator.next().return
46   SA  -{F}java.util.Collection.data
          ->{O}java.util.AbstractList.iterator().this
          <{R}java.util.AbstractList.iterator().return
          -{F}java.util.Iterator.data
47   SA  -{F}java.util.Collection.data
          ->{O}java.util.AbstractList.listIterator(int).this
          <{R}java.util.AbstractList.listIterator(int).return
          -{F}java.util.Iterator.data
48   SA  -{F}java.util.Collection.data
          ->{O}java.util.Collection.iterator().this
          <{R}java.util.Collection.iterator().return
          -{F}java.util.Iterator.data
49   SA  -{F}java.util.Collection.data
          ->{O}java.util.List.iterator().this
          <{R}java.util.List.iterator().return
          -{F}java.util.Iterator.data
50   SA  -{F}java.util.Collection.data ->{O}java.util.Set.iterator().this
          <{R}java.util.Set.iterator().return -{F}java.util.Iterator.data
```

A.2. Concern Intent Specification

As part of our experiment on the JHotDraw case study, the CODEX tool was run several times on two different versions of the case study, but always using the concern intent specification shown in listing A.2.

Listing A.2: Specification of concern intents in the JHotDraw case study

```
1   concern Clipboard {
2     sink CH.ifa.draw.util.Clipboard.getClipboard().return;
3     source CH.ifa.draw.util.Clipboard.getClipboard().return;
```

```
4     sink CH.ifa.draw.util.Clipboard.getContents().return;
5     }
6     concern DrawRendering {
7     source CH.ifa.draw.framework.DrawingView
            .paint(java.awt.Graphics).g;
8     source CH.ifa.draw.framework.DrawingView
            .drawAll(java.awt.Graphics).g;
9     source CH.ifa.draw.framework.DrawingView .draw(java.awt.Graphics,
            CH.ifa.draw.framework.FigureEnumeration).g;
10    source CH.ifa.draw.standard.CompositeFigure
            .draw(java.awt.Graphics).g;
11    source CH.ifa.draw.standard.CompositeFigure
            .draw(java.awt.Graphics,
            CH.ifa.draw.framework.FigureEnumeration).g;
12    source CH.ifa.draw.standard.StandardDrawingView
            .paintComponent(java.awt.Graphics).g;
13    source CH.ifa.draw.framework.DrawingView
            .drawDrawing(java.awt.Graphics).g;
14    source CH.ifa.draw.framework.DrawingView
            .drawHandles(java.awt.Graphics).g;
15    source CH.ifa.draw.framework.DrawingView
            .drawBackground(java.awt.Graphics).g;
16    }
17    concern DrawingTitle {
18    sink CH.ifa.draw.application.DrawApplication
            .getDrawingTitle().return;
19    sink CH.ifa.draw.contrib.MDI_DrawApplication
            .getDrawingTitle().return;
20    sink java.awt.Frame.setTitle(java.lang.String).param0;
21    sink javax.swing.JInternalFrame .setTitle(java.lang.String).param0;
22    }
23    concern FigureChange {
24    subconcern FigureChange.Events;
25    source CH.ifa.draw.framework.Figure
            .addFigureChangeListener(CH.ifa.draw.framework
            .FigureChangeListener).l;
26    source CH.ifa.draw.framework.Figure
            .addToContainer(CH.ifa.draw.framework
            .FigureChangeListener).c;
27    source CH.ifa.draw.framework.FigureChangeListener
            .figureInvalidated(CH.ifa.draw.framework
            .FigureChangeEvent).this;
28    source CH.ifa.draw.framework.FigureChangeListener
            .figureChanged(CH.ifa.draw.framework
            .FigureChangeEvent).this;
29    source CH.ifa.draw.framework.FigureChangeListener
            .figureRemoved(CH.ifa.draw.framework
            .FigureChangeEvent).this;
30    source CH.ifa.draw.framework.FigureChangeListener
            .figureRequestRemove(CH.ifa.draw.framework
            .FigureChangeEvent).this;
```

```
31      source CH.ifa.draw.framework.FigureChangeListener
                .figureRequestUpdate(CH.ifa.draw.framework
                .FigureChangeEvent).this;
32      sink CH.ifa.draw.framework.FigureChangeListener
                .figureInvalidated(CH.ifa.draw.framework
                .FigureChangeEvent).this;
33      sink CH.ifa.draw.framework.FigureChangeListener
                .figureChanged(CH.ifa.draw.framework
                .FigureChangeEvent).this;
34      sink CH.ifa.draw.framework.FigureChangeListener
                .figureRemoved(CH.ifa.draw.framework
                .FigureChangeEvent).this;
35      sink CH.ifa.draw.framework.FigureChangeListener
                .figureRequestRemove(CH.ifa.draw.framework
                .FigureChangeEvent).this;
36      sink CH.ifa.draw.framework.FigureChangeListener
                .figureRequestUpdate(CH.ifa.draw.framework
                .FigureChangeEvent).this;
37      }
38      concern FigureChange.Events {
39      source CH.ifa.draw.framework.FigureChangeListener
                .figureInvalidated(CH.ifa.draw.framework
                .FigureChangeEvent).e;
40      source CH.ifa.draw.framework.FigureChangeListener
                .figureChanged(CH.ifa.draw.framework .FigureChangeEvent).e;
41      source CH.ifa.draw.framework.FigureChangeListener
                .figureRemoved(CH.ifa.draw.framework .FigureChangeEvent).e;
42      source CH.ifa.draw.framework.FigureChangeListener
                .figureRequestRemove(CH.ifa.draw.framework
                .FigureChangeEvent).e;
43      source CH.ifa.draw.framework.FigureChangeListener
                .figureRequestUpdate(CH.ifa.draw.framework
                .FigureChangeEvent).e;
44      sink CH.ifa.draw.framework.FigureChangeListener
                .figureInvalidated(CH.ifa.draw.framework
                .FigureChangeEvent).e;
45      sink CH.ifa.draw.framework.FigureChangeListener
                .figureChanged(CH.ifa.draw.framework .FigureChangeEvent).e;
46      sink CH.ifa.draw.framework.FigureChangeListener
                .figureRemoved(CH.ifa.draw.framework .FigureChangeEvent).e;
47      sink CH.ifa.draw.framework.FigureChangeListener
                .figureRequestRemove(CH.ifa.draw.framework
                .FigureChangeEvent).e;
48      sink CH.ifa.draw.framework.FigureChangeListener
                .figureRequestUpdate(CH.ifa.draw.framework
                .FigureChangeEvent).e;
49      }
50      concern FigureZOrder {
51      sink CH.ifa.draw.framework.Figure.getZValue().return;
52      sink CH.ifa.draw.standard.OrderedFigureElement .getZValue().return;
53      }
54      concern Mouse.Click {
```

```
55      source java.awt.event.MouseListener
               .mouseClicked(java.awt.event.MouseEvent).param0;
56      source java.awt.event.MouseListener
               .mousePressed(java.awt.event.MouseEvent).param0;
57      source java.awt.event.MouseListener
               .mouseReleased(java.awt.event.MouseEvent).param0;
58    }
59    concern Mouse.Move {
60      source java.awt.event.MouseListener
               .mouseEntered(java.awt.event.MouseEvent).param0;
61      source java.awt.event.MouseListener
               .mouseExited(java.awt.event.MouseEvent).param0;
62      source java.awt.event.MouseMotionListener
               .mouseDragged(java.awt.event.MouseEvent).param0;
63      source java.awt.event.MouseMotionListener
               .mouseMoved(java.awt.event.MouseEvent).param0;
64    }
65    concern Persistency.Reader {
66      source CH.ifa.draw.util.StorableInput .readStorable().this;
67      sink CH.ifa.draw.util.StorableInput.readBoolean().return;
68      sink CH.ifa.draw.util.StorableInput.readColor().return;
69      sink CH.ifa.draw.util.StorableInput.readDouble().return;
70      sink CH.ifa.draw.util.StorableInput.readInt().return;
71      sink CH.ifa.draw.util.StorableInput .readStorable().return;
72      sink CH.ifa.draw.util.StorableInput.readString().return;
73    }
74    concern Persistency.Reference {
75      sink CH.ifa.draw.util.StorableOutput.fMap;
76      sink CH.ifa.draw.util.StorableInput.fMap;
77      source CH.ifa.draw.util.StorableOutput
               .map(CH.ifa.draw.util.Storable).this;
78      source CH.ifa.draw.util.StorableOutput
               .map(CH.ifa.draw.util.Storable).storable;
79      source CH.ifa.draw.util.StorableOutput
               .mapped(CH.ifa.draw.util.Storable).return;
80      source CH.ifa.draw.util.StorableOutput
               .mapped(CH.ifa.draw.util.Storable).storable;
81      source CH.ifa.draw.util.StorableOutput
               .writeRef(CH.ifa.draw.util.Storable).storable;
82      source CH.ifa.draw.util.StorableInput
               .map(CH.ifa.draw.util.Storable).storable;
83      source CH.ifa.draw.util.StorableInput
               .map(CH.ifa.draw.util.Storable).this;
84      sink CH.ifa.draw.util.StorableInput .retrieve(int).return;
85      sink CH.ifa.draw.util.StorableInput.retrieve(int).ref;
86      source CH.ifa.draw.util.StorableInput .retrieve(int).this;
87    }
88    concern Persistency.Writer {
89      source CH.ifa.draw.util.StorableOutput
               .writeStorable(CH.ifa.draw.util.Storable).this;
90      source CH.ifa.draw.util.StorableOutput .writeBoolean(boolean).b;
```

```
91    source CH.ifa.draw.util.StorableOutput
              .writeColor(java.awt.Color).c;
92    source CH.ifa.draw.util.StorableOutput .writeDouble(double).d;
93    source CH.ifa.draw.util.StorableOutput.writeInt(int).i;
94    source CH.ifa.draw.util.StorableOutput
              .writeStorable(CH.ifa.draw.util.Storable).storable;
95    source CH.ifa.draw.util.StorableOutput
              .writeString(java.lang.String).s;
96    }
97    concern StorageFormatManager {
98    sink CH.ifa.draw.application.DrawApplication
              .getStorageFormatManager().return;
99    sink CH.ifa.draw.util.StorageFormatManager .myStorageFormats;
100   sink CH.ifa.draw.util.StorageFormatManager
              .findStorageFormat(javax.swing.filechooser
              .FileFilter).return;
101   sink CH.ifa.draw.util.StorageFormatManager
              .findStorageFormat(javax.swing.filechooser
              .FileFilter).findFileFilter;
102   source CH.ifa.draw.util.StorageFormatManager
              .registerFileFilters(javax.swing.JFileChooser).this;
103   }
104   concern ToolActivation {
105   subconcern ToolActivation.Actions;
106   sink CH.ifa.draw.framework.Tool.isActive().return;
107   sink CH.ifa.draw.framework.Tool.isEnabled().return;
108   sink CH.ifa.draw.framework.Tool.isUsable().return;
109   sink CH.ifa.draw.standard.AbstractTool
              .EventDispatcher.myRegisteredListeners;
110   sink CH.ifa.draw.framework.ToolListener
              .toolEnabled(java.util.EventObject).this;
111   sink CH.ifa.draw.framework.ToolListener
              .toolDisabled(java.util.EventObject).this;
112   sink CH.ifa.draw.framework.ToolListener
              .toolUsable(java.util.EventObject).this;
113   sink CH.ifa.draw.framework.ToolListener
              .toolUnusable(java.util.EventObject).this;
114   sink CH.ifa.draw.framework.ToolListener
              .toolActivated(java.util.EventObject).this;
115   sink CH.ifa.draw.framework.ToolListener
              .toolDeactivated(java.util.EventObject).this;
116   }
117   concern ToolActivation.Actions {
118   source CH.ifa.draw.framework.ToolListener
              .toolEnabled(java.util.EventObject).this;
119   source CH.ifa.draw.framework.ToolListener
              .toolDisabled(java.util.EventObject).this;
120   source CH.ifa.draw.framework.ToolListener
              .toolUsable(java.util.EventObject).this;
121   source CH.ifa.draw.framework.ToolListener
              .toolUnusable(java.util.EventObject).this;
```

```
122    source CH.ifa.draw.framework.ToolListener
              .toolActivated(java.util.EventObject).this;
123    source CH.ifa.draw.framework.ToolListener
              .toolDeactivated(java.util.EventObject).this;
124    }
125    concern Undo {
126      subconcern Undo.Actions;
127      subconcern Undo.Activities;
128      sink CH.ifa.draw.util.Undoable.undo().this;
129      sink CH.ifa.draw.util.Undoable.redo().this;
130      sink CH.ifa.draw.util.UndoManager.undoStack;
131      sink CH.ifa.draw.util.UndoManager.redoStack;
132      sink CH.ifa.draw.util.UndoManager.isUndoable().return;
133      sink CH.ifa.draw.util.UndoManager.isRedoable().return;
134      sink CH.ifa.draw.framework.DrawingEditor .getUndoManager().return;
135    }
136    concern Undo.Actions {
137      source CH.ifa.draw.util.Undoable.undo().this;
138      source CH.ifa.draw.util.Undoable.redo().this;
139    }
140    concern Undo.Activities {
141      sink CH.ifa.draw.standard.AbstractHandle
              .setUndoActivity(CH.ifa.draw.util.Undoable)
              .newUndoableActivity;
142      sink CH.ifa.draw.standard.AbstractTool
              .setUndoActivity(CH.ifa.draw.util.Undoable)
              .newUndoableActivity;
143      sink CH.ifa.draw.standard.AbstractCommand
              .setUndoActivity(CH.ifa.draw.util.Undoable)
              .newUndoableActivity;
144    }
```

A.3. CoDEx Project File

This sections shows the CoDEx project file used for the object-sensitive run with separation of superimposed roles.

Listing A.3: Sample CoDEx project file

```
1    <ProjectWorkflow name="run_jhd53_O_RS">
2      <Action name="parse source code"
              class="codex.extraction.recoder.FactExtractorImpl">
```

Appendix A. JHotDraw Experiment Details

```
3      <Parameter name="input" value="JhotDraw/5.3/src/"/>
4      <Parameter name="library_input" value="lib_used.txt"/>
5      <Parameter name="split_roles" value="true"/>
6      <Parameter name="relation_edge"
               value="codex.core.graph.SumWeightRelationEdge"/>
7      <Parameter name="composite_edge"
               value="codex.core.graph.SumWeightCompositeEdge"/>
8    </Action>
9    <Action name="export concern graph"
             class="codex.export.GMLGraphExporter">
10     <Parameter name="path_name" value="out/jhd53/O_RS_graph.gml"/>
11     <Parameter name="relations">
12       <Element name="SA" type="double" value="100"/>
13       <Element name="PA" type="double" value="100"/>
14       <Element name="OCA" type="double" value="100"/>
15       <Element name="RVA" type="double" value="100"/>
16       <Element name="EA" type="double" value="100"/>
17       <Element name="PI" type="double" value="100"/>
18       <Element name="OCI" type="double" value="100"/>
19       <Element name="RVI" type="double" value="100"/>
20       <Element name="CFD" type="double" value="100"/>
21       <Element name="CID" type="double" value="100"/>
22       <Element name="CED" type="double" value="100"/>
23     </Parameter>
24   </Action>
25   <Action name="extract concern extents"
             class="codex.analysis.ConcernExtentExtractor">
26     <Parameter name="concern_definitions"
               value="jhotdraw_concerns.xml"/>
27     <Parameter name="sensitivity" value="object"/>
28     <Parameter name="relations">
29       <Element name="SA" type="double" value="100"/>
30       <Element name="PA" type="double" value="100"/>
31       <Element name="OCA" type="double" value="100"/>
32       <Element name="RVA" type="double" value="100"/>
33       <Element name="EA" type="double" value="100"/>
34       <Element name="PI" type="double" value="100"/>
35       <Element name="OCI" type="double" value="100"/>
36       <Element name="RVI" type="double" value="100"/>
37       <Element name="CFD" type="double" value="100"/>
38       <Element name="CID" type="double" value="100"/>
39       <Element name="CED" type="double" value="100"/>
40     </Parameter>
41     <Parameter name="graph_compactor"
               value="codex.core.graph.HierarchicGraphCompactor"/>
42   </Action>
43   <Action name="export graph statistics"
             class="codex.export.StatisticsExporter">
44     <Parameter name="path_name" value="out/jhd53/O_RS_stats.txt"/>
45   </Action>
46   <Action name="export concern skeletons"
             class="codex.export.GMLConcernExporter">
```

```
47      <Parameter name="path_name" value="out/jhd53/O_RS_concerns/"/>
48      <Parameter name="relations">
49       <Element name="SA" type="double" value="100"/>
50       <Element name="PA" type="double" value="100"/>
51       <Element name="OCA" type="double" value="100"/>
52       <Element name="RVA" type="double" value="100"/>
53       <Element name="EA" type="double" value="100"/>
54       <Element name="PI" type="double" value="100"/>
55       <Element name="OCI" type="double" value="100"/>
56       <Element name="RVI" type="double" value="100"/>
57       <Element name="CFD" type="double" value="100"/>
58       <Element name="CID" type="double" value="100"/>
59       <Element name="CED" type="double" value="100"/>
60      </Parameter>
61     </Action>
62     <Action name="export concern elements"
             class="codex.export.ConcernElementsExporter">
63      <Parameter name="path_name" value="out/jhd53/O_RS_concerns.txt"/>
64     </Action>
65     <Action name="evaluate identification accuracy"
             class="codex.eval.AccuracyEvaluator">
66      <Parameter name="reference_file" value="prj/ref_jhd53.txt"/>
67      <Parameter name="concern_file"
             value="out/jhd53/O_RS_concerns.txt"/>
68      <Parameter name="output_file"
             value="out/jhd53/O_RS_accuracy.txt"/>
69     </Action>
70    </ProjectWorkflow>
```

A.4. Detailed Experiment Results

The following tables present detailed size and accuracy measurements for each of the identified concern skeletons, collected for insensitive, context-sensitive and object-sensitive runs of the CODEX tool on both versions of the JHotDraw case study.

Concern Name	Ref. Size	JHD 5.3 I				JHD 5.3 C				JHD 5.3 O			
		Size	Prec.	Rec.	F$_1$	Size	Prec.	Rec.	F$_1$	Size	Prec.	Rec.	F$_1$
Clipboard	10	9	0.89	0.8	0.84	9	0.89	0.8	0.84	7	1	0.7	0.82
DrawRendering	85	75	1	0.88	0.94	75	1	0.88	0.94	75	1	0.88	0.94
DrawingTitle	46	36	0.81	0.63	0.71	36	0.81	0.63	0.71	27	1	0.59	0.74
FigureChange	140	1289	0.11	0.97	0.19	1274	0.11	0.97	0.19	700	0.18	0.89	0.3
FigureChange.Events	64	61	1	0.95	0.98	61	1	0.95	0.98	61	1	0.95	0.98
FigureZOrder	11	15	0.73	1	0.85	15	0.73	1	0.85	8	1	0.73	0.84
Mouse.Click	44	44	1	1	1	44	1	1	1	44	1	1	1
Mouse.Move	31	31	1	1	1	31	1	1	1	31	1	1	1
Persistency.Reader	83	1093	0.06	0.81	0.11	1092	0.06	0.81	0.11	48	0.9	0.52	0.66
Persistency.Reference	22	1626	0.01	0.82	0.02	1626	0.01	0.82	0.02	19	0.95	0.82	0.88
Persistency.Writer	75	1456	0.05	0.93	0.09	1439	0.05	0.93	0.09	87	0.8	0.93	0.86
StorageFormatManager	35	669	0.04	0.71	0.07	668	0.04	0.71	0.07	24	0.88	0.6	0.71
ToolActivation	81	748	0.08	0.78	0.15	747	0.08	0.78	0.15	71	0.83	0.73	0.78
ToolActivation.Actions	18	19	0.95	1	0.97	19	0.95	1	0.97	19	0.95	1	0.97
Undo	359	873	0.33	0.81	0.47	872	0.33	0.81	0.47	278	0.99	0.77	0.86
Undo.Actions	154	92	0.97	0.58	0.72	92	0.97	0.58	0.72	92	0.97	0.58	0.72
Undo.Activities	81	49	0.96	0.58	0.72	49	0.96	0.58	0.72	49	0.96	0.58	0.72

Table A.1: Size and accuracy measurements for JHotDraw 5.3, no separation of superimposed roles

Concern Name	Ref. Size	JHD 5.3 I RS				JHD 5.3 C RS				JHD 5.3 O RS			
		Size	Prec.	Rec.	F_1	Size	Prec.	Rec.	F_1	Size	Prec.	Rec.	F_1
Clipboard	10	9	0.89	0.8	0.84	9	0.89	0.8	0.84	7	1	0.7	0.82
DrawRendering	85	75	1	0.88	0.94	75	1	0.88	0.94	75	1	0.88	0.94
DrawingTitle	46	36	0.81	0.63	0.71	36	0.81	0.63	0.71	27	1	0.59	0.74
FigureChange	140	176	0.74	0.93	0.82	176	0.74	0.93	0.82	176	0.74	0.93	0.82
FigureChange.Events	64	61	1	0.95	0.98	61	1	0.95	0.98	61	1	0.95	0.98
FigureZOrder	11	15	0.73	1	0.85	15	0.73	1	0.85	8	1	0.73	0.84
Mouse.Click	44	44	1	1	1	44	1	1	1	44	1	1	1
Mouse.Move	31	31	1	1	1	31	1	1	1	31	1	1	1
Persistency.Reader	83	868	0.06	0.61	0.11	868	0.06	0.61	0.11	48	0.9	0.52	0.66
Persistency.Reference	22	1504	0.01	0.82	0.02	1504	0.01	0.82	0.02	19	0.95	0.82	0.88
Persistency.Writer	75	1350	0.05	0.95	0.1	1329	0.05	0.95	0.1	89	0.8	0.95	0.87
StorageFormatManager	35	588	0.04	0.71	0.08	588	0.04	0.71	0.08	24	0.88	0.6	0.71
ToolActivation	81	617	0.1	0.78	0.18	617	0.1	0.78	0.18	71	0.83	0.73	0.78
ToolActivation.Actions	18	19	0.95	1	0.97	19	0.95	1	0.97	19	0.95	1	0.97
Undo	359	762	0.38	0.81	0.52	762	0.38	0.81	0.52	279	0.99	0.77	0.87
Undo.Actions	154	93	0.97	0.58	0.73	93	0.97	0.58	0.73	93	0.97	0.58	0.73
Undo.Activities	81	49	0.96	0.58	0.72	49	0.96	0.58	0.72	49	0.96	0.58	0.72

Table A.2: Size and accuracy measurements for JHotDraw 5.3, with separation of superimposed roles

Concern Name	Ref. Size	JHD 5.4 I				JHD 5.4 C				JHD 5.4 O			
		Size	Prec.	Rec.	F_1	Size	Prec.	Rec.	F_1	Size	Prec.	Rec.	F_1
Clipboard	10	9	0.89	0.8	0.84	9	0.89	0.8	0.84	7	1	0.7	0.82
DrawRendering	164	127	1	0.77	0.87	121	1	0.74	0.85	121	1	0.74	0.85
DrawingTitle	47	956	0.05	0.96	0.09	946	0.05	0.96	0.09	30	0.87	0.55	0.68
FigureChange	160	216	0.69	0.93	0.79	216	0.69	0.93	0.79	203	0.67	0.84	0.74
FigureChange.Events	75	72	0.99	0.95	0.97	72	0.99	0.95	0.97	71	0.99	0.93	0.96
FigureZOrder	11	20	0.55	1	0.71	20	0.55	1	0.71	10	0.8	0.73	0.76
Mouse.Click	63	61	1	0.97	0.98	61	1	0.97	0.98	61	1	0.97	0.98
Mouse.Move	44	41	1	0.93	0.96	41	1	0.93	0.96	41	1	0.93	0.96
Persistency.Reader	115	2061	0.04	0.71	0.08	1702	0.05	0.71	0.09	799	0.09	0.63	0.16
Persistency.Reference	18	2271	0.01	0.83	0.01	2261	0.01	0.83	0.01	1562	0.01	0.83	0.02
Persistency.Writer	98	2198	0.04	0.9	0.08	2178	0.04	0.9	0.08	1463	0.06	0.9	0.11
StorageFormatManager	34	612	0.04	0.71	0.07	604	0.04	0.71	0.08	337	0.06	0.62	0.11
ToolActivation	76	776	0.05	0.55	0.1	766	0.05	0.55	0.1	454	0.09	0.55	0.16
ToolActivation.Actions	18	19	0.95	1	0.97	19	0.95	1	0.97	19	0.95	1	0.97
Undo	375	1100	0.28	0.81	0.41	1089	0.28	0.81	0.42	739	0.39	0.77	0.52
Undo.Actions	156	105	0.96	0.65	0.77	105	0.96	0.65	0.77	105	0.96	0.65	0.77
Undo.Activities	87	49	0.96	0.54	0.69	49	0.96	0.54	0.69	49	0.96	0.54	0.69

Table A.3: Size and accuracy measurements for JHotDraw 5.4, no separation of superimposed roles

Concern Name	Ref.	JHD 5.4 I RS				JHD 5.4 C RS				JHD 5.4 O RS			
	Size	Size	Prec.	Rec.	F_1	Size	Prec.	Rec.	F_1	Size	Prec.	Rec.	F_1
Clipboard	10	9	0.89	0.8	0.84	9	0.89	0.8	0.84	7	1	0.7	0.82
DrawRendering	164	127	1	0.77	0.87	121	1	0.74	0.85	121	1	0.74	0.85
DrawingTitle	47	873	0.05	0.96	0.1	866	0.05	0.96	0.1	30	0.87	0.55	0.68
FigureChange	160	197	0.73	0.9	0.81	197	0.73	0.9	0.81	186	0.72	0.83	0.77
FigureChange.Events	75	72	0.99	0.95	0.97	72	0.99	0.95	0.97	71	0.99	0.93	0.96
FigureZOrder	11	20	0.55	1	0.71	20	0.55	1	0.71	10	0.8	0.73	0.76
Mouse.Click	63	61	1	0.97	0.98	61	1	0.97	0.98	61	1	0.97	0.98
Mouse.Move	44	41	1	0.93	0.96	41	1	0.93	0.96	41	1	0.93	0.96
Persistency.Reader	115	1763	0.04	0.57	0.07	1384	0.05	0.57	0.09	622	0.09	0.5	0.15
Persistency.Reference	18	2106	0.01	0.83	0.01	2103	0.01	0.83	0.01	1309	0.01	0.83	0.02
Persistency.Writer	98	2065	0.04	0.9	0.08	2037	0.04	0.9	0.08	1375	0.06	0.9	0.12
StorageFormatManager	34	588	0.04	0.71	0.08	581	0.04	0.71	0.08	260	0.08	0.62	0.14
ToolActivation	76	728	0.06	0.55	0.1	721	0.06	0.55	0.11	387	0.11	0.55	0.18
ToolActivation.Actions	18	19	0.95	1	0.97	19	0.95	1	0.97	19	0.95	1	0.97
Undo	375	899	0.33	0.79	0.47	892	0.33	0.79	0.47	411	0.69	0.75	0.72
Undo.Actions	156	99	0.96	0.61	0.75	99	0.96	0.61	0.75	99	0.96	0.61	0.75
Undo.Activities	87	49	0.96	0.54	0.69	49	0.96	0.54	0.69	49	0.96	0.54	0.69

Table A.4: Size and accuracy measurements for JHotDraw 5.4, with separation of superimposed roles

Bibliography

[Aho 86] Alfred V. Aho, Ravi Sethi & Jeffrey D. Ullman. Compilers: principles, techniques, and tools. Addison-Wesley Longman Publishing Co., Inc., Boston, MA, USA, 1986.

[Andersen 94] L. O. Andersen. *Program Analysis and Specialization for the C Programming Language*. PhD thesis, University of Copenhagen, 1994.

[Antoniol 05] G. Antoniol & Y.-G. Gueheneuc. *Feature identification: a novel approach and a case study*. In Software Maintenance, 2005. ICSM'05. Proceedings of the 21st IEEE International Conference on, pages 357–366, Sept. 2005.

[Batory 92] Don Batory & Sean O'Malley. *The design and implementation of hierarchical software systems with reusable components*. ACM Trans. Softw. Eng. Methodol., vol. 1, no. 4, pages 355–398, 1992.

[Batory 03] Don Batory, Jacob Neal Sarvela & Axel Rauschmayer. *Scaling step-wise refinement*. In ICSE '03: Proceedings of the 25th International Conference on Software Engineering, pages 187–197, Washington, DC, USA, 2003. IEEE Computer Society.

[Ben-Menachem 97] M. Ben-Menachem & G. S. Marliss. Software quality: Producing practical, consistent software. International Thomson Computer Press, first edition, 1997.

[Biggerstaff 93] T. J. Biggerstaff, B. G. Mitbander & D. Webster. *The concept assignment problem in program understanding*. In Proceedings of the International Conference on Software Engineering (ICSE), pages 482–498, Los Alamitos, CA, USA, 1993. IEEE Computer Society Press.

Bibliography

[Bohner 96]   S. A. Bohner & R. S. Arnold.   Software change impact analysis. IEEE Computer Society Press, Los Alamitos, CA, USA, 1996.

[Breu 03]   Silvia Breu & Jens Krinke.   *Aspect Mining Using Dynamic Analysis.* GI-Softwaretechnik-Trends, vol. 23, no. 2, pages 21–22, May 2003.

[Breu 04]   S. Breu & J. Krinke.   *Aspect mining using event traces.* In Automated Software Engineering, 2004. Proceedings. 19th International Conference on, pages 310–315, Sept. 2004.

[Breu 06]   Silvia Breu & Thomas Zimmermann.   *Mining Aspects from Version History.* In ASE '06: Proceedings of the 21st IEEE/ACM International Conference on Automated Software Engineering, pages 221–230, Washington, DC, USA, 2006. IEEE Computer Society.

[Brooks 83]   R. Brooks.   *Towards a Theory of the Comprehension of Computer Programs.* International journal of man-machine studies, vol. 18, no. 66, pages 543–554, 1983.

[Bruntink 04]   Magiel Bruntink, Arie van Deursen, Tom Tourwe & Remco van Engelen. *An Evaluation of Clone Detection Techniques for Identifying Crosscutting Concerns.* In ICSM '04: Proceedings of the 20th IEEE International Conference on Software Maintenance, pages 200–209, Washington, DC, USA, 2004. IEEE Computer Society.

[Bruntink 05]   Magiel Bruntink, Arie van Deursen, Remco van Engelen & Tom Tourwe. *On the Use of Clone Detection for Identifying Crosscutting Concern Code.* IEEE Trans. Softw. Eng., vol. 31, no. 10, pages 804–818, 2005.

[Ceccato 05]   M. Ceccato, M. Marin, K. Mens, L. Moonen, P. Tonella & T. Tourwe. *A Qualitative Comparison of Three Aspect Mining Techniques.* In Proceedings of the International Workshop on Program Comprehension (IWPC), pages 13–22, 2005.

[Ceccato 06]   M. Ceccato, M. Marin, K. Mens, L. Moonen, P. Tonella & T. Tourwé. *Applying and combining three different aspect Min-*

ing Techniques. Software Quality Control, vol. 14, no. 3, pages 209–231, 2006.

[Chen 00] Kunrong Chen & Václav Rajlich. *Case Study of Feature Location Using Dependence Graph*. In IWPC '00: Proceedings of the 8th International Workshop on Program Comprehension, pages 241–247, Washington, DC, USA, 2000. IEEE Computer Society.

[Choi 93] Jong-Deok Choi, Michael Burke & Paul Carini. *Efficient flow-sensitive interprocedural computation of pointer-induced aliases and side effects*. In POPL '93: Proceedings of the 20th ACM SIGPLAN-SIGACT symposium on Principles of programming languages, pages 232–245, New York, NY, USA, 1993. ACM.

[Clements 01] Paul Clements & Linda Northrop. Software product lines: practices and patterns. Addison-Wesley Longman Publishing Co., Inc., Boston, MA, USA, 2001.

[Colyer 04] A. Colyer & A. Clement. *Large-scale AOSD for Middleware*. In Proceedings of the International Conference on Aspect-Oriented Software Development (AOSD), pages 56–65. ACM, Mar 2004.

[Corbi 89] T. A. Corbi. *Program understanding: challenge for the 1990's*. IBM Syst. J., vol. 28, no. 2, pages 294–306, 1989.

[Czarnecki 00] Krzysztof Czarnecki & Ulrich W. Eisenecker. Generative programming: methods, tools, and applications. ACM Press/Addison-Wesley Publishing Co., New York, NY, USA, 2000.

[Dijkstra 82] Edsger W. Dijkstra. *On the Role of Scientific Thought*. In Selected Writings on Computing: A Personal Perspective, pages 60–66. Springer-Verlag, 1982. ISBN 0-387-90652-5.

[Eaddy 07] Marc Eaddy, Alfred Aho & Gail C. Murphy. *Identifying, Assigning, and Quantifying Crosscutting Concerns*. In ACoM '07: Proceedings of the First International Workshop on Assessment of Contemporary Modularization Techniques, page 2, Washington, DC, USA, 2007. IEEE Computer Society.

[Eisenbarth 01]   Thomas Eisenbarth, Rainer Koschke & Daniel Simon. *Feature-Driven Program Understanding Using Concept Analysis of Execution Traces.* In Proceedings of the 9th International Workshop on Program Comprehension, pages 300–309. IEEE Computer Society Press, 2001.

[Eisenbarth 03]   Thomas Eisenbarth, Rainer Koschke & Daniel Simon. *Locating Features in Source Code.* IEEE Trans. Softw. Eng., vol. 29, no. 3, pages 210–224, 2003.

[Emami 94]   Maryam Emami, Rakesh Ghiya & Laurie J. Hendren. *Context-sensitive interprocedural points-to analysis in the presence of function pointers.* In PLDI '94: Proceedings of the ACM SIGPLAN 1994 conference on Programming language design and implementation, pages 242–256, New York, NY, USA, 1994. ACM.

[Erlikh 00]   L. Erlikh. *Leveraging Legacy System Dollars for E-Business.* IT Professional, vol. 2, no. 3, pages 17–23, 2000.

[Ferrante 87]   Jeanne Ferrante, Karl J. Ottenstein & Joe D. Warren. *The program dependence graph and its use in optimization.* ACM Trans. Program. Lang. Syst., vol. 9, no. 3, pages 319–349, 1987.

[Gallagher 91]   Keith Brian Gallagher & James R. Lyle. *Using Program Slicing in Software Maintenance.* IEEE Trans. Softw. Eng., vol. 17, no. 8, pages 751–761, 1991.

[Gallagher 06]   K. Gallagher, D. Binkley & M. Harman. *Stop-List Slicing.* In Source Code Analysis and Manipulation, 2006. SCAM '06. Sixth IEEE International Workshop on, pages 11–20, Sept. 2006.

[Gamma 95]   E. Gamma, R. Helm, R. Johnson & J. Vlissides. Design patterns. Addison-Wesley Professional, 1995.

[Ganter 99]   B. Ganter & R. Wille. Formal concept analysis - mathematical foundations. Springer, 1999.

[Gold 05]   N. E. Gold, M. Harman, D. Binkley & R. M. Hierons. *Unifying program slicing and concept assignment for higher-level executable source code extraction.* Software Practice and Experience, vol. 35, no. 10, pages 977–1006, 2005.

[Goos 97]   Gerhard Goos.   Vorlesungen über informatik, volume 1: Grundlagen und funktionales Programmieren.   Springer-Verlag, second edition, 1997.

[Gosling 05] J. Gosling, B. Joy, G. Steele & G. Bracha.   The java language specification. Addison-Wesley, third edition, 2005.

[Gotel 94]   O. C. Z. Gotel & C. W. Finkelstein. *An analysis of the requirements traceability problem.*   In Requirements Engineering, 1994., Proceedings of the First International Conference on, pages 94–101, Apr 1994.

[Hammer 09a] Christian Hammer. *Information Flow Control for Java - A Comprehensive Approach basedon Path Conditions in Dependence Graphs.* PhD thesis, Universität Karlsruhe, 2009.

[Hammer 09b] Christian Hammer & Gregor Snelting. *Flow-Sensitive, Context-Sensitive, and Object-sensitive Information Flow Control Based on Program Dependence Graphs.* International Journal of Information Security, vol. 8, no. 6, pages 399–422, December 2009. Supersedes ISSSE and ISoLA 2006.

[Hannemann 01] Jan Hannemann & Gregor Kiczales. *Overcoming the Prevalent Decomposition of Legacy Code.* In Proceedings of the ICSE Workshop on Advanced Separation of Concerns, 2001.

[Harman 02] M. Harman, N. Gold, R. Hierons & D. Binkley. *Code Extraction Algorithms which Unify Slicing and Concept Assignment.* In WCRE '02: Proceedings of the Ninth Working Conference on Reverse Engineering (WCRE'02), page 11, Washington, DC, USA, 2002. IEEE Computer Society.

[Harrison 93] William Harrison & Harold Ossher. *Subject-oriented programming: a critique of pure objects.* SIGPLAN Not., vol. 28, no. 10, pages 411–428, 1993.

Bibliography

[Harrison 04] William Harrison, Harold Ossher, Stanley Sutton Jr. & Peri Tarr. *Concern Modeling in the Concern Manipulation Environment.* IBM Research Report RC23344, 2004.

[Hartigan 75] John A. Hartigan. Clustering algorithms. John Wiley & Sons, New York, NY, USA, 1975.

[Hayes 03] Brian Hayes. *The Post-OOP Paradigm.* American Scientist, vol. 91, no. 2, page 106, Mar/Apr 2003.

[Himsolt 97] Michael Himsolt. The graphlet system (system demonstration), volume 1190 of *Lecture Notes in Computer Science*, pages 233–240. Springer-Verlag, 1997.

[Horwitz 88] S. Horwitz, T. Reps & D. Binkley. *Interprocedural slicing using dependence graphs.* SIGPLAN Not., vol. 23, no. 7, pages 35–46, 1988.

[Horwitz 90] S. Horwitz, T. Reps & D. Binkley. *Interprocedural slicing using dependence graphs.* ACM Trans. Program. Lang. Syst., vol. 12, no. 1, pages 26–60, 1990.

[IEEE 90] IEEE. *IEEE Standard Glossary of Software Engineering Terminology.* IEEE Std 610.12-1990, 1990.

[Inc. 97] Sun Microsystems Inc. *Code Conventions for the Java Programming Language.* http://java.sun.com/docs/ codeconv/-CodeConventions.pdf, 1997.

[Ishio 07] Takashi Ishio, Ryusuke Niitani, Gail Murphy & Katsuro Inoue. *A Program Slicing Approach for Locating Functional Concerns.* Rapport technique, SE Lab, Dept. of Computer Science, Osaka University, 2007.

[Janzen 03] Doug Janzen & Kris De Volder. *Navigating and querying code without getting lost.* In AOSD '03: Proceedings of the 2nd international conference on Aspect-oriented software development, pages 178–187, New York, NY, USA, 2003. ACM.

[Johnson 02] Rod Johnson. Expert one-on-one j2ee design and development. Wrox Press Ltd., Birmingham, UK, 2002.

184

[Jones 91] C. Jones. Applied software measurement: assuring productivity and quality. McGraw-Hill, Inc., New York, NY, USA, 1991.

[Kam 77] John B. Kam & Jeffrey D. Ullman. *Monotone data flow analysis frameworks.* Acta Informatica, vol. 7, no. 3, pages 305–317, 1977.

[Kiczales 97] G. Kiczales, J. Lamping, A. Menhdhekar, C. Maeda, C. Lopes, J. M. Loingtier & J. Irwin. *Aspect-Oriented Programming.* In M. Akşit & S. Matsuoka, editeurs, Proceedings European Conference on Object-Oriented Programming, volume 1241, pages 220–242. Springer-Verlag, Berlin, Heidelberg, and New York, 1997.

[Kildall 73] Gary A. Kildall. *A unified approach to global program optimization.* In POPL '73: Proceedings of the 1st annual ACM SIGACT-SIGPLAN symposium on Principles of programming languages, pages 194–206, New York, NY, USA, 1973. ACM.

[Koschke 05] Rainer Koschke & Jochen Quante. *On dynamic feature location.* In ASE '05: Proceedings of the 20th IEEE/ACM international Conference on Automated software engineering, pages 86–95, New York, NY, USA, 2005. ACM.

[Koskinen 04] J. Koskinen. *Software Maintenance Costs.* http:// users.jyu.fi/~koskinen/smcosts.htm, Sept 2004.

[Kotonya 98] Gerald Kotonya & Ian Sommerville. Requirements engineering - processes and techniques. John Wiley & Sons, 1998.

[Kozaczynski 94] Wojtek Kozaczynski & Jim Q. Ning. *Automated program understanding by concept recognition.* Automated Software Engineering, vol. 1, no. 1, pages 61–78, Mar 1994.

[Krinke 03] Jen Krinke. *Advanced Slicing of Sequential and Concurrent Programs.* PhD thesis, Universität Passau, 2003.

[Krinke 06] Jens Krinke. *Mining Control Flow Graphs for Crosscutting Concerns.* In WCRE '06: Proceedings of the 13th Working Conference on Reverse Engineering, pages 334–342, Washington, DC, USA, 2006. IEEE Computer Society.

[Kuttruff 09]   Volker Kuttruff. *Realisierung von Softwareproduktlinien durch Komposition von Belangimplementierungen.* PhD thesis, Universität Karlsruhe, Fakultät für Informatik, 2009.

[Lai 99]   Albert Lai & Gail C. Murphy. *The Structure of Features in Java Code: An Exploratory Investigation.* In MDSOC'99: OOPSLA'99 Workshop on Multi-dimensional Separation of Concerns in Object-Oriented Systems, 1999.

[Lai 02]   A. Lai & G. Murphy. *Behavioural Concern Modelling for Software Change Tasks.* In Proceedings of the IEEE International Conference on Software Maintenance, pages 112–121, Los Alamitos, CA, USA, 2002. IEEE Computer Society.

[Lehman 74]   M. M. Lehman. *Programs, Cities, Students - Limits to Growth?* In Imperial College of Science and Technology Inaugural Lecture Series, volume 9, pages 211–229. University of London, 1974.

[Lientz 80]   B. P. Lientz & E. B. Swanson. Software maintenance management. Addison-Wesley Longman Publishing Co., Inc., Boston, MA, USA, 1980.

[Liu 08]   Y. Liu & A. Milanova. *Static Analysis for Inference of Explicit Information Flow.* In Proceedings of the ACM SIGPLAN-SIGSOFT Workshop on Program Analysis for Software Tools and Engineering (PASTE), 2008.

[Liu 09]   Y. Liu & A. Milanova. *Practical Static Analysis for Inference of Security-related Program Properties.* In Proceedings of the International Conference on Program Comprehension (ICPC). IEEE, 2009.

[Ludwig 01]   A. Ludwig. *Recoder.* http://recoder.sourceforge.net/, 2001.

[Ludwig 02]   Andreas Ludwig. *Automatische Transformation großer Softwaresysteme.* PhD thesis, University of Karlsruhe, Dec 2002.

[Maletic 00]   J. I. Maletic & A. Marcus. *Using latent semantic analysis to identify similarities in source code to support program understanding.* In Tools with Artificial Intelligence, 2000. ICTAI

2000. Proceedings. 12th IEEE International Conference on, pages 46–53, 2000.

[Maletic 01] J. I. Maletic & A. Marcus. *Supporting program comprehension using semantic and structural information*. In ICSE '01: Proceedings of the 23rd International Conference on Software Engineering, pages 103–112, Washington, DC, USA, 2001. IEEE Computer Society.

[Marcus 03] A. Marcus & J. I. Maletic. *Recovering documentation-to-source-code traceability links using latent semantic indexing*. In Software Engineering, 2003. Proceedings. 25th International Conference on, pages 125–135, May 2003.

[Marcus 04] Andrian Marcus, Andrey Sergeyev, Vaclav Rajlich & Jonathan I. Maletic. *An Information Retrieval Approach to Concept Location in Source Code*. In WCRE '04: Proceedings of the 11th Working Conference on Reverse Engineering, pages 214–223, Washington, DC, USA, 2004. IEEE Computer Society.

[Marcus 05] Andrian Marcus, Vaclav Rajlich, Joseph Buchta, Maksym Petrenko & Andrey Sergeyev. *Static Techniques for Concept Location in Object-Oriented Code*. In IWPC '05: Proceedings of the 13th International Workshop on Program Comprehension, pages 33–42, Washington, DC, USA, 2005. IEEE Computer Society.

[Marin 04] Marius Marin, Arie van Deursen & Leon Moonen. *Identifying Aspects Using Fan-In Analysis*. In WCRE '04: Proceedings of the 11th Working Conference on Reverse Engineering, pages 132–141, Washington, DC, USA, 2004. IEEE Computer Society.

[Marin 05] Marius Marin, Leon Moonen & Arie van Deursen. *A Classification of Crosscutting Concerns*. In ICSM '05: Proceedings of the 21st IEEE International Conference on Software Maintenance, pages 673–676, Washington, DC, USA, 2005. IEEE Computer Society.

[Marin 06] Marius Marin, Leon Moonen & Arie van Deursen. *A common framework for aspect mining based on crosscutting concern sorts*. In WCRE '06: Proceedings of the 13th Working Conference on Reverse Engineering, pages 29–38, Washington, DC, USA, 2006. IEEE Computer Society.

[Marin 07] M. Marin, A. van Deursen & L. Moonen. *Identifying Crosscutting Concerns Using Fan-in Analysis*. ACM Transactions on Software Engineering and Methodology, vol. 17, no. 1, pages 1–37, 2007.

[Martin 96a] Robert C. Martin. *Interface Segregation Principle*. The C++ Report, vol. 8, Aug. 1996.

[Martin 96b] Robert C. Martin. *The Liskov substitution principle*. The C++ Report, vol. 8, pages 14, 16–17, 20–23, Mar. 1996.

[Mens 08a] Kim Mens, Andy Kellens & Jens Krinke. *Pitfalls in Aspect Mining*. In WCRE '08: Proceedings of the 2008 15th Working Conference on Reverse Engineering, pages 113–122, Washington, DC, USA, 2008. IEEE Computer Society.

[Mens 08b] T. Mens & S. Demeyer. Software evolution. Springer Publishing Company, Inc., 2008.

[Milanova 02] A. Milanova, A. Rountev & B. G. Ryder. *Parameterized Object Sensitivity for Points-to and Side-Effect Analyses for Java*. In Proceedings of the ACM SIGSOFT International Symposium on Software Testing and Analysis (ISSTA)), pages 1–11. ACM, 2002.

[Milanova 05] A. Milanova, A. Rountev & B. G. Ryder. *Parameterized Object Sensitivity for Points-to Analysis for Java*. ACM Transactions on Software Engineering and Methodology (TOSEM), vol. 14, no. 1, pages 1–41, Jan 2005.

[Moad 90] J. Moad. *Maintaining the competitive edge*. DATAMATION, vol. 36, no. 4, pages 61–62, 64, 66, Feb 1990.

[Murphy 01] Gail C. Murphy, Albert Lai, Robert J. Walker & Martin P. Robillard. *Separating features in source code: an exploratory study*. In ICSE '01: Proceedings of the 23rd International Conference on Software Engineering, pages 275–284, Washington, DC, USA, 2001. IEEE Computer Society.

[Naveh 03]   B. Naveh. *JGraphT*. http://www.jgrapht.org/, 2003.

[Nielson 99]   F. Nielson, H. R. Nielson & C. Hankin. Principles of program analysis. Springer-Verlag New York, Inc., Secaucus, NJ, USA, 1999.

[Ossher 99]   Harold Ossher & Peri Tarr. *Multi-Dimensional Separation of Concerns in Hyperspace*. IBM Research Report RC21452, 1999.

[Ottenstein 84]   Karl J. Ottenstein & Linda M. Ottenstein. *The program dependence graph in a software development environment*. In SDE 1: Proceedings of the first ACM SIGSOFT/SIGPLAN software engineering symposium on Practical software development environments, pages 177–184, New York, NY, USA, 1984. ACM.

[Parnas 72]   D. L. Parnas. *On the criteria to be used in decomposing systems into modules*. Communications of the ACM, vol. 15, no. 12, pages 1053–1058, 1972.

[Poshyvanyk 06]   Denys Poshyvanyk, Yann-Gael Gueheneuc, Andrian Marcus, Vaclav Rajlich & Giuliano Antoniol. *Combining Probabilistic Ranking and Latent Semantic Indexing for Feature Identification*. In ICPC '06: Proceedings of the 14th IEEE International Conference on Program Comprehension, pages 137–148, Washington, DC, USA, 2006. IEEE Computer Society.

[Poshyvanyk 07a]   Denys Poshyvanyk, Yann-Gael Gueheneuc, Andrian Marcus, Giuliano Antoniol & Vaclav Rajlich. *Feature Location Using Probabilistic Ranking of Methods Based on Execution Scenarios and Information Retrieval*. IEEE Trans. Softw. Eng., vol. 33, no. 6, pages 420–432, 2007.

[Poshyvanyk 07b]   Denys Poshyvanyk & Andrian Marcus. *Combining Formal Concept Analysis with Information Retrieval for Concept Location in Source Code*. In ICPC '07: Proceedings of the 15th IEEE International Conference on Program Comprehension, pages 37–48, Washington, DC, USA, 2007. IEEE Computer Society.

[Pressman 01]   R. S. Pressman. Software engineering: A practitioner's approach. McGrap-Hill, fifth edition, 2001.

[Putnam 97] L. H. Putnam & W. Myers. Industrial strength software: Effective management using measurement. Institute of Electrical & Electronics Engineering, 1997.

[Rajan 05] H. Rajan & K. J. Sullivan. *Classpects: unifying aspect- and object-oriented language design.* In Software Engineering, 2005. ICSE 2005. Proceedings. 27th International Conference on, pages 59–68, May 2005.

[Reps 97] T. Reps. *Program analysis via graph reachability.* In Proceedings of the International Symposium on Logic Programming (ILPS), pages 5–19, Cambridge, MA, USA, 1997. MIT Press.

[Reps 98] T. Reps. *Program analysis via graph reachability.* Information and Software Technology, vol. 40, no. 11–12, pages 5–19, 1998.

[Robillard 99] Martin P. Robillard & Gail C. Murphy. *Migrating a Static Analysis Tool to AspectJ.* In MDSOC'99: OOPSLA'99 Workshop on Multi-dimensional Separation of Concerns in Object-Oriented Systems, 1999.

[Robillard 02] Martin P. Robillard & Gail C. Murphy. *Concern graphs: finding and describing concerns using structural program dependencies.* In ICSE '02: Proceedings of the 24th International Conference on Software Engineering, pages 406–416, New York, NY, USA, 2002. ACM.

[Robillard 03] M. P. Robillard & G. C. Murphy. *Automatically inferring concern code from program investigation activities.* In Automated Software Engineering, 2003. Proceedings. 18th IEEE International Conference on, pages 225–234, Oct. 2003.

[Robillard 07] Martin P. Robillard & Gail C. Murphy. *Representing concerns in source code.* ACM Trans. Softw. Eng. Methodol., vol. 16, no. 1, page 3, 2007.

[Roy 07] Chanchal Kumar Roy, Mohammad Gias Uddin, Banani Roy & Thomas R. Dean. *Evaluating Aspect Mining Techniques: A Case Study.* In ICPC '07: Proceedings of the 15th IEEE International Conference on Program Comprehension, pages 167–176, Washington, DC, USA, 2007. IEEE Computer Society.

[Safyallah 06] Hossein Safyallah & Kamran Sartipi. *Dynamic Analysis of Software Systems using Execution Pattern Mining*. In ICPC '06: Proceedings of the 14th IEEE International Conference on Program Comprehension, pages 84–88, Washington, DC, USA, 2006. IEEE Computer Society.

[Shepherd 04] D. Shepherd, E. Gibson & L. Pollock. *Design and evaluation of an automated aspect mining tool*. In SERP '04: Proceedings of the International Conference on Software Engineering Research and Practice, pages 601–607, 2004.

[Shepherd 05a] David Shepherd, Jeffrey Palm, Lori Pollock & Mark Chu-Carroll. *Timna: a framework for automatically combining aspect mining analyses*. In ASE '05: Proceedings of the 20th IEEE/ACM international Conference on Automated software engineering, pages 184–193, New York, NY, USA, 2005. ACM.

[Shepherd 05b] David Shepherd, Tom Tourwé & Lori Pollock. *Using language clues to discover crosscutting concerns*. SIGSOFT Softw. Eng. Notes, vol. 30, no. 4, pages 1–6, 2005.

[Smaragdakis 99] Yannis Smaragdakis & Don S. Batory. *Building Product-Lines with Mixin-Layers*. In Proceedings of the Workshop on Object-Oriented Technology, page 197, London, UK, 1999. Springer-Verlag.

[Smaragdakis 02] Yannis Smaragdakis & Don Batory. *Mixin layers: an object-oriented implementation technique for refinements and collaboration-based designs*. ACM Trans. Softw. Eng. Methodol., vol. 11, no. 2, pages 215–255, 2002.

[Sochos 06] Periklis Sochos, Matthias Riebisch & Ilka Philippow. *The Feature-Architecture Mapping (FArM) Method for Feature-Oriented Development of Software Product Lines*. In ECBS '06: Proceedings of the 13th Annual IEEE International Symposium and Workshop on Engineering of Computer Based Systems, pages 308–318, Washington, DC, USA, 2006. IEEE Computer Society.

[Sochos 07] Periklis Sochos. *The Feature-Architecture Mapping Method for Feature-Oriented Development of Software Product Lines*.

PhD thesis, Technische Universität Ilmenau, Fakultät für Informatik und Automatisierung, 2007.

[Sommerville 06] I. Sommerville. Software engineering. International computer science series. Addison-Wesley Pub. Co., 8th edition, Jun 2006.

[Sridharan 05] Manu Sridharan, Denis Gopan, Lexin Shan & Rastislav Bodík. *Demand-driven points-to analysis for Java.* In OOPSLA '05: Proceedings of the 20th annual ACM SIGPLAN conference on Object-oriented programming, systems, languages, and applications, pages 59–76, New York, NY, USA, 2005. ACM.

[Steensgaard 96] Bjarne Steensgaard. *Points-to analysis in almost linear time.* In POPL '96: Proceedings of the 23rd ACM SIGPLAN-SIGACT symposium on Principles of programming languages, pages 32–41, New York, NY, USA, 1996. ACM.

[Sutton-Jr. 05] S. M. Sutton-Jr. & I. Rouvellou. *Concern Modeling for Aspect-Oriented Software Development.* In R. E. Filman, T. Elrad, S. Clarke & M. Aksit, editeurs, Aspect-Oriented Software Development, chapitre 21. Addison-Wesley, 2005.

[Tar 99] P. Tar, H. Ossher, W. Harrison & S. M. Sutton-Jr. *N Degrees of Separation: Multi-Dimensional Separation of Concerns.* In Proceedings of the International Conference on Software Engineering (ICSE), May 1999.

[Tarr 04] Peri Tarr, William Harrison & Harold Ossher. *Pervasive Query Support in the Concern Manipulation Environment.* IBM Research Report RC23343, 2004.

[Tip 95] Frank Tip. *A Survey of Program Slicing Techniques.* Journal of Programming Languages, vol. 3, pages 121–189, 1995.

[Tonella 04a] Paolo Tonella & Mariano Ceccato. *Aspect Mining through the Formal Concept Analysis of Execution Traces.* In WCRE '04: Proceedings of the 11th Working Conference on Reverse Engineering, pages 112–121, Washington, DC, USA, 2004. IEEE Computer Society.

[Tonella 04b] Paolo Tonella & Mariano Ceccato. *Migrating Interface Implementation to Aspects.* In ICSM '04: Proceedings of the 20th IEEE International Conference on Software Maintenance, pages 220–229, Washington, DC, USA, 2004. IEEE Computer Society.

[Tourwé 04] Tom Tourwé & Kim Mens. *Mining Aspectual Views using Formal Concept Analysis.* In SCAM '04: Proceedings of the Source Code Analysis and Manipulation, Fourth IEEE International Workshop, pages 97–106, Washington, DC, USA, 2004. IEEE Computer Society.

[Trifu 05] Mircea Trifu & Volker Kuttruff. *Capturing Nontrivial Concerns in Object-Oriented Software.* In Proceedings of the 12-th Working Conference on Reverse Engineering, pages 99–108. IEEE, Nov 2005.

[Trifu 08] M. Trifu. *Using Dataflow Information for Concern Identification in Object-Oriented Software Systems.* In Proceedings of the 12-th European Conference on Software Maintenance and Reengineering, pages 193–202. IEEE, Apr 2008.

[Trifu 09] M. Trifu. *Improving the Dataflow-Based Concern Identification Approach.* In Proceedings of the 13-th European Conference on Software Maintenance and Reengineering. IEEE, Mar 2009.

[van der Spek 08] Pieter van der Spek, Steven Klusener & Pierre van de Laar. *Towards Recovering Architectural Concepts Using Latent Semantic Indexing.* In CSMR '08: Proceedings of the 2008 12th European Conference on Software Maintenance and Reengineering, pages 253–257, Washington, DC, USA, 2008. IEEE Computer Society.

[van Rijsbergen 79] C. J. van Rijsbergen. Information retrieval. Dept. of Computer Science, University of Glasgow, second edition edition, 1979.

[Weihl 80] William E. Weihl. *Interprocedural data flow analysis in the presence of pointers, procedure variables, and label variables.* In POPL '80: Proceedings of the 7th ACM SIGPLAN-SIGACT symposium on Principles of programming languages, pages 83–94, New York, NY, USA, 1980. ACM.

[Weiser 79] Mark David Weiser. *Program slices: formal, psychological, and practical investigations of an automatic program abstraction method.* PhD thesis, University of Michigan, Ann Arbor, MI, USA, 1979.

[Weiser 82] Mark Weiser. *Programmers use slices when debugging.* Commun. ACM, vol. 25, no. 7, pages 446–452, 1982.

[Weiser 84] Mark Weiser. *Program Slicing.* IEEE Transactions on Software Engineering, vol. 10, no. 4, pages 352–357, 1984.

[Wiegers 03] Karl Eugene Wiegers. Software requirements. Microsoft Press, Redmond, WA, USA, 2003.

[Wieringa 95] Roel Wieringa. *An introduction to requirements traceability.* Rapport technique, Faculty of Mathematics and Computer Science, Vrije Universiteit Amsterdam, 1995.

[Wilde 03] Norman Wilde, Michelle Buckellew, Henry Page, Vaclav Rajlich & LaTreva Pounds. *A comparison of methods for locating features in legacy software.* Journal of Systems and Software, vol. 65, no. 2, pages 105–114, 2003.

[Xu 05] Baowen Xu, Ju Qian, Xiaofang Zhang, Zhongqiang Wu & Lin Chen. *A brief survey of program slicing.* SIGSOFT Softw. Eng. Notes, vol. 30, no. 2, pages 1–36, 2005.

[yWorks 00] yWorks. *yEd Graph Editor.* http://www.yworks.com, 2000.

[Zhang 03a] C. Zhang & H. A. Jacobsen. *Quantifying Aspects in Middleware Platforms.* In Proceedings of the International Conference on Aspect-Oriented Software Development (AOSD), pages 130–139. ACM, 2003.

[Zhang 03b] C. Zhang & H. A. Jacobsen. *Refactoring Middleware with Aspects.* IEEE Transactions on Parallel and Distributed Systems, vol. 14, no. 11, pages 1058–1073, Nov 2003.

[Zhang 03c] Charles Zhang & Hans-Arno Jacobsen. *A Prism for Research in Software Modularization Through Aspect Mining.* Technical Communication, 2003.

[Zhang 04] Charles Zhang & Hans-Arno Jacobsen. *PRISM is research in aSpect mining.* In OOPSLA '04: Companion to the 19th annual ACM SIGPLAN conference on Object-oriented programming systems, languages, and applications, pages 20–21, New York, NY, USA, 2004. ACM.

[Zhang 07] Charles Zhang & Hans-Arno Jacobsen. *Efficiently mining crosscutting concerns through random walks.* In AOSD '07: Proceedings of the 6th international conference on Aspect-oriented software development, pages 226–238, New York, NY, USA, 2007. ACM.